Passenger Rail

The Transportation Alternative

Walton W. Loevy

PublishAmerica
Baltimore

© 2005 by Walton W. Loevy.
All rights reserved. No part of this book may be reproduced, stored in a retrieval system or transmitted in any form or by any means without the prior written permission of the publishers, except by a reviewer who may quote brief passages in a review to be printed in a newspaper, magazine or journal.

First printing

ISBN: 1-4137-6168-2
PUBLISHED BY PUBLISHAMERICA, LLLP
www.publishamerica.com
Baltimore

Printed in the United States of America

For my father.

TABLE OF CONTENTS

PREFACE — 7
PART ONE: Roadway Gridlock and Rail Mass Transportation — 11
  CHAPTER 1: Congestion Mitigation Misconception — 13
  CHAPTER 2: Modes of Transportation and City Planning — 18
  CHAPTER 3: From the Past, an Electric Train of the Future — 27
    California's Ambitious High-Speed Rail Project — 32
PART TWO: Viable Commuter Railroads — 43
  CHAPTER 4: From the Private Sector to Government Subsidy — 45
    Maryland Area Rail Commuter — 48
  CHAPTER 5: Peninsula Commute Service — 58
    A CarLink to Caltrain — 70
  CHAPTER 6: Chicagoland Commuter Rail Network — 75
    Innovations to Maximize Service, Minimize Loss — 78
    The Rock Island District — 83
    Illinois Central and Metra Electric — 85
    Metra Improves Stations and Expands Service — 89
  CHAPTER 7: Trinity Railway Express — 95
PART THREE: Adapting to Serve Regional and Commuter Rail — 103
  CHAPTER 8: Passenger Rail and the Struggling Interurban — 105
    The South Shore Line — 107
    Freight on the South Shore Line — 114
    The South Shore in Transition — 117
    The Future of Northern Indiana Commuter Rail Service — 124
  CHAPTER 9: Amtrak: The Intercity Commuter Railroad — 127
    Regional Passenger Rail in California — 134
    Amtrak, the Freight Railroads, and Positive Train Control — 140
    Transformation of the Alton Route — 147
PART FOUR: Revitalization of Street Railways and New Light Rail — 155
  CHAPTER 10: Modernization, Tourism, or New Start — 157
    Southeastern Pennsylvania Transportation Authority — 160
    Norristown High Speed Line — 166
  CHAPTER 11: New Orleans Regional Transit Authority — 170
    Riverfront Streetcar Line — 175
    Canal Street Line — 178
  CHAPTER 12: Denver Regional Transportation District — 182

CHAPTER 13: Kenosha Transit Electric Streetcar 197
PART FIVE: Planning Commuter Rail on the Front Range 201
   CHAPTER 14: The Reluctant Return of Passenger Rail 203
      The Kite Route 206
   CHAPTER 15: The Kite Route, the Rocket, and Other Lines 217
      Commuter Rail and Tourism 222
   CHAPTER 16: A Public Rail Transportation Revolution 227
ENDNOTES 231
BIBLIOGRAPHY 253

PREFACE

Transportation of any sort is fundamental to any civilization or culture. Even if walking an average three miles per hour is the most that can be obtained, mobility is crucial to survival. Through invention and technology, faster and better ways to travel have been developed. From the horsecart to the train, to the automobile and airplane, developments in transportation have literally shaped the way people live. Transportation is a critical component that effects how communities are designed and built. From the high-density inner cities to the sprawling suburbs, most often geography and transportation determine the direction city planning and urban development will take.

Technological advancements move forward, leaving outmoded technologies behind. The evolution from horsecart to airplane or even spaceship seems a logical progression. Therefore, when the automobile superseded the trolley car and passenger train as people's preferred commuting option, an assumption was made that rail transportation would forever be obsolete. Ironically, the extreme popularity of the automobile began to effect its viability during peak-hour travel periods in major cities. As logic would dictate, a new technology would have to be developed to take its place. Yet, the durability and resilience of an old technology has been chosen in city after city as the preferred transportation alternative to the automobile. Light rail, the modern term for electric streetcar, and commuter rail, what was once just a local passenger train, were being reintroduced in cities that at one time thought to do away with the flanged wheel and steel rail. Passenger trains were also showing their desirability between cities, as regional and medium-haul trains competed against busy roadways and congested airports.

Along with light rail and commuter rail, passenger trains fit into two additional categories, they being intercity passenger rail and high-speed rail. Distances, the railroad infrastructure, its rolling stock and the type of service it was to provide, often determined which category a particular train best fit into. For instance, most light rail and high-speed lines were electrified, with only a few exceptions. Yet, light rail vehicles operated comparatively slowly and in many cases on city streets. These trains were designed to be people movers and were not intended to travel great distances. In contrast, electrified high-speed trains on a dedicated right-of-way could best be utilized connecting cities 100 to 500 miles apart. Intercity passenger trains operated this way also, but in North America, they were typically diesel powered and operated at speeds far less than the 125 mile per hour minimum that defined high-speed rail. Commuter trains were designed to be heavy-rail trains similar to intercity passenger and high-speed rail, even electrified in some cases. But unlike the other two, commuter rail was intended to serve shorter distances with less time between trains, connecting cites and suburbs within a heavily populated region. Moreover, the type of patron who often rode the trains further defined the type of train and its service. Commuter trains were intended to serve regular passengers who traveled very frequently. Intercity trains served more infrequent patrons who typically traveled farther than the average commuter.

What these differences in trains and rail service reflect is an entire history of rail transportation and its development, in search of the most viable and cost effective way to transport people. Some experiments succeeded, such as electrification, while others failed, for example the cable car and interurban lines. Experiments also took place in public policy, to determine what was to be the role of government in providing transportation for the masses.

For the most part, passenger rail in North America existed precariously in the hands of the private sector. Often public-private partnerships for passenger rail were difficult to negotiate without compromises being made by both the passenger rail agency and the railroad. Hauling freight for most for-profit railroads offered a far greater opportunity to make money than transporting passengers. This was also true during the height of rail travel, even though enough people were captive to riding passenger trains to justify the service.

Despite the high operating costs per passenger mile, public investment through frugally allocated government subsidy came to be a key component in the renaissance of passenger rail and rail mass transit. Taxpayer supported government subsidy, spurred on by the demands of the voters to no longer be stuck in traffic, was responsible for the rail resurgence.

New and innovative technologies may be able to disguise modern rail as part of a progressive evolution in transportation. But the revolution in rail travel can be found in people's attitude and appreciation for a 19th-century technology that was once thought to be outmoded.

PASSENGER RAIL

A Metra control cab car leads a Chicago-bound train, with the locomotive pushing, past the interlocking tower in South Barrington, Illinois, on May 21, 1997. Former Chicago & North Western bi-level cars on the Union Pacific Northwest Line, crossed the Elgin, Joliet & Eastern, a planned future commuter rail route for Chicago's Metra.

PART ONE

Roadway Gridlock and
Rail Mass Transportation

CHAPTER ONE

Congestion Mitigation Misconception

More is better. Bigger is better. According to the Surface Transportation Policy Project, increasing the number of streets and highways, or increasing the capacity of those roads, is the most popular solution to correcting automobile traffic congestion in the United States. Representing a national network of over 250 organizations, the non-profit Surface Transportation Policy Project was devoted to improving transportation throughout the nation. According to their studies, road building has failed as an effective measure to combat automobile traffic congestion. Frustrated with pouring billions of dollars into roads without the benefit of a significant decline in congestion, the U.S. government and a number of states have been exploring transportation alternatives to the automobile. One increasingly popular transportation alternative is rail.

"It turns out that the most common response to congestion, road building, is just making things worse," said Roy Kienitz, the executive director of the Surface Transportation Policy Project. "We don't need more of the same. We need new solutions that give people a way to avoid traffic jams." (1)

Based on information provided by the Texas Transportation Institute, the Surface Transportation Policy Project determined that severe congestion is not the result of too few streets and highways. Rather, congestion levels increased slightly within cities which added the most highway space per resident than those that built or widened fewer roads. Instead, sprawl city planning combined with a dependence on a single mode of transportation has brought daily commuters to a crawl in major metropolitan areas throughout the country.

For example, from 1983 to 1990, the sprawling suburbs of major U.S. cities influenced an average 69 percent increase in driving, according to the Surface Transportation Policy Project. As people abandoned limited and antiquated transit systems and began making longer trips by automobile, traffic congestion increased. Actual population growth was responsible for only 13 percent of the increase in automobile use. "Sprawl is making just about everyone drive farther and more often, and that fills up the roads," said Kienitz. (2)

In 1998, the federal government provided $5.8 billion to be used to build new highways or add lanes to existing ones. That figure increased to $9 billion in 1999. For fiscal year 2002, the U.S. Senate approved the final version of transportation appropriations, which came to be $32.9 billion to be spent on roads and $13 billion for aviation. Money for mass transit increased marginally from almost $6 billion in 1999, to $6.7 billion for 2002. (3) "By real numbers, far more people are driving cars than taking transit," said the president of the American Highway Users Alliance, William D. Fay. (4) "Most travel in the U.S. is still taking place over highways."(5)

The belief that more asphalt is the solution to severe automobile traffic congestion continued to permeate. Adding traffic lanes to increase roadway capacity seemed a logical concept. Although most transportation funding has gone toward road building, new money for transportation alternatives has been offered to the states by the federal government.

A true renaissance for rail and other transportation alternatives began with the Intermodal Surface Transportation Efficiency Act of 1991, otherwise known as ISTEA (iced tea). State governments, led by their departments of transportation, were issued block grants by the federal government to spend on transportation at their discretion. Flexible funding for such programs as the Congestion Mitigation and Air Quality Improvement program (CMAQ), and the Surface Transportation Program (STP), was available specifically to combat severe automobile traffic congestion in cities. Although many states still chose to use ISTEA and other grant money on roads, states like Washington, California and Illinois chose to embrace rail as a transportation alternative to the automobile. Before ISTEA, according to the Surface Transportation Policy Project, only about $3 billion was allocated to the states for public transportation in 1990, which included buses, trolleys and trains. Since 1990, money for transit more than doubled. (6)

From 1996 to 1999, transit ridership in the United States increased by more than 15 percent. According to the American Public Transportation Association (APTA), ridership on public transit increased 4.5 percent in 1999 compared to 1998. Meanwhile, automobile travel increased only 2 percent.(7) Between 1999 and the year 2000, transit ridership continued to rise by 3.5 percent. Automobile travel staggered at an increase of only 0.047 percent growth. For the third year in a row, public transportation use increased faster on a percentage basis than automobile use. "These figures show that a decades-old trend of declining transit and increasing driving has been reversed," said Kienitz. "Driving isn't shrinking, but it's not growing, either.... Before we can say Americans have made a wholesale change in the way they travel, the trend has to hold over ten years. Still, this is change both on paper, in statistics, and in people's minds. And it's a reason to pay attention.(8)

In New York City, for example, daily trips on bus, subway and commuter rail systems averaged 5.1 million in 1997. By the year 2000, daily trips averaged 7.2 million, according to New York's Metropolitan Transportation Authority. Nationwide public transportation use was at its highest in 1946, according to APTA. Travel in the United States on buses, trolleys and trains peaked at 23.4 billion trips that year. In 1972, ridership was at its lowest at 6.5 billion trips. Travel on public mass transit vehicles steadily increased beginning in 1995, to 9.4 billion trips in 1999, about the level it was back in 1960. (9)

Local transportation planners observed the eagerness with which people in some metropolitan areas were willing to abandon their cars to ride rail mass transit. For example, when TRAX light rail trolleys began operating in January 2000 in Salt Lake City, Utah, transportation planners estimated daily ridership to be no more than 14,000 patrons. Actual ridership on TRAX trolleys averaged almost 20,000 daily commuters. "People are going into town again who haven't been there for years," said John Inglish, general manager for the Utah Transit Authority. (10)

Despite this and other rail transportation success stories throughout North America, the prospect of operating a light rail line or commuter railroad for profit remained too elusive for the private sector to back such projects financially. Therefore, transportation alternatives such as rail depended on government subsidy. Similar to highways and aviation, rail mass transit and passenger rail as a transportation alternative would not be forthcoming without government involvement. Yet, according to the Surface Transportation Policy Project, almost 90 percent of flexible federal transportation funding went to traditional highway projects as the nation moved slower and slower into the 21st century. Less than 7 percent was actually spent on providing new modes of transportation. As a result, the driving public had little or no choice but to add to the traffic congestion on major street and highway arterials in those North American cities which offered no viable alternatives. (11)

To understand the renaissance of rail mass transit and passenger rail, a firm explanation of what causes severe automobile traffic congestion must be made clear. More than just too many automobiles on too few roadways, geography and city planning are other contributing factors. Significant also is an historical context to understanding how severe congestion came to be and how trains and trolleys lost favor with the public in the first place. The history of such commuter railroads as Maryland's MARC, Caltrain in San Francisco, Metra in Chicago, and Indiana's South Shore Line serve as examples of how private sector passenger railroading was almost abandoned in favor of other modes. These government subsidized transit agencies turned failing commuter rail services into modern transportation alternatives.

From an understanding of why people are stuck in traffic to an historical context that explains how mobility has changed over time, a careful analysis of modern rail mass transportation is then required. Examples, ranging from California high-speed rail to New Orleans streetcars, cover a wide spectrum of the different kinds of rail transportation, their uses and applications. Intercity high-speed rail projects represented the future of medium-haul rail transportation as potentially preferable to flying or driving. Within heavily populated regions, Denver RTD and the Trinity Railway Express in Dallas promised to restore mobility in places where roadway travel was at one time the only option. Further, more than basic commuter service was being offered by transit agencies in Philadelphia, New Orleans, and Kenosha, Wisconsin. An effort to combine history and tourism with commuting was taking place to increase ridership and improve transit's image by making streetcars fun to ride. Finally, taking the lessons learned from mobility-challenged regions and their solutions to restore mobility, a strategy for passenger rail on Colorado's Front Range is considered. Stalled plans for commuter rail along the eastern edge of the Rocky Mountains inspired an analysis of what could be done. If tried and true tactics combined with innovative new ideas are applied, a new and potentially successful transportation alternative could restore the region's rapidly deteriorating mobility.

Although other examples of successful passenger rail and rail mass transit initiatives exist, these case studies provide a general overview of the changes in transportation which have taken place across the United States. Each offers a unique perspective on how to approach the problems of implementing and providing viable train or trolley service, while at the same time reflecting an overall trend toward rail transportation. That trend is based on a background of years of automobile oriented transportation and city planning. Understanding how roadways became congested, and how poor urban planning contributed to Americans being stuck in traffic, is fundamental to understanding the resurgence of passenger rail.

PASSENGER RAIL

Billboards for new housing developments advertise to automobile drivers as they pass under the Burlington Northern Santa Fe triple-track raceway. Homes were for sale in an Aurora, Illinois, subdivision named Concord Valley. In October 1995, slant nosed F40PH-2M 199 powered an Aurora-bound express through Naperville, but did not stop.

CHAPTER TWO

Modes of Transportation and City Planning

Transportation planning is a fundamental component of urban planning. How a community is planned and built is often dependent on the primary mode of transportation envisioned for that society. For example, cities were once constructed with the pedestrian and horse cart in mind. Business and residential areas were built within close proximity to each other because the fastest and most efficient modes of transportation, the foot and the hoof, were very limited in speed and capacity. The development of railroads and street railways enabled cities to expand while also decreasing in density. New residential areas were built outside of what became a city's central business district. Rail mass transit was the fastest and most efficient mode of transportation available, which enabled people to live away from the part of town where they worked and shopped.

The automobile was the next major development. It provided a significantly faster and more efficient mode of transportation within cities. This enabled city development to sprawl. Not only did residential areas move farther away from the central business district, but businesses were able to move away as well. Businesses discovered that they could succeed by moving out of the congested central business district and into the less dense suburbs. This caused central business districts in many large cities to be reduced in size and importance. The railroads were especially affected, since they were originally built to serve the central business districts of most North American cities. Large numbers of people stopped riding trains and trolley cars to downtown. In many cases, they drove their automobiles from suburb to neighboring suburb, avoiding the central business district entirely.

Well-established rail companies bore other financial burdens as well. Stock and bond holders rightfully demanded financial returns for their investments in rail transportation. Tax burdens, including bridge maintenance requirements and paving assessments for street railways, added costs and took away from profits. Further, there was an unwillingness among most people to accept a fare increase to ride a streetcar above the time-honored five cent charge. Therefore, many rail lines and street railways were abandoned, even further isolating metropolitan central business districts. Nine million Americans moved to the suburbs during the mid-1950s. Also in 1950, an automobile accessible regional shopping center was established in Seattle, Washington. It was the world's first suburban mall, with many more to follow. (12)

June 28, 1956, marked the beginning of the Interstate Highway System, later named the Dwight D. Eisenhower System of Interstate and Defense Highways. President Eisenhower signed legislation authorizing construction of 41,000 miles of high speed, limited access highway. The interstates were designed for the convenience of automobile travel by civilians in peace time or the quick and easy deployment of troops and military equipment in war time. But even interstate highways, particularly in cities, could not end urban traffic congestion. Roads funded by government subsidy, which once enabled the automobile to move about freely, became congested within major metropolitan areas. Further, there were not enough tax dollars or real estate acres available to build and maintain the kinds of roads necessary to keep up with the demand. The automobile was choking on its own popularity. In stop-and-go traffic, the automobile was no longer fast and efficient, pleasant and comfortable.

The Texas Transportation Institute determined that only 34 percent of the nation's major roads were congested in 1982, compared to 59 percent in 2001. Only 18 U.S. cities suffered from severe automobile traffic congestion problems in 1988. The top five cities at that time with the most severe congestion were Los Angeles and San Francisco, California; Chicago, Illinois; Miami, Florida; and Washington, D.C. By 2001, Los Angeles and the San Francisco-Oakland area still ranked number one and number two respectively, demonstrating that efforts to increase road building failed to make a significant difference in relieving congestion on California's West Coast. Automobile traffic congestion levels in Denver, Colorado, ranked third in 2001, according to the Texas Transportation Institute's annual mobility study. Miami maintained its position at number four, and Phoenix, Arizona, and Chicago tied for fifth. The mobility study was conducted based on information provided by various state and local agencies and the Federal Highway Administration. (13)

The causes for increased automobile use nationally were identified as an increase in suburban living, inadequate public transportation to the suburbs, the scattering of jobs, and more women in the work place. By 1997, automobile traffic congestion ranked second behind crime as the social problem which Americans said bothered them the most. Alternatives had to be explored. Ironically, old-fashioned rail became a viable way in which large cities could mitigate the effects of severe automobile traffic congestion and its impact on the public.

To encourage the expansion of rail mass transit in Toronto, Canada, statistical studies were undertaken during the late 1980s to measure the impacts of such a rail service. The study found that a typical traffic lane can carry no more than 1,000 persons per hour driving and riding in automobiles. If the same traffic lane were reserved for mass transit vehicles only, persons per hour capacity would increase to 5,500. (14) Regarding commuter railroads, according to the Association of American Railroads, a one-way track of a double track mainline can accommodate the same number of passengers as does a highway of ten lanes. Moreover, a twelve lane freeway requires a right-of-way that is almost 225 feet wide, if built to interstate highway standards. A double track railroad right-of-way needs only to be 50 feet wide. Beginning as an experimental operation in May of 1967, the government of Ontario, operating as Toronto's GO Transit, succeeded in luring many suburban commuters out of their automobiles and onto its trains. About 2.5 million Canadians rode GO Transit that first year. A major advantage was the commuter railroad's space to capacity ratio versus roadways. (15)

The first major requirement in operating a successful rail commuter line is the development of an acceptable and expandable infrastructure. This includes the right-of-way, the track on which the trains are to run, adequate station stops with plentiful parking, and trains to run on that infrastructure. Second, the railroad must provide convenient and frequent scheduling of arriving and departing trains. The third requirement is marketing. People must be made aware that a viable transportation alternative to driving is available. Once these things are accomplished, a viable passenger rail alternative is possible.

As transportation planners throughout major metropolitan areas considered the use of rail mass transit as an alternative to severe automobile traffic congestion, they were generally persuaded by five important decision-making guidelines: 1) identify and study all possible modes of transportation; 2) evaluate the advantages, disadvantages, and consequences of each transportation alternative; 3) evaluate social values and goals; 4) determine the best modes available to meet specific transportation needs; 5) select a mode of transportation which will most likely meet the needs of the public, within the limits of predetermined financial boundaries. Transportation planners used guidelines such as these to determine whether or not subsidized rail mass transit is the most appropriate transportation alternative for their large city. The transportation objective of Chicago, Illinois, was stated clearly in the Chicago Area Transportation Study of 1962. "It does not matter, basically, whether people in urban areas move by bus, automobile, suburban railroad, or elevated-subway train, as long as the main purpose is achieved." (16)

Commuter rail, light rail, and intercity passenger rail experienced a rebirth at the turn of the 21st century. For instance, people took 40 million trips on GO Transit during the year 2000, setting a record high for ridership on Toronto commuter trains and continuing a four-year trend. Further, this movement toward better subsidized mass transit helped revitalize the once abandoned central business districts of many communities, large and small. (17)

A major contributor to traffic congestion is urban sprawl. Neighborhoods and businesses are built oriented to major thoroughfares, including interstate highways. Thus interstates and other major arterials generate the growth that makes them quickly exceed capacity. Housing, commercial, and industrial uses are attracted to major thoroughfares. The busier the roads become, the more all sorts of uses, commercial and residential, strive to locate along them. Roads generate the growth that makes them obsolete.

The Interstate Highway System was originally designed to solely connect U.S. cities, each city accessed by one or just a few interchanges. As interstates became urbanized, more interchanges were built, effectively turning urban interstates into major local streets. More people are encouraged to use interstates because developers build along or near these supposedly high speed automobile expressways.

Automobile traffic congestion is caused by a high number of travelers, usually commuting alone, using the most popular roads at the most popular times. Too many people using the most popular form of transportation, the automobile, converge on an increasingly inadequate street or highway arterial crowded beyond its designed capacity. Often roads are built without the foresight that population growth can cause a significant increase in automobile use greater than the actual increase in population. Rapid growth creates a swamping effect which inhibits the ability of local governments to keep up with, or control, automobile traffic congestion. As a result, government-funded projects to accommodate increased automobile traffic are completed long after the original need first developed. Such projects include widening existing streets and highways or building new ones. The problem with accommodating increased automobile use with road building is that the expensive expansion of roadways is only a temporary solution. In time, traffic will surpass the new road's capacity, making it again inadequate. This is the conundrum which has kept cities such as Los Angeles and San Francisco at the top of the list of the nation's most congested urban areas for well over a decade, despite continued road building efforts.

Urban sprawl is the result of the popularity of low density living. This kind of suburban living could be mass transit accessible if areas of business were centralized. City activity centers, however, sprawl with the neighborhoods. This effectively replaces a city's real downtown with multiple shopping centers, typically located at interstate interchanges and along other major thoroughfares throughout the outlying suburbs. If businesses and neighborhoods are scattered, people cannot conveniently travel in large numbers utilizing the same mass transit system. The financial commitment required to connect all of the neighborhoods, businesses, and shopping centers with mass transit is prohibitive in haphazardly sprawling communities. The city of Toronto, Ontario, considered the idea of developing "planned" communities in an effort to better deal with the problem of population growth. Toronto visualized three possible strategies: "spread," "central," and "nodal." (18)

Many North American cities often embraced the spread strategy. The spread strategy is no strategy at all. Rather, municipalities allow land developers to build businesses and neighborhoods in proximity to one another, spread out over a large land area, connected by massive roads and freeways. This encourages automobile use and typically leads to traffic congestion problems no matter how many roads are built or how much existing roads are expanded.

Directly opposed to urban sprawl is the central strategy. The idea is to build and rebuild within existing metropolitan areas, concentrating population growth in high-density housing and neighborhoods. Automobile use is usually restricted by the condensed nature of high-density building, resulting in a greater dependence on public transportation. This strategy is criticized, however, by the fact that people often prefer not to live so close together or near the industrialized parts of the city.

The term "nodal" means a swelling as opposed to spreading. The idea behind the nodal strategy is to centralize businesses into a few big clusters, but allow residential suburban sprawl. All businesses and neighborhoods would be automobile accessible. An effort would be made, however, to encourage the use of public transportation. People living in sprawled out neighborhoods could access a rail mass transit line equipped with local park & ride stops along the transit route. They would then take the train or trolley into a centralized business district.

Other city planning strategies include the "hub and spoke" and "mixed-use" approach. Chicago, Illinois, offers an excellent example of hub and spoke planning. Suburban villages fan out from a major city along railroads and major roadways. Those Chicago suburbs located along commuter rail routes offer a mass transportation mobility option not available to roadway-access-only communities.

In some ways Chicago's suburban villages embraced an unofficial version of mixed use city planning as well, also described as New Urbanism. Each community has its own local grocery store and other businesses to serve nearby residences, while major businesses are clustered in downtown Chicago. However, New Urbanism is truly defined as residential, business and entertainment outlets existing together, all within walking distance or connected by mass transit. People still have to drive to get around within many of Chicago's suburbs. Further, as automobile-oriented suburbs grow and attract businesses out of the major inner cities, "cross commuting" between suburbs becomes a factor in causing severe automobile traffic congestion.

Cross commuting occurs when people live in one suburban community and work in another. If a person lives in community "A" but goes to work in community "B," and if another person lives in community "B" but works in community "A," these people are said to be "cross commuting." (19) Each new suburban community adds to the web of cross commuters. Congestion relieving strategies such as mass transit or ride sharing become less feasible. If people lived, worked and played within the same local area, cross commuting would be significantly reduced. Although people will always travel outside of their immediate community from time to time, the strategy behind mixed-use New Urbanism is to encourage less travel between work, home, and local services. Cross commuting also encourages driving alone. More than any other factor, single occupancy vehicles contribute the most to peak-hour traffic congestion.

When people commuting through severe congestion reach their level of maximum tolerance, they do one of three things, depending on what options are available to them. They either choose a new travel route, commute at off-peak hours, or find a different transportation option other than driving alone. Therefore, alternatives such as ride sharing, cycling or mass transit offer the most value and encourage a significant number of users when the preferred mode of transportation, a personal automobile, is no longer available.

The potential of ride sharing to significantly reduce high traffic levels is greatest if large numbers of people participate. Like mass transit, however, the drawback of ride sharing is that people would have to give up having a car conveniently available for immediate use. People also have to coordinate their schedules with others in order to make ride sharing work. This is not always convenient since people's schedules often fluctuate. Frequent service on a mass transit system can often accommodate people's varying schedules better than ride sharing.

On some freeways, local governments designate the farthest left lane or lanes for HOV, or High Occupancy Vehicle use only. Automobiles carrying two or more people, depending on the law, are the only ones permitted to use these lanes. The risk of designating an HOV lane is that, if it fails to attract vehicles, it could lead to increased traffic congestion. A mass of lone drivers may be creeping along in the right lanes while the HOV lanes remain largely unused. Further, vehicles with multiple passengers in HOV lanes still have to cross regular traffic to enter or exit the freeway.

Another idea is to establish a system of toll roads to discourage commuting during peak-hour travel times. The thought being that people would use alternative free-access roads that were not as popular or use mass transit to avoid paying the toll. However, even if the added expense of tolls discourages some people from driving, people will often adjust to the financial burden of paying tolls. They would have to adjust to paying a transit fare if they chose that alternative anyway. Imposing a huge tax on gasoline would also fail to discourage driving for the same reason. People would get used to paying the inflated rate. Moreover, traditional toll booths cause lines to form, further contributing to the problem of congestion. Tolls are usually intended to help pay off the expense of new or privately built highways, not to discourage driving.

Roadway traffic congestion threatens mobility, but it also threatens air quality. As it takes longer for people to drive to their destinations, more emissions are produced from combustion-engine vehicles. This is particularly true when cars are stopped in traffic with the motor idling. In an effort to help state governments meet air quality standards established by the Clean Air Act of 1990, the federal government created the Congestion Mitigation and Air Quality Improvement program, or CMAQ. According to the Surface Transportation Policy Project, by the turn of the 21st century, 42 percent of federal funding through CMAQ went toward long-term solutions. These included, but were not limited to, the creation or expansion of mass transit systems. Fifty percent of CMAQ funding went into short-term air quality solutions such as emissions testing. However, state governments spent about eight percent on road expansion projects, arguing that more and bigger street and highway arterials would relieve traffic congestion and thus improve air quality. The Surface Transportation Policy Project did not recognize road expansion as a responsible use of CMAQ money towards the reduction of air pollution created by automobiles. (20)

California was one of the leading states in the nation to fund major road building projects before the age of congestion and air quality concerns. With the world's seventh largest economy and the nation's largest state population, California became a leader in the trend to embrace rail mass transit and passenger rail by the turn of the 21st century. The state's population was expected to grow from about 34 million residents in 2002, according to the California Department of Finance, to an estimated 50 million by 2030. (21) State officials were aware that such a sizable number of automobiles on area roadways could not be accommodated. To preserve mobility throughout California, a $25 billion 700-mile electrified high-speed rail network was proposed. A $10 billion bond initiative, which required voter approval, was signed by Governor Gray Davis in September 2002. It was to be one of the most ambitious of the nation's proposed passenger rail initiatives. (22)

Automobile traffic congestion is an almost impossible problem to solve, especially since building higher capacity roads encourages more people to commute alone in their cars. Mass transit, rail or otherwise, is only a partial solution to severe roadway congestion. Rather, it offers people an alternative to driving, if they choose to take it. People are truly "stuck" in traffic only when driving is their only transportation option.

The three car garage to be built onto this new suburban home in Arvada, Colorado, suggests metro Denver's primary mode of transportation, the automobile. But is it sustainable? Sprawl city planning contributes to severe automobile traffic congestion and discourages mass transit use.

CHAPTER THREE

From the Past, an Electric Train of the Future

Electrically-propelled rail rapid transit is no stranger to California. Despite its reputation for massive street and highway construction throughout the 20th century, California at one time had two of the country's best electric interurban railways. A nearly complete passenger rail infrastructure was in place to serve the state's population. Railroads built around 1900 were designed to easily add capacity with anticipated urban development. Northern Californians were whisked between cities at 73 miles per hour on the Sacramento Northern. In Southern California, Pacific Electric patrons enjoyed seven and a half minute headways on the busiest routes.

An electric interurban railway, the Sacramento Northern was one of the most far reaching of the nation's intercity passenger rail short lines. Built to high standards for hauling both passenger and freight trains, through trains traversed 183 miles between San Francisco and Chico via Sacramento. The interurban was widely known for a fast, comfortable ride and excellent service.

The oldest portion of the route was built by a predecessor interurban, the Northern Electric. A line powered by electrified third rail was built south from Chico to Oroville and then on to Sacramento via Marysville. Trains began operating to Oroville and Marysville in 1906. Frequent through rail service to Sacramento was inaugurated on September 7, 1907.

A second Sacramento Northern predecessor, the Oakland Antioch & Eastern, built an electric interurban northeast from Oakland, a city across the San Francisco Bay from San Francisco, to Sacramento. The interurban was built to very high standards compared to most other electrified short lines throughout the country. This was true despite no bridge being built across the Sacramento River north of the junction at West Pittsburg. An open-dock ferry was employed to shuttle up to six rail cars from one side of the river to the other. Through service between Oakland and Sacramento began on September 3, 1913.

In 1928, the two mainlines and their branches were consolidated under common ownership by steam railroad Western Pacific. The railroad's purpose behind the merger was to use its interurban subsidiary, the Sacramento Northern, as a feeder route for freight traffic. Despite being under Western Pacific control, the interurban maintained a separate identity because electric operations were largely incompatible with a steam railroad. Sacramento Northern freight and passenger trains operated in the streets of many of the communities served. Interurban cars shared track with local streetcars in Chico, Marysville and Sacramento.

Between cities, speed was of the essence as 73 mile-per-hour interurban cars were assigned to such trains as the "Comet" and the "Meteor." Even with the ferry crossing, the trip between Oakland and Sacramento could be made in under three hours. Service was top notch, especially on those occasions when observation dining cars were added to some mainline trains.

Despite its reputation for excellent service, the Sacramento Northern began suffering from competition with steam railroad Southern Pacific, the rising popularity of the automobile, the stock market crash of October 1929, and the ensuing depression that followed during the Thirties. Direct rail access to San Francisco, which began in early 1939, was not enough to reverse the decision by railroad management to gradually discontinue all passenger service. By November 1940, commuter rail service had been reduced to San Francisco-Pittsburg, short of the ferry crossing over the Sacramento River. This service ended on June 30, 1941, although freight service for parent Western Pacific continued.

The Pacific Electric interurban was a conglomerate of predecessor railroads, the larger systems originating in the Los Angeles area, including an original 1901 Pacific Electric. The oldest line, completed from Los Angeles to Pasadena in 1895, was acquired from the Los Angeles Pacific by Henry Huntington in 1898. Henry Huntington was the primary founder of Pacific Electric, who also served as president of steam railroad Southern Pacific. He was the nephew of C.P. Huntington, a powerful investor who was famous for helping to build the Central Pacific, the railroad's original name before it was changed to Southern Pacific.

Following its official 1901 charter, Henry Huntington's Pacific Electric began constructing a number of major routes, including lines that served Covina, San Pedro, Long Beach, and Newport Beach. Huntington shared ownership of Pacific Electric and other interurban properties with the Southern Pacific. Eight interurban railroads, all under common control, were merged in September 1911. They were Pacific Electric, Los Angeles Pacific, Huntington's Los Angeles Interurban, Los Angeles & Redondo, and four smaller interurbans that were also Huntington properties in San Bernardino.

Operated more like a suburban electrified railroad than a typical interurban, the new Pacific Electric ran the most modern equipment at relatively high speeds with frequent headways on the busiest routes. The bulk of the system operated over private right-of-way with station stops, although trains in certain areas did operate on city streets. Street running occurred in Glendale, Pasadena, Santa Monica, Hollywood, and in downtown Los Angeles leading out primarily to the western lines. A complete suburban rail mass transit network was in place, well ahead of anticipated population growth. Once a connection was built between the Los Angeles core system and the lines in San Bernardino, Pacific Electric was then arguably a true intercity rail carrier. The 58 mile line to San Bernardino opened for through service on July 11, 1914.

By 1915, Pacific Electric was one of the finest of the nation's electric interurban railways. It built or acquired 760 route miles, including lines shared with other railroads, and had over a thousand miles of track during the peak of its existence. The California Railroad Commission estimated that the investment made to create Pacific Electric, the nation's largest interurban electric railway, was about $100 million. That was nearly ten percent of the total amount invested in all U.S. interurban lines. (23)

Revenue income increased until 1923, as rail traffic rose sharply due to a boom in urban development. The encroachment of the automobile, however, began negatively effecting passenger ridership for both Pacific Electric and Southern Pacific. After 1924, parent Southern Pacific began losing interest in local passenger service, including its interurban subsidiary. But it took the Depression to slice Pacific Electric's revenues in half. Between 1938 and 1941, Pacific Electric management significantly cut passenger service, as recommended by the California Railroad Commission. California was being built for automobiles. Neighborhood and business development was scattering, making mass transit for rail or bus far less viable.

As was typical of U.S. interurbans, Pacific Electric also hauled freight, especially to interchange with the Southern Pacific. But about 75 percent of the railroad's revenue had come from hauling passengers. Even by as late as 1953, freight service contributed to only half of the total revenue earned by the company. This was during a time when the nation's remaining interurbans relied heavily, if not exclusively, on the revenues gained by hauling freight. The only Pacific Electric passenger service left by then called at Long Beach and San Pedro, and also served Bellflower, Hollywood and Burbank. (24)

In 1954, Pacific Electric sold the remainder of its passenger rail service to Metropolitan Coach Lines, but retained ownership of the tracks and right-of-way to continue hauling freight. Metropolitan Coach Lines never intended to continue operating passenger trains, but attempted to abandon them in favor of operating buses. Local protest did delay the abandonment of some service for a while. The last Pacific Electric rail route to have passenger service was the line to Long Beach. It was abandoned by the Los Angeles Metropolitan Transportation Authority, a public agency, on April 9, 1961.

Local electrified rail rapid transit service would not return between Los Angeles and Long Beach until 1991. The Long Beach line, designated the Blue Line, was the first new light rail route to open in the Los Angeles area. After 30 years of automobile dominance, a major rail mass transit initiative was being implemented by the Southern California Regional Rail Authority. Los Angeles light rail, marketed as Metrorail, would become part of a complex, integrated web of subways, light rail, bus routes, and full-sized commuter rail. The six-county Southern California Regional Rail Authority (SCRRA) was comprised of representatives from Los Angeles, Ventura, Orange, Riverside, San Bernardino, and San Diego counties. By 1995, the Los Angeles Metropolitan Transportation Authority had developed a $75 billion 20-year plan to have 95 miles of new light rail built. The ambitious Los Angeles area transit plan also included improvements to bus service. (25)

"We have a very immature transportation system in Los Angeles," said former Metropolitan Transportation Authority chief executive officer Joseph Drew. "We're going to have to work hard to catch up." (26) More than a year after it opened, Metrorail's Blue Line surpassed ridership projections by 20 to 25 percent. (27)

Voter-approved passenger rail bond funds, from Propositions 108 and 116, were released by the California Transportation Commission to begin implementing SCRRA commuter rail projects in Southern California. The first $66.8 million allocated would enable three new commuter rail lines to be developed from Los Angeles Union Station to Moorpark, Santa Clarita, and Pomona. The new service was marketed as Metrolink. Amtrak was contracted to operate the trains, which were pressed into service on October 26, 1992. Utilizing upgraded track shared with Amtrak and the existing freight railroads, the entire system would radiate from Union Station and serve about 60 stations along 400 miles of railroad. The project was expected to take over 30 years to complete. (28)

At least two former Pacific Electric lines were purchased from the Southern Pacific by SCRRA for Metrolink commuter service. Diesel-powered bi-level commuter trains accessed Los Angeles Union Station via the old Pacific Electric State Street line and the Baldwin Park Branch. The old Baldwin Park line was in a serious state of disrepair and had to be rebuilt from the below-roadbed foundation on up. A portion of the old Santa Fe Pasadena line was also purchased to finish the connection between Los Angeles and San Bernardino. Commuter trains switched onto the former Santa Fe Railway east of Claremont to complete their 56.6 mile journey. Metrolink's share of the cost was $125 million to purchase and upgrade a conglomeration of lines that served the same purpose as Pacific Electric's Los Angeles-San Bernardino line built back in 1914. A grand opening in San Bernardino on May 15, 1993, celebrated the introduction of Metrolink rail service, which began transporting commuters to and from Los Angeles the following day. (29)

"The mistake everyone makes is to think in terms of either subways or buses, instead of looking at the whole array of systems Los Angeles needs because of its unique commuting patterns. Subways, buses, light rail, ride-sharing, staggered work hours—we may need all of them," said Richard Katz, former chairman of the California Assembly transportation committee. (30)

Although not alone, California unknowingly traded its future mobility by embracing the automobile as its single primary mode of local transportation. By the turn of the 21st century, government officials were actively looking for ways to break California free from the dominance of freeways. Commuter rail and light rail were just the start of what government officials had in mind for the future of state wide passenger rail.

The Sacramento Northern and Pacific Electric interurbans failed, as did so many other passenger railroads across the country, because the automobile became the preferred choice for local travelers. Without the need for a transportation alternative, California could easily give up its interurbans for roadways. Sprawl city planning and scattered development challenged Metrorail and Metrolink to reconnect Los Angeles with its outlaying suburbs by rail. Nonetheless, as people demanded their political leaders to provide a rail alternative to severe automobile traffic congestion, Los Angeles and other parts of California were being reconnected by passenger rail. To free

Californians from mobility problems caused by congestion, government officials were seriously considering asking those same citizens to approve the spending of billions of dollars for a massive high-speed rail initiative. The reason political leaders considered such a highly controversial proposal was they believed that a majority of California voters might say yes.

California's Ambitious High-Speed Rail Project

To meet its clean air goals and offer a solution to crowded airports and congested roadways within the state, California considered electrified high-speed passenger rail as a possible transportation supplement. In conjunction with other modes of transportation, high-speed rail was to give Californians more mobility without contributing significantly to the problem of air pollution. Electric passenger trains were envisioned to be California's most viable solution.

"The existing transportation infrastructure will be more efficient and productive with high-speed trains, which will rely on the freeway, highway, urban transit, and conventional rail networks for access," stated the California High-Speed Rail Authority's Final High-Speed Train Plan. (31) "The Authority's legislative mandate is to develop a high-speed train system that is coordinated with the state's existing transportation network, particularly intercity rail and bus lines, commuter rail lines and urban rail transit lines." (32)

True high-speed rail is defined as electrically propelled rail transport traveling at speeds greater than 150 miles per hour. To be viable, trains connect major metropolitan areas which are about 100 to 500 miles apart. To travel safely at such high velocities, the railroad right-of-way must be completely grade separated. This means that other forms of transportation, such as roads for automobile traffic or conventional railroad lines, must bridge over or pass under the high-speed guideway. No road/railroad grade crossings would be built. Also, no conventional trains would operate on the dedicated electric railway. Slower trains not built to the standards of the high-speed rail infrastructure could disrupt the synergy of high-speed operations and impose a potential safety hazard. Given the problem of incompatibility, connectivity at stations to conventional passenger rail was a priority for the California High-Speed Rail Authority.

The high-speed guideway must be built as straight as possible and utilize the most modern and sophisticated signaling and automatic train control systems. Based on proven high-speed rail systems in other countries, fast electric trains are safer and much more energy efficient than automobiles or airplanes, according to the Final High-Speed Train Plan. By the end of the 20th century, an overall five billion passengers traveled safely on such trains as the 186 mile-per-hour bullet train, introduced in Japan in 1964, the French TGV introduced in 1981, and the 1991 German ICE trains. (33)

The governor of California and the state legislature authorized the establishment of the California Intercity High-Speed Rail Commission in 1993. The commission was charged with developing the framework for implementing 200 mile-per-hour high-speed rail within the state. The state legislature then created the California High-Speed Rail Authority in 1996 to develop a plan to finance, construct, and operate an intercity high-speed passenger rail system. The plan that was developed described a 700-mile network serving California's largest cities.

By the year 2020, the Final High-Speed Train Plan projected that approximately 32 million intercity passengers and ten million commuters would be riding the new high-speed trains. During peak travel periods, trains would operate 15-minutes apart, on average, throughout the system. At full capacity, trains would operate three minutes apart, although the Final High-Speed Train Plan projected that, even by the year 2050, the rail network would be carrying less than half its designed passenger capacity. (34)

In contrast, at least three California airports were expected to experience increasing capacity problems over the course of 20 years, including San Francisco International (SFO), Los Angeles International (LAX), and Lindberg Field in San Diego. From 1997 to 2016, the number of aircraft passengers in California was expected to increase by 50 percent. An estimated 80 percent increase was expected from 1997 to 2050. Airport expansion was uncertain, however, given California's noise pollution restrictions and other environmental impact concerns. (35) Thomas Windmuller of the International Air Transport Association, a former airline vice president, said, "Even to the extent that high-speed rail does take customers from airlines on individual, relatively short-haul routes, in doing so, valuable (take-off and landing) slots are freed up for airlines to devote to the relatively more profitable longer-haul routes." (36)

The environmental impacts that airports impose have rendered them incompatible within civic centers or neighborhoods. As a result, airports are typically built away from central business districts and where people live. In contrast, railroad stations tend to coexist well within living and working environments. This improves people's accessibility to passenger rail without compromising their livelihood and may actually cause an increase to the value of adjacent property. The positive impact of high-speed rail stations on surrounding land values, according to the California Intercity High-Speed Rail Commission's High-Speed Rail Summary Report & 20-Year Action Plan, was projected to be $1.7 to $2 billion through 2020. (37)

"In combination with appropriate local land use policies, the increased accessibility afforded by the high-speed service could encourage more intensive development and may lead to higher property values around stations," stated the Final High-Speed Train Plan. Moreover, the actual development of station stops as multi-use business and retail centers could be an asset that benefits the railroad. The potential non-rail fare revenue generated at each of the 23 proposed train stations systemwide was projected to range from $730,000 to $1.8 million annually. (38)

The high-speed rail double track guideway would be built with sidings at station stops. The sidings would allow express and other trains to pass stopped trains without disruption. High-level boarding platforms at stations would facilitate the boarding and detraining of passengers. High platforms and other station amenities would meet the requirements of disabled passengers as stipulated by the Americans with Disabilities Act of 1990. Ten-car, ADA-compliant electric trainsets were expected to seat 650 passengers. Trains would operate between 100 and 150 miles-per-hour within urban areas, but possibly exceed 200 miles-per-hour between major cities.

The first segment of the $25 billion high-speed rail network would be built between San Francisco and Los Angeles, via Fresno and Bakersfield in the San Joaquin Valley. Extensions off the core system to Sacramento and San Diego would eventually be constructed, according to the Final High-Speed Train Plan. By then 90 percent of California's heavily populated regions would be served by electrified high-speed rail. The metropolitan centers of Sacramento, Los Angeles, San Diego, and the San Francisco Bay Area would be served, as well as cities within the San Joaquin Valley and elsewhere. "Implementation of the high-speed rail system would show that the State is committed to making the infrastructure investments necessary to sustain economic growth and quality of life," stated the Summary Report & Action Plan. (39)

State officials estimated that $14.7 billion would be necessary just to connect San Francisco and Los Angeles with high-speed rail, the nation's busiest air route. Fast passenger trains would compete directly with the airlines for patronage between major cities. But secondary markets, which are marginally served by the airlines, would benefit greatly from being located on or near high-speed rail lines. "We will get residents from all over California," said Bakersfield mayor Harvey Hall. "They can find affordable housing here and commute to downtown Los Angeles in less than an hour." Bakersfield is located in the San Joaquin Valley, 112 miles north of Los Angeles. (40)

According to the Summary Report & Action Plan, secondary travel markets, such as Bakersfield and Fresno, received inadequate service from commercial airlines. Expensive and infrequent flights made air travel from the San Joaquin Valley less desirable, a problem that high-speed rail could at least mitigate as a transportation alternative. Further, within the San Joaquin Valley in particular, thick ground fog and other weather problems frequently disrupted airline and automobile travel. Trains are rarely effected by climate conditions such as rain or fog and therefore operate much more reliably.

Instead of competing with the airlines for passengers in secondary markets, electric trains were intended to serve them. The trains would take away the need for airlines to serve regional airports. International airports, near or at capacity, would be able to reduce regional air service, allowing for an increase in more lucrative transcontinental and international flights. Even without a high-speed rail alternative, a decline in intrastate flights could occur as the potential demand for long-distance air service increases. Severe automobile traffic congestion and reduced regional air service would mean fewer transportation options for California travelers.

San Francisco International Airport (SFO) was located on the proposed core rail system between San Francisco and Los Angeles. Los Angeles International Airport (LAX), however, was not. The proposed core rail system would terminate at Los Angeles Union Station, an important rail hub in Southern California and identified as the busiest passenger terminal on the proposed high-speed network. More rail passengers were already using Los Angeles Union Station in 1999 than in 1949.

Once fully operational, the California high-speed rail system was expected to divert approximately 45 percent of the traveling public from flying to riding the rails. This especially included regional air travel. To ride high-speed trains between San Francisco and Los Angeles was expected to be about half the cost of comparable airfare. Intercity rail fares would be based on a 20-dollar boarding fee, plus an additional charge per mile. The boarding fee for commuters would be $5, plus miles. The Final High-Speed Train Plan also estimated that 42 percent of intercity and trans-state automobile travel, including trips to the airport, would be diverted. By the year 2020, over 13 million intercity travelers annually were expected to give up driving to become rail passengers. Further, electric trains were expected to generate intrastate travel that would not exist without a rail option. People who would otherwise prefer not to travel were expected to account for approximately six percent of high-speed rail ridership. This would mean two million more passengers annually, riding the trains. (41)

Beginning with an environmental impact study, the entire high-speed rail system was expected to take 16 years to construct before becoming fully operational. The initial San Francisco-Los Angeles core system could be completed in less than half that time. Despite the complexity and geographic size of the project, Californians could begin benefitting from their rail investment relatively quickly. On the same scale as California's water and highway projects, the Final High-Speed Train Plan projected the cost of construction to be $12 million per mile in rural areas. In urban areas, where the guideway would have to be elevated in places, the possible cost estimate was projected to exceed $70 million per mile. (42)

To reduce construction costs, conventional rail lines could be converted for high-speed passenger service wherever possible. Otherwise, separate high-speed rail lines would be built parallel to conventional rail lines, utilizing much the same right-of-way. Where space is limited, an elevated guideway could be built above conventional rail lines. According to the Final High-Speed Train Plan, using existing railroad right-of-way for high-speed rail was expected to help reduce construction costs by up to $499 million. Existent right-of-way purchases were estimated to cost about $2.5 billion. (43)

The entire rail system's total estimated construction cost of $25 billion could be offset by operating revenues generated between San Francisco and Los Angeles. However, the California High-Speed Rail Authority determined that a quarter-cent temporary statewide sales tax would be required to build the base system. It would remain in effect until projected passenger revenues exceeded operating and maintenance costs. Local governments would not be required to contribute financially to the construction and operation of the base system. Only if desired enhancements such as a new track alignment or station amenities were requested would local community support be required.

"Californians like the concept of a high-speed train system and are willing to support it, even with the prospect of a tax increase," stated the Final High-Speed Train Plan. (44) "As daunting as building a high-speed train network in California may seem, proceeding in stages is within the political, policy and procedural grasp of the state and regional agencies today." (45)

State officials estimated that 300,000 jobs would be created by the high-speed rail project, which would spur economic growth and generate about $300 million for the state in annual revenue. Critics argued, however, that California's budget deficit of nearly $24 billion for 2003 would make initial construction of the project cost prohibitive. (46)

Although 25 to 30 billion dollars is a significant amount of money, the cost to build traditional high-speed rail would be less than a proposed "maglev" system. Magnetic levitating trains, or mag-lev, glide friction free above a magnetically-opposed guideway. Their attraction is speed, which could be potentially greater than the 150 to 200 mile-per-hour velocity of electrified rail. A maglev test train in Japan reached 340 miles per hour. The cost is higher still, however. Transrapid, a German maglev manufacturer, estimated that an average maglev system could be built for about $40 to $60 million per mile. The cost would increase depending on the difficulty of the terrain being navigated, especially if construction took place through a densely populated urban area. According to Amtrak, the cost to upgrade existent trackage for 150 mile-per-hour speeds was $5 million or less per mile. "A maglev system's massive cost prevents its use in any location in which, one, private money is at stake, or two, public authority is even remotely accountable to the electorate," said public policy and civil engineering professor James Moore at the University of Southern California. (47)

Therefore, although costly, electrified high-speed rail was not the most expensive transportation alternative to be reviewed, but possibly the better cost/value option. Also, traditional rail was a proven technology as a result of over a century and a half of development and application. At the start of the 21st century, maglev was still highly experimental.

Critics were also concerned that, if the high-speed train proved popular, urban development would sprawl along the rail route. Agricultural lands would be depleted, especially in the San Joaquin Valley between Fresno and Bakersfield. True, the interstate highway system has shown that developers are attracted to the most popular transportation lanes, especially where large numbers of people converge onto a single arterial. Therefore, proper zoning would be required to protect land designated for light to moderate development or as open space. Historically, roads have attracted more urban development than railroads. This is in part because roadways have easy-on easy-off access. Development could be moderately controlled depending on how many station stops are built and where they are located.

The final program Environmental Impact Report (EIR)/Environmental Impact Statement (EIS) was expected to be completed in 2004. The purpose of such a report/statement was to specifically determine the effect a high-speed rail system would have on the environment and quality of life. It reflected a sincere effort to find solutions to concerns raised by the communities involved. An evaluation of possible locations for train stations was part of the process. Nevertheless, proper zoning laws offered a better solution to directly control urban sprawl than limiting the number of station stops.

Developing an Environmental Impact Report/Statement was part of the $14.7 billion necessary to build and begin operating high-speed trains over the 400-mile line between San Francisco and Los Angeles. This included improving feeder lines connecting to the high-speed rail corridor, such as light rail, commuter rail, and intercity passenger lines. "This launches a new era of transportation in this state," said California Governor Gray Davis in 2002. "High-speed rail will keep Californians moving faster, cleaner and cheaper than ever before." (48)

Through federal transit grants, the financial burden to cover the capital costs of the project could be significantly reduced for California taxpayers. In 1998, Congress enacted the nation's second guaranteed funding authorization for transportation, the Transportation Equity Act for the 21st Century (TEA-21). Transportation in the U.S. was authorized $41 billion, including $36 billion in guaranteed federal funding. This kind of funding guarantee was intended to ensure that federal Highway Trust Fund money be used for transportation, including bus and rail mass transit. TEA-21 succeeded the original authorization legislation, the Intermodal Surface Transportation Efficiency Act of 1991 (ISTEA). (49)

Federal and state funding for California high-speed rail could be joined by private investment through franchises, vendor financing, or other contracts. For example, according to the Final High-Speed Train Plan, parking facilities would be contracted out to for-profit businesses. Businesses would pay to build and landscape parking lots or garages as long as the prospect to make money existed. Profits could be generated in the form of payments by the passenger railroad or by charging people to park their cars. The High-Speed Rail Authority was expected to reduce construction costs by $190 million by turning over the responsibility of building and maintaining parking facilities to private ventures. (50)

The highest projected ridership and revenue levels were to be generated between San Francisco and Los Angeles. The core rail system was expected to attract 35 percent of all high-speed rail passengers. Trips to and from the San Joaquin Valley to San Francisco or Los Angeles would account for 17 percent of systemwide ridership. Another 17 percent were expected to ride between Los Angeles and San Diego. Ridership and revenue was projected to nearly double once high-speed trains were operating off the core system to Sacramento and San Diego. By the year 2020, 42 million passengers were expected to generate $888 million in annual revenue. Annual operating and maintenance costs were to be about $550 million, allowing for a passenger revenue surplus. By 2050, the Final High-Speed Train Plan projected that over 47 million passengers would bring in $1.3 billion in transit fare revenue. (51)

An additional source of revenue could be generated by hauling express packages or lightweight freight. Specialized freight cars for hauling mail, parcels, packages, and other light freight could be added to regularly scheduled passenger trains. Dedicated medium-weight freight trains could operate primarily at night so as to not interfere with regular passenger trains. Designed to the same specifications as high-speed passenger trains, dedicated freight trains would operate at a maximum speed of 125 miles-per-hour. High-value or time sensitive products such as electronics or perishables could be shipped, if dedicated loading and unloading facilities were built. The Summary Report & Action Plan estimated that hauling light and medium-weight freight on high-speed trains could net $20 million per year. (52) Freight trains would be introduced only after passenger service was established and with money not included as part of base project estimates. By the year 2045, the Final High-Speed Train Plan estimated that a possible $34.1 million could be generated annually just by hauling light freight on passenger trains. High-speed rail freight also had the potential to remove some truck traffic off congested parallel roadways. (53)

To maximize service and offer flexible schedules to the traveling public, five different types of trains would serve California's high-speed rail network. Express, semi-express, suburban-express, regional, and local service were all planned. There would be 20 trans-state express trains each weekday connecting the three most populated cities in Northern California with the two biggest cities in the southern part of the state. Express trains would operate from San Francisco, San Jose, or Sacramento to Los Angeles or San Diego and vice-versa. With no intermediate stops, travel times would be competitive with the airlines. Between the downtown areas of San Francisco and Los Angeles, an Express train was expected to need only two-and-a-half hours to complete its journey. Add traveling to the station and time to check baggage, and the average trip would require an estimated three hours and twenty minutes, about the same as flying.

"The Los Angeles-to-San Francisco air corridor is already the busiest in the world, and our highways are clogged. But we're never going to be able to relieve this gridlock by building more highway lanes or more airport runways," said Chairman Rod Diridon of the California High-Speed Rail Authority. The travel time average for an automobile between San Francisco and Los Angeles was almost seven hours. (54)

Twelve weekday semi-express trains would operate like non-stop express trains but stop to serve major cities within the San Joaquin Valley. Cities like Modesto, Fresno, and Bakersfield would be served by otherwise non-stop semi-express trains. Suburban-express trains would operate like commuter trains within metropolitan areas, but run as non-stop express trains between cities. There would be 20 suburban-express trains operating locally within the San Francisco Bay Area and the metropolitan area of Los Angeles. Between these cities and their outlying suburbs, no intermediate stops in the San Joaquin Valley would be served.

There were expected to be 22 regional trains each weekday. Some would connect Sacramento and San Francisco. Other morning trains would fan out from the San Joaquin Valley to San Francisco or to Los Angeles and San Diego, then return to the San Joaquin Valley in the evening. Finally, twelve local trains each weekday would stop at all stations or operate in "skip-stop" fashion based on demand. Faster local trains would serve higher-demand stations by skipping low-demand stations. Stations with fewer boarding passengers would be served by alternate local trains that stopped at each and every station. Schedules were to be determined based on travel times, plus two minutes at each station for boarding and detraining passengers. As standard with high-speed rail systems in other countries, schedules were to allow a six percent recovery time to compensate for minor delays between stations.

"As California's population grows, traffic will get worse and the state's economy will suffer unless we do something to relieve pressures on our transportation system," said state senator Jim Costa of Fresno. "We need high-speed rail to complement our existing automobile, air and rail transportation systems." (55)

As part of California's overall transportation network, high-speed rail was envisioned as a supplement to other modes of transportation. The two primary modes which the state largely depended on, the automobile and the airplane, were overburdened. Although California had been making significant investments in conventional passenger rail to serve its population, a faster and more efficient means of transportation was desired. A clean-air electrified high-speed rail system was envisioned to move more people quickly and easily between major city centers and other intermediary communities. California was already a leader in establishing new rail mass transit as a transportation alternative. With the introduction of high-speed passenger rail, the Golden State would once again be an example to other states looking for ways to alleviate their transportation mobility problems.

Learning when to embrace a rail transportation alternative to the automobile or airplane, whether inner-city light rail, regional commuter rail, or high-speed passenger rail, can be a challenge for any municipality or government. Often times mobility has to all but disappear before a transportation alternative is considered. Even then, more years of severe automobile traffic congestion are endured before the new rail system is fully operational. Reorienting communities toward rail mass transit or passenger rail as part of a community or regional development master plan can be even more challenging. But when states such as California attempt to pioneer innovative and new technologies for rail, other state governments should be watching.

In an age when the automobile has enabled sprawl city planning to reduce the viability of mass transit, finding an alternative to the driving public's otherwise preferred mode of transportation can be difficult. But when mobility is compromised due to an over dependence on the most popular mode, an alternative must be found. In some cases, an entirely new transportation infrastructure must be developed. Further, new philosophies for redesigning communities must be adopted to revitalize the functionality of mass transit. In California, light rail, commuter rail and high-speed rail were just a few of the many ways the state and its municipalities were able to reinvent how people lived and traveled. The underlying purpose behind establishing transportation and urban development strategies was to improve people's quality of life. Despite political controversy, government officials were getting voter approval to develop plans that were meant to restore mobility using rail. Arguably, a new golden age of passenger railroading was dawning in a true Sacramento Northern – Pacific Electric tradition.

On the former Santa Fe Surf Line between Los Angeles and San Diego, Amtrak California F59PHI 463 pulls an Amfleet *Pacific Surfliner* train through San Juan Capistrano, California, in March 2002. The Surf Line could be integrated into the California High-Speed Rail Authority's 200-mph electrified high-speed rail network.

PART TWO

Viable Commuter Railroads

CHAPTER FOUR

From the Private Sector to Government Subsidy

The purpose of high-speed rail is to provide a mode of transportation which offers a high volume of passengers reduced travel time at high velocity. The advantage compared to the automobile is a greater number of passengers traveling at a faster speed. The advantage of speed, henceforth, is most meaningful when distances traveled are greater than 100 miles. In California, high-speed rail was intended to connect cities 100 to 500 miles apart. In the Los Angeles area, light rail and commuter rail operated shorter distances in a densely populated region. Extreme speeds were not necessary, although high capacity was. The person-per-mile capacity of Metrorail trolleys and Metrolink commuter trains offered high volumes of commuters an efficient peak hour alternative to low capacity automobiles. However, just like for streets and highways, government money had to be available for such a rail transportation alternative to exist.

Commuter rail and light rail lines haul passengers using vehicles with flanged wheels on steel rails, similar to any conventional railroad. Both serve basically the same purpose—to carry the commuting public from home to work and back again. But each is as different as they are similar. A light rail system is designed to connect a city's downtown business district with its surrounding suburbs using streetcar-type lightweight equipment. Streetcars, or light rail vehicles, are designed to offer convenient service by street running and making frequent stops. A commuter railroad provides a different kind of service. Full-sized passenger trains link a major central city to more distant suburbs and other cities. Although light rail can do this too, distance or a desire for more passenger-per-mile capacity can often determine the need for commuter trains as opposed to light rail. Further, very few commuter railroads are street running. The few that take to the streets do not function very well as a streetcar service.

According to the American Public Transportation Association (APTA), the higher frequency of commuter train service compared to intercity trains, and the use of large capacity passenger cars, define a commuter railroad. Intercity trains, which operate at most a few times a day, provide more spacious and sometimes luxurious accommodations for passengers who, more often than not, are going to be traveling many miles more than the average commuter. Commuter trains are also defined by the APTA as hauling at least 50 percent or more passengers who ride regularly at least three times a week. (56)

Before the need for government subsidy, commuter and intercity passenger trains often operated along with freight trains under the control of one company. When the nation's railroads threatened to severely reduce passenger rail service, some passenger trains were taken over by government agencies. Both passenger and freight trains were typically dispatched by the host railroad, even well into the age of government-operated trains. Right-of-way and track maintenance were often the responsibility of the host railroad as well. From time to time these factors put commuter and intercity passenger trains at a disadvantage. Whether the host railroad chose to prioritize its own trains over scheduled passenger trains, or did not maintain its rail line for faster passenger train speeds, the passenger railroad was often at the mercy of the rail line provider. The proper dispatching of trains and a well maintained railroad were important factors that contributed to a passenger railroad's reliability, and therefore its viability.

Commuter rail viability is also directly the result of proper funding, marketing, and to a certain degree, city planning. When businesses are located near commuter rail stations and neighborhoods are built around park & ride access points, such easy access makes commuter rail attractive. The hassle of driving or flying must be greater than taking the train before people will consider using a rail alternative. In the United States, regional governments invested in rail mass transportation sporadically. Passenger rail systems which were generously funded could provide better service and were better marketed than those systems which were not properly funded.

Commuter railroads were doing well at the turn of the 21st century. According to the American Public Transportation Association, 411 million passenger trips were taken on commuter trains during the year 2000. Patronage was up 5.2 percent compared to 1999. "Easy-to-use quality public transportation such as commuter rail provides access, freedom, and mobility," said William W. Millar, president of the APTA. (57)

The increase in commuter rail ridership was attributed to better investment by local, state and federal governments, resulting in expanded commuter rail service and improved customer service. Severe automobile traffic congestion also contributed greatly toward people's desire to ride commuter trains. The 68 largest metropolitan areas in the United States, according to *Rail Magazine*, saw automobile traffic congestion nearly triple between 1982 and 1999. Between 1996 and the year 2000, 21 states made capital investments in rail projects totaling more than $850 million. (58)

Maryland Area Rail Commuter, or MARC, was created as a result of the transition of passenger rail from the private sector to subsidized government ownership. Local passenger trains on the old Baltimore & Ohio and Pennsylvania railroads would eventually make the transition to publicly owned and operated commuter trains. People continued to use the same passenger rail service but with a different purpose. Instead of being the only way to really travel, as it was during the 19th century, passenger rail became Maryland's accepted alternative for travel.

Expansive road and highway networks demonstrated California's commitment toward serving the driving public. Despite an extreme dedication to road building on the West Coast, the only commuter railroad west of the Mississippi River for much of the 20th century survived into the next century. The Peninsula Corridor, originally built between San Francisco and San Jose, endured difficult times as California tried to build itself out of traffic jams with more roadways. Finally, under Caltrain, this former Southern Pacific commuter rail line became a fixture as part of the state's new determination to find an alternative to the automobile.

Chicago, Illinois, had a variety of commuter railroads serving its outlying suburbs since the glory days of passenger railroading in America. As in Maryland and California, Chicago-area commuter rail came under the control of a government agency, marketed as Metra. Since automobile traffic congestion in northeastern Illinois continued to be severe, Metra was able to provide a significant and viable transportation alternative. Frequent and extensive rail service made the success of Chicago's commuter rail system second only to New York's Long Island Rail Road.

Northern Texas commuters in the Dallas-Fort Worth "Metroplex" traveled exclusively on street and highway arterials for more than 60 years. Although Dallas and Fort Worth were connected by rail, the only passenger trains were operated by the nation's intercity passenger railroad, Amtrak. Due to their scheduling for long-distance service, Amtrak trains were not practical for daily commuter use. Otherwise, the only trains traveling between these two cities were carrying bulk commodity freight. As freight trains continued to pass stranded motorists on parallel congested roadways, a return to the days when people rode interurban trains was being considered. Through the efforts of public transportation authorities in Dallas and Fort Worth and the effected municipalities in the Metroplex, commuter rail returned to northern Texas in the form of the Trinity Railway Express.

The existence of these commuter railroads reflected a central theme. Road building failed to solve the problem of severe automobile traffic congestion. In an effort to restore mobility within heavily populated metropolitan areas, federal, state and local governments invested extensively in commuter rail and other viable forms of mass transportation. Looking ahead to a world stuck in traffic, the traveling public was willing to invest hard-earned dollars through taxation to get out of this predicament.

Maryland Area Rail Commuter

Chartered on February 28, 1827, the Baltimore & Ohio was the first railroad built in the United States. The B&O provided regional commuter and long-distance passenger trains until federal and state government agencies took over such services. The railroad between Baltimore, Maryland, and Washington, D.C., was the oldest U.S. rail line to have continuous passenger train operations. These trains were challenged by automobile travel and regional airline service.

In an effort to reduce costs and streamline commuter service, the Baltimore & Ohio, like so many other railroads, purchased rail diesel cars during the 1950s. Built by the Budd Company, rail diesel cars were bi-directional self-propelled passenger cars which could operate as a single unit or in multiple unit sets. Assigning a standard passenger locomotive to a two or three car train underutilized the power of the locomotive which was costly to maintain. Lower-horsepower rail diesel cars promised reduced maintenance and allowed standard locomotives to be assigned to more power-demanding trains. Intended for short-haul and branch line service, the efficiency of a rail diesel car was greater than a locomotive and passenger car, but offered about the same passenger capacity. With operator controls at either end, turning the train was not required as was usually the case with a locomotive and cars. The railroad's answer to reduced train sizes and fewer riders was the rail diesel car.

Three primary versions of the rail diesel car were offered by the Budd Company to cost-conscience railroads. The most popular was the 90-seat

RDC-1 coach. Several railroads also purchased the 71-seat RDC-2, which came equipped with a small baggage room. A railway post office could be built into the baggage area of a 49-seat RDC-3, a coach-baggage combine. One of the least popular versions was the non-passenger, baggage and railway post office RDC-4. Short haul and branch line routes could rarely utilize the full benefits of a railway post office and large baggage area. Moreover, the lack of any passenger capacity made the RDC-4 impractical as a single unit.

To further combat a steady decline in both passenger and freight revenue, railroads like the Baltimore & Ohio sought to combine with other railroads. Managements hoped that larger, more efficiently operated rail systems could better compete with other railroads and the encroaching automobile, airline and trucking industries. In 1960, the Interstate Commerce Commission (ICC) received an application by the Chesapeake & Ohio Railroad to purchase the majority of B&O stock shares. Once permission was granted, the C&O purchased a controlling 61 percent of the B&O by the following year. Later, the ICC granted the C&O official control of the B&O, a merger agreement that was finalized on February 4, 1963. Nonetheless, the B&O continued to operate separately, even obtaining loans from the C&O to improve its rolling stock. The ICC then granted the 11,000-mile B&O/C&O permission to take control of the 800-mile Western Maryland Railway in March 1968. The combined rail system became known as Chessie System, although separate corporate identities remained. (59)

Also in 1968, the Baltimore & Ohio converted RDC-2 combines into snack bar rail diesel cars for Baltimore-Washington rush hour trains. The former baggage area was used as a kitchen. The forward part of the passenger area contained the bar, tables and booths. Due to increasing costs to operate commuter trains, snack bar service ended on October 7, 1968. Annual losses to the B&O for maintaining commuter service had increased to about $525,000 by 1969. (60)

National and regional passenger rail service was failing in the private sector despite many corporate mergers. A federally mandated solution was required to keep money-losing passenger trains operating. Despite the encroachment of the automobile, government agencies believed that rail service was still a necessity for many communities nationally. For a state to take control over regional passenger rail service, the federal government required the state to develop a transportation "action plan." Federal legislation thus required the creation of Maryland's Department of

Transportation, or "MDOT," in 1970. MDOT was responsible for "the development and maintenance of a continuing, comprehensive, and integrated transportation planning process." (61)

Threatened by the impending discontinuance of local passenger service by Chessie System's B&O in 1974, the state of Maryland agreed to provide some financial support to help offset regional commuter operation deficits. A year later, an operating agreement with the railroad established that the state would pay the entire operating deficit and purchase rolling stock. A major federal grant, provided by the Urban Mass Transportation Administration, was awarded to MDOT in 1978. The grant was to pay 80 percent of the cost for capital improvements which were intended to modernize commuter rail service on the B&O. The state of Maryland was required to cover the remaining 20 percent.

Capital improvements began with the purchase of ten used rail diesel cars. Through the 80/20 percent purchase agreement with the federal government, Maryland paid $753,400 (20 percent) for the purchase and rehabilitation of the rail diesel cars in 1980. (62) Eventually other rail diesel cars were commissioned into Maryland commuter service. The Maryland State Railroad Administration paid $15.8 million to purchase and rehabilitate 32 passenger coaches and five locomotives, a program that was completed in June 1982. The locomotives were former Baltimore & Ohio "F7" streamlined diesels rebuilt by Morrison Knudsen. New to the refurbished F9PH units, as they were redesignated, were 350-kilowatt generators designed to provide electric light and heat to the passenger cars. (63)

Over on the Pennsylvania Railroad, declining revenues inspired a reluctant merger with the also ailing New York Central in 1968. Things went from bad to worse for the new Penn Central, which in 1970 lost $325.8 million. In bankruptcy, Penn Central sold its electrified New York to Washington high-speed rail line to fledgling Amtrak, following the creation of the National Railroad Passenger Corporation in 1971. (64)

Penn Central was one of several bankrupt northeast railroads in 1976 which were merged into the Consolidated Rail Corporation. Conrail, the marketing name for Consolidated Rail, took responsibility for operating commuter trains in the New York, Baltimore and Washington areas. In Maryland, the financial burden of commuter operations was almost immediately handed over to the newly created Maryland State Railroad Administration. The administration was formed in 1976, by the executive order of the governor, to oversee railroad contracts such as the operating agreements established with the Baltimore & Ohio Railroad and Conrail. The administration's other responsibilities included the procurement of rolling stock and the authority to apply for and manage any money provided by the federal government for commuter rail.

Conrail was relieved of its responsibility to operate Northeast Corridor commuter trains as a result of the Northeast Rail Services Act of 1981. In 1983, a new operating agreement was established between the state and Amtrak to continue electric commuter rail operations between Baltimore and Washington. At about this time a marketing study was conducted by the Maryland State Railroad Administration. The study led to the 1983 creation of the marketing name MARC. The name Maryland Area Rail Commuter (MARC) was devised to give MDOT commuter rail its own identity. In 1992, the Maryland State Railroad Administration was absorbed into the Maryland Mass Transit Administration (MTA), which oversaw bus and rail transit throughout the state.

Maryland's MTA provided bus, subway, light rail, commuter rail and freight railroad assistance, through either direct operations or contracted arrangements. Responsibilities also included financial, technical and administrative assistance to local mass transportation systems in the city of Baltimore and throughout Maryland. In accordance with state legislation, as long as ticket sales made up at least 50 percent of a bus or rail line's annual revenue, MTA was required to continue transit operations. Moreover, MTA was restricted from providing mass transportation to areas where farebox revenue was projected to recover less than 50 percent of the cost to operate. (65)

The 187-mile MARC Train Service operated under contract over rail lines owned by Amtrak and CSX. The B&O/C&O parent Chessie System was merged with the Seaboard System, following Interstate Commerce Commission approval on November 1, 1980. A mammoth CSX (Chessie-Seaboard) railroad was the result. It took almost seven years, however, to officially merge the B&O into CSX Transportation in 1987.

Three primary MARC commuter rail routes served Baltimore, Washington, six Maryland counties and a portion of northeastern West Virginia. The Camden Line, owned by CSX, was the Baltimore & Ohio's original main line between Baltimore and Washington. Diesel-powered MARC trains operated between Union Station in Washington, D.C., and Camden Station in Baltimore. Trains also powered by diesels served the former B&O Brunswick Line, which operated from Washington Union

Station, northwest through Brunswick, Maryland, to Martinsburg, West Virginia. MARC trains were stored and serviced in Brunswick. The extension westward from Brunswick to Martinsburg opened for service in 1989.

In July 1989, all five MARC diesels were overhauled for "push-pull" service. The work was done at the CSX rail facilities in Huntington, West Virginia. To equip a locomotive for push-pull operation was to enable it to haul or push a train in the forward or reverse directions with equal ability. When the locomotive is pulling, the train operates normally with the engine crew in the cab of the engine. When the locomotive is pushing, the engine crew controls the train from the last passenger car, which is equipped with a "control cab." Special cables run through the entire length of the train to connect the control cab to the engine. In some cases, retired locomotives have their engines removed and are retrofitted to become control cab cars themselves. Push-pull eliminates the need for a passenger railroad to turn the locomotive on a turntable or entire trains on a wye to go back the other way. This and other innovations made commuter railroads nationwide faster and more efficient.

Electric-powered MARC trains provided commuter service on Amtrak's northeast corridor from Union Station in Washington, D.C., north through Penn Station in Baltimore, to Perryville, Maryland. Service from Baltimore to Perryville was introduced in 1989. Perryville is located on the east bank of the Susquehanna River.

The expansion of MARC commuter service to Perryville and Martinsburg reflected a trend which was effecting the entire nation. People were continuing to move out of the big cities and into the suburbs. Between 1980 and 1995, the city of Baltimore lost over eight percent of its population. Employment also dropped by eight percent, according to the Mass Transit Administration. A 1998 MTA Revenue and Passenger Report determined that ridership on all MTA transit services, including commuter rail, had been in a gradual decline until the trend reversed in 1996. People began looking at MARC trains and other MTA transit alternatives as a way to avoid the troubles associated with driving. Further, Baltimore light rail, introduced in 1992, was making the Baltimore metropolitan area more attractive to commuters and businesses. Commuters in 1996 took 94.2 million trips using MTA supported mass transit. In 1999, people made 101.4 million trips, an increase in ridership of 7.6 percent. (66) On average, over 20,000 passengers were riding MARC's 187-mile tri-route commuter rail system every weekday. (67)

"In an age when companies can do business from anywhere in the world, they're locating in the best places to live and work," said Maryland Governor Parris N. Glendening, in the year 2000. (68) "By 2020, the Baltimore-Washington region will add 1.7 million people, 1.1 million jobs, and 250,000 cars on the roads. We cannot pave our way out of the congestion such growth brings. An efficient commuter rail system is critical." (69)

Although the population of the city of Baltimore was expected to continue to drop through the year 2020, according to MTA, suburban populations were still on the rise. From 1980 to 1995, the population of Baltimore's suburbs increased 24.7 percent. MTA projected suburban population growth to increase another 19 percent from 1995 through 2020. (70) One of Governor Glendening's goals for the year 2020 was for MTA ridership levels on bus, light rail and MARC trains to reach one million trips a day. Transit ridership would have to increase by 83 percent. "The MTA and other agencies are planning to revitalize neighborhoods, stimulate prosperity, and improve the quality of life for all Marylanders. MARC's contribution to this initiative is through the Smart Growth Transit Program," said the governor. (71)

In January 2000, Governor Glendening announced an initiative to spend over $1 billion on transit in addition to Maryland's regular capital transportation projects. Almost a year later, Glendening added another $750 million to that initiative through the six-year Smart Growth Transit Program. Integrating transit as part of city and regional development was one way the governor intended to improve people's quality of life. (72)

By this time, MARC's five original streamlined passenger diesels had been retired as motive power and replaced with newer equipment. The original MDOT rail diesel cars had long since been retired. Although the service they provided was antiquated compared to some of the more modern trains used at the turn of the 21st century, the older refurbished equipment helped the state of Maryland successfully fill the gap between failed passenger rail in the private sector and viable government subsidized commuter rail. By the year 2000, MARC's 32 locomotives, including electric engines, and 102 commuter passenger cars made up 81 trains each weekday.

Of the governor's $1.75 billion for mass transportation, $103 million was to help MARC purchase new bi-level cars, which had more room to carry passengers than standard coaches. (73) Only a few years earlier, MARC received its first 50 148-seat bi-level cars, built by Kawasaki of Yonkers, New York. The money was also going to help extend MARC train service out to Frederick, Maryland. Frederick was located north of Washington, D.C., and west of Baltimore. A Rail Capital Grant was given to MARC by the federal government for fiscal year 2001, worth $15 million. (74)

Since the late 1980s, residents in the city and county of Frederick had access to MARC commuter trains through Meet-the-MARC shuttle service. TransIT Services of Frederick County provided shuttle bus service to and from the Point of Rocks station on the Brunswick Line. Offered was convenient drop-off and pick-up interchange with three Washington, D.C.-bound MARC trains in the morning and five returning trains in the evening. The popular shuttle service experienced a 31 percent ridership increase in 2000, according to TransIT, over the previous year. (75)

Although a fine example of a well coordinated bus-to-rail transit service, the people of Frederick were to be better served with direct rail access provided by MARC. Commuter trains would diverge from the Brunswick Line at Point of Rocks to head northeast on the old Baltimore & Ohio mainline toward Baltimore. At Frederick Junction, MARC trains would turn north up a four mile branch line to terminate in Frederick.

The first revenue run on the new 13.5 mile Frederick Extension, inaugurating weekday commuter rail service, took place on the morning of Monday, December 17, 2001. Push-pull MARC trains called at the East Street Station in downtown Frederick and at a suburban station in Monocacy, where an 800-space parking lot was provided. Frederick was Maryland's second largest municipality with a population of about 54,000.

Requiring five years and $56 million, the majority of the cost to build the Frederic Extension was paid for by the federal government, about $44 million. State funding covered the rest. A mere 230 passengers rode each day during the first month of operation. That average increased to 280 by late spring. Since no rail line directly connected Frederick to Washington, D.C., the round-about routing via a new wye connection at Point of Rocks meant rail travel one way took about 90 minutes. Despite the circuitous rail alignment, an estimated 1600 daily passengers were expected to be using the three weekday round-trip trains by 2005. (76)

Three Meet-the-MARC shuttles from various points in the Frederick area interchanged with commuter trains at the downtown Frederick station. Bus passengers were expected to pay one dollar per one way trip, unless they had paid in advance to ride MARC. Anyone possessing a train ticket or monthly pass for rail service to or from the Frederick area could ride the Meet-the-MARC shuttle without charge.

Maryland's Smart Growth Transit Program initiative was to help MTA upgrade and modernize all of its transportation services, including commuter rail. The MTA was to get $53 million to install real-time schedule information displays at bus and rail stations. (77) Also, the system for collecting fares was to be modernized. As machines that collected tokens and change became obsolete, computer technology offered an opportunity to implement a system which utilized fare cards. A magnetic strip card encoded with a monetary value was viewed as advantageous for both the daily commuter and the transit agency. Instead of fumbling for tokens or change, a single swipe of the card would reduce a pre-paid amount, already credited to the card, by one fare. The card was designed to work as long as it had money on it. Also, the turnstile or farebox could determine if the card holder was making a transfer from one train or bus to another. It automatically deducted the appropriate transfer fare, if any, from the amount of credit stored on the card. More than just a transit card, a fare card could be used as a cash card with which people could pay for parking meters, pay phones or taxis. If a station contained retailers, the card could be used for shopping. The more flexible the fare cards, the more people were likely to use them.

With a token system, the average transit rider bought $9 worth at a time. Fare card users were likely to put $30 to $50 on the card. Depending on the card's flexibility, $100 or more might be put on a card. This could be financially advantageous to the transit agency. Effectively, people would be giving the transit agency a short-term interest-free loan at the time of purchase. Fare cards could develop into a significant source of income if enough people purchased and used the cards. The Maryland Mass Transit Administration was given $90 million to restructure fare collection, and an additional $50 million to install Smart Card fare technology. "Our goal must be to make mass transit not just an option, but the preferred transportation option for commuters, shoppers and other travelers," said Governor Glendening. (78)

Other opportunities for MTA mass transit through the Smart Growth Transit Program included $267 million for the development and operation of new transit routes and services. Another $133 million was designated for the expansion of existent mass transit. This included expanding the "Access to Jobs" program, which offered people more job opportunities through better transportation. Finally, $157 million was given to MTA to upgrade and improve infrastructure necessities. These included maintaining and improving facilities and equipment, and the purchase of new buses, light rail vehicles and commuter passenger cars. (79) A significant financial source for this and other transportation projects throughout the state of Maryland came from a state Transportation Trust Fund, a source of invested interest-building capital from which to draw. By 2002, MARC had 26 diesel locomotives and ten electric engines to pull 282 conventional and bi-level commuter cars over its expanded 200 mile rail network.

Although Maryland Area Rail Commuter was not one of the larger commuter railroads in the country, it represented the kind of viable transportation alternative necessary to mitigate the problems associated with severe automobile traffic congestion on East Coast roadways. A profound transformation took place during the 30-plus years since the creation of MDOT. From simple beginnings using refurbished rail diesel cars to bi-level push-pull commuter trains, this change in rolling stock reflected a change in philosophy. Subsidized Baltimore-Washington commuter rail service was originally a hold-over stop gap measure to keep some commuter trains operating after they were shed by the private sector. Since then, significant investments were made to make MARC and other MTA transit services an attractive alternative to stop-and-go driving. From service expansions to Martinsburg, Perryville and Frederick, to advanced fare card technology, MARC train service had become modern and efficient. It was a stark contrast to the days of the old rail diesel cars. Although people had been riding trains over some of these same lines since as early as the 1830s, the technology was proving itself worthy by revolutionizing how people traveled beyond the year 2000. But to attract riders to rail transportation, the state of Maryland had to embrace a philosophy which not all states shared. That a viable mass transit or passenger rail network must receive proper public funding to be a success.

Reconditioned streamliner-era locomotives and passenger coaches filled the gap between private sector commuter rail and government agency-controlled services. A former Baltimore & Ohio F7, rebuilt as MARC F9PH 7185, leads a Brunswick-bound commuter train past the Point of Rocks, Maryland, station in August 1986.

CHAPTER FIVE

Peninsula Commute Service

Similar to the Baltimore-Washington corridor on the East Coast was California's Peninsula Corridor between San Francisco, San Jose and Gilroy on the West Coast. The West's only established commuter rail service west of the Mississippi River for much of the 20th century was the Peninsula Corridor. Through government subsidy, Caltrain continued the tradition of transporting passengers to and from the various communities which dotted this important rail route, connecting people to the major metropolitan centers of San Jose and San Francisco. Although it operated in obscurity during the boom years of the automobile, in an age of severe automobile traffic congestion, the importance of Caltrain's Peninsula Corridor has been amplified. By preserving the right-of-way and service during passenger rail's lean years, San Francisco, San Jose and their surrounding areas had the infrastructure already in place to offer a rail transportation alternative to the automobile.

The Peninsula Corridor was named for the body of land on which San Francisco was located. The town of San Francisco was officially established in 1847, just a year before gold was discovered 120 miles to the northeast. By the time California became a state in 1850, San Francisco had more than 20,000 residents. This important port and trade center needed to be connected to the then state capital of San Jose by the fastest and most efficient mode of transportation available. A railroad was first proposed in January 1851.

The San Francisco and San Jose Railroad Company was incorporated in 1860. The building of the railroad was financed by the three counties which the rail line would traverse. They were San Francisco, San Mateo and Santa Clara counties. Regular rail service began on the Peninsula Corridor on October 18, 1863. Trains operated between San Francisco and Mayfield, later California Avenue, in Palo Alto. Following a two hour train trip to Mayfield, passengers transferred to a horse-driven stagecoach for the ride down to San Jose. Rails connected San Jose to San Francisco on January 16,

1864. Shortly thereafter, two passenger trains began operating in each direction every weekday.

In 1870, the San Francisco and San Jose Railroad was absorbed into what would eventually become the Southern Pacific Railway. The busy Peninsula Corridor was made double track in 1904. The successful operation of passenger trains by the Southern Pacific lasted until after World War II.

In an effort to modernize Peninsula Commute Service, as the Southern Pacific called it, ten new "Gallery" cars were purchased, to be delivered beginning in June 1955. Bi-level Gallery cars were designed to have seats on a protruding walkway above the first-floor row of seats on either side of the main corridor. The floor of the second level was incomplete so that people on the first-floor would not have to stand or walk hunched over. Resembling gallery seats on balconies such as in a theater, but in a long corridor like a shooting gallery, these bi-level cars were aptly named. The immediate success of the Gallery car inspired the Southern Pacific to order 21 more in January 1956.

No new Gallery cars were purchased for commute service until 1968. Fifteen were built for the Southern Pacific by Pullman, an order worth more than $3 million, completed in 1969. This increased the railroad's commuter fleet to 46 bi-level cars and 55 standard coaches. Similar to the original fleet of 31 Gallery cars, the new cars seated 160 passengers and were air-conditioned. The doors were designed so that three passengers could board or detrain simultaneously. No control cab cars were built since the Peninsula Corridor was operated conventionally with no push-pull service. Diesel engines from Southern Pacific's motive power pool pulled the commute trains. All locomotives assigned to the corridor were equipped with steam generators to heat passenger cars. (80)

In 1969, approximately 11,000 passengers a day rode on 44 weekday trains on Southern Pacific's 47-mile commuter rail line between San Francisco and San Jose. Over half of those trains operated during peak travel periods in the morning and late afternoon. On weekends, 24 commute trains operated on Saturdays, 18 on Sundays. Weekday service began at 5:05 AM. With the exception of one rush hour train which originated in San Francisco, all commute trains originated in San Jose. During peak travel periods trains ran from three to 19 minutes apart. Trains operating at off-peak hours ran anywhere from 55 minutes to two hours and 35 minutes apart. Weekday commute service ended for the day at 12:35 AM. (81)

The Southern Pacific used a zone fare system to standardize fare collection from commuters traveling along the Peninsula Corridor. The suburban territory was divided into six zones with three or four stations in each zone. A rider could detrain at any station within the zone for which the purchaser had bought a ticket.

The one Peninsula Corridor commute train to operate beyond San Jose in 1969 was Southern Pacific's "Del Monte." Southbound, the Del Monte served as a rush hour commute train but with three additional through cars to Pacific Grove near Monterey, 120 miles south of San Francisco. The three cars assigned were standard long-distance passenger cars, one of which was a parlor-lounge snack car. Northbound, the three-car intercity train picked up Gallery cars in San Jose and operated as a mid-morning local to Southern Pacific's Third Street terminal. This passenger terminal, located at Third and Townsend, replaced the original downtown station at 18th and Valencia streets in 1915.

The Del Monte was discontinued with the formation of Amtrak on May 1, 1971. Also, Southern Pacific's passenger trains to and from Los Angeles were taken off the Peninsula Corridor by Amtrak and moved to another line, running San Jose to Oakland. With the beginning of Amtrak, which took over intercity passenger rail operations nationwide, passenger trains on the Peninsula Corridor were from then on exclusively commuter rail.

Peninsula Commute Service declined as fast, high-capacity roads encouraged Californians to commute by automobile. Parallel U.S. Highway 101 contributed to Southern Pacific's annual commuter rail losses. By 1976, commuter trains hauling a mere 8,000 daily passengers were costing the railroad about $9 million a year. (82) The Southern Pacific argued with the state Public Utilities Commission over fares and minimum service levels. Finally, in 1977, the Southern Pacific petitioned for the discontinuance of Peninsula Commute Service, wanting to get out of passenger railroading entirely. When the Public Utilities Commission said no, the petition went to the Interstate Commerce Commission. In the meantime, the three peninsula counties of San Francisco, San Mateo and Santa Clara partially subsidized commuter tickets through a temporary Fare Stabilization Plan. This action helped reverse a long decline in ridership by reducing the amount of fare charged to individual commuters.

Following several months of negotiations, the Southern Pacific agreed to run commuter trains under contract if most of the operating costs were covered by public agencies. The three counties, which originally financed the building of the Peninsula Corridor, joined with the California Department of Transportation to finance continued commuter rail. The California Department of Transportation, or Caltrans, assumed responsibility for Peninsula Commute Service when the new agreement went into effect on July 1, 1980. Caltrans was solely responsible for adding new station stops to the corridor and other capital improvements.

Population growth within the Silicon Valley area around San Jose encouraged Caltrans to expand reverse-commute service out of San Francisco in October 1981. A new morning train from the six-year-old Fourth Street terminal in San Francisco, and its evening counterpart, increased the number of weekday trains from 44 to 46. Evening reverse-commute trains left the Cahill Street terminal in San Jose, built in 1935. More reverse-commute trains were added in 1986, a year after a major rolling stock upgrade program began. Modernization and improved rail service was how "Caltrain" planned to attract riders off increasingly congested California roadways. Caltrain was Caltrans' new marketing name for Peninsula Commute Service.

"Society has changed. Most homes depend on two incomes, which means two people commuting to work," said Chuck Harvey, chief operating officer for Caltrain. "Work schedules are changing and the core job center is no longer in San Francisco, in fact there are many places of industry throughout the Bay Area. That means the Caltrain service must be flexible, frequent and dependable." (83)

In June 1985, the first of 18 new passenger diesels were introduced into commuter rail service. They were built by General Motors' Electro-Motive Division (EMD) and designated F40PH-2 units. They were equipped with Head-End Power (HEP) to supply electric light and heat to the passenger cars and were push-pull capable. At the same time, the first of 63 new Sumitomo Gallery cars arrived to introduce push-pull operation on the Peninsula Corridor. A bi-level cab car with controls linked to the locomotive enabled the engine crew to operate the train in the reverse direction with equal ability. Peninsula commute trains from then on were bi-directional. An additional pair of F40PH-2 passenger diesels were built by EMD in 1987 to handle Caltrain's growing passenger car fleet. The Gallery car was proving to be highly cost-effective in its durability and flexibility with relatively few maintenance requirements. Caltrans purchased ten more Gallery cars for a total of 73, including 21 cab control cars. Ridership at this time was approximately 455,000 passenger trips per month. Reverse-commuting was also on the rise. To evaluate the future of Peninsula Commute Service, a three-county Peninsula Corridor Study Joint Powers Board was created.

On June 5, 1990, California voters approved a $1.99 billion bond initiative known as Proposition 116: "The Clean Air and Transportation Improvement Bond Act of 1990." It included a gradual nine cent per gallon gas tax increase. The passage of this bond issue represented a breakthrough for rail mass transit. Instead of the gas tax going exclusively toward more road building, Californians voted for a rail alternative. People were willing to pay more in taxes in order to ride trolleys and trains. (84)

Through the Joint Powers Board, the three involved counties purchased the Peninsula Corridor from the Southern Pacific in December 1991. Although the Southern Pacific retained trackage rights to operate freight trains in the corridor, the right-of-way, track and infrastructure were sold to the Joint Powers Board for $242.3 million. (85) An additional $4 million was spent to acquire trackage rights over Southern Pacific-owned track for 34 miles south of San Jose to Gilroy. Amtrak was chosen to replace Southern Pacific as Caltrain operator beginning on July 1, 1992. (86)

The number of commute trains increased from 54 to 60 trains per weekday when Caltrain operations were turned over to Amtrak. This included four weekday trains on the extension to Gilroy which also opened at the same time. South of downtown San Jose, Tamien Station was opened to connect Caltrain to the Santa Clara County light rail system. All 26 commuter stations, 20 passenger engines and 73 Gallery cars were deeded to the Joint Powers Board by Caltrans.

An unusual pilot program began in September of 1992 to allow bicycles on commute trains. The idea was to enable cyclists better commuting flexibility and access to various recreational cycling opportunities. Cyclists who were twelve years old or older, with a Caltrain-issued bicycle permit, could use the train to access the San Francisco Bay area, the Redwood Forest, and other trails and landmarks near commute stations. Although a cyclist was required to pay regular fare, there was no additional charge to bring a bicycle. A Gallery car equipped for bicycle transport had racks which could hold twelve bikes.

This was a first in U.S. commuter rail operations. By March 1995, at least 8,000 cyclists had received bicycle permits, with approximately 400 of them riding commute trains each day. Initially, the bicycle experiment led to some resistance by train crews, and cycle groups wanted the poorly publicized permit requirement dropped. (87) The bicycle program was nonetheless popular, so on November 24, 1995, Caltrain doubled the number of bikes allowed per train from twelve to twenty-four. New racks were installed in the cab control cars at the suggestion of train crews. Cab cars became primary bicycle cars. Secondary rack-equipped cars were provided whenever possible. They were usually located second car from the engine. Bicycles were permitted on several off-peak weekday trains and on all weekend and holiday trains. During the early days of the program, cyclists were not to bring their bikes on rush-hour trains.

Bicycle use as an alternative mode of transportation was gaining momentum. In San Francisco alone, new walking and biking trails were in the planning or construction phases, including the Industrial City Rail-Trail and the Mission Creek Bike Path and Greenbelt. The expanding bicycle program allowed passengers to bring their bikes on every train, every day and without a permit. By the year 2002, almost 2,000 bicycles were riding the commute trains each weekday. (88)

The 77-mile Peninsula Corridor between San Francisco and Gilroy had 35 commuter stations by this time, seven of which were listed on the National Register of Historic Places. The oldest passenger depot was in Santa Clara, which celebrated its 130th anniversary of continuous passenger rail service in January 1994. On the 20th of August that same year, the Amtrak/Caltrain passenger terminal in San Jose reopened following a year of reconstruction and restoration. It was renamed the San Jose Diridon Station. This plus other rebuild and upgrade programs made stations and commute trains wheelchair accessible by July 1995. The work was done in compliance with the Americans with Disabilities Act of 1990.

In contrast, the zone fare system had not changed on the Peninsula Corridor since the days of the Southern Pacific. It just got larger with the addition of more stations and the extension to Gilroy. Caltrain had nine zones with two to seven stations in each zone. They were labeled "SF," then one through eight. There was hourly weekday service to zones seven and eight between San Jose and Gilroy, but no weekend service. In June 1996, Caltrain recorded that the annual number of passenger trips reached 7.4 million, the highest annual ridership total since 1958. (89)

As a result of the transportation mandate included in Proposition 116, the state of California and population-saturated local governments had the opportunity to make the Golden State a leader in the renaissance of rail mass transit and passenger rail. With aid from the federal government, tax dollars invested in rail helped to mobilize those parts of the state which were increasingly congested by automobile use. Once a threatened commuter rail line during the 1970s, Caltrain's 79 mile-per-hour Peninsula Corridor was able to provide a modern and efficient alternative to driving. Without the necessary subsidies for capital investment, Peninsula Commute Service could not have been made viable.

In March 1998, 20 new Gallery cars were ordered from Nippon Sharyo, a Japanese rail car manufacturer. Six were control cab cars. Later that year, in December, Caltrain received the first of three new passenger diesels from the Boise Locomotive Company. The new locomotives from Boise, Idaho, cost almost $2 million each. They joined a fleet of 20 EMD-built diesels, which were being overhauled by Alstom Transport of Montreal, Quebec, for about $15 million. The Canadian company's rebuild contract was awarded by Caltrain to give the F40PH-2 units another decade of use. (90)

Alstom was also awarded a $35 million contract to begin the overhaul and refurbishment of Caltrain's older Gallery cars, which had been operated continuously since 1985. Included as part of the overhaul were larger luggage areas for the benefit of multimodal passengers who used Caltrain and shuttle buses to go to airports. Aluminum two-shelf racks with space underneath for larger bags were to be installed on 26 overhauled Gallery cars. Each commuter train was to have at least one car with dedicated space for luggage. "With the increasing number of people who take Caltrain to the San Francisco and San Jose airports, we have seen a greater need for a luggage area," said Walt Stringer, Caltrain operations manager. "Overall ridership has grown, too, and the luggage area also gets bulky items out of the way of other passengers." (91)

Caltrain recognized its role as a long-distance transportation provider through its multimodal interchange with nearby airports. Shuttle buses connected the San Francisco (SFO) and San Jose international airports with commute trains at the Millbrae and Santa Clara stations respectively. A significant advantage to government-controlled commuter rail was its relationship to government-controlled bus systems. Some shuttle bus services were open to the public and free of charge, based on destination and sponsorship. For the purpose of connectivity with rail and air transport, free shuttles served train stations and air terminals. Other buses served specific communities or operated directly to specific businesses. The shuttle bus program received its support from participating employers, local communities, the Peninsula Corridor Joint Powers Board, and the Bay Area Air Quality Management District Transportation Fund for Clean Air. Through diversified shuttle connections, Caltrain was able to offer multimodal interchange for improved commuter mobility. Between bicycles, buses, trains and airplanes, Peninsula Corridor commuters were able to utilize a highly flexible transportation network.

Caltrain passengers could also transfer to Bay Area Rapid Transit (BART) light rail trains at the Millbrae intermodal station to access San Francisco International Airport or light rail line destinations downtown. Millbrae was one of four stations to open along a new 8.7-mile BART light rail extension. Each station had bus and park and ride access. Construction of the $1.5 billion light rail extension to SFO and Millbrae began in May 1998 and took almost five years to complete. Opening day was Sunday, June 22, 2003. As many as 70,000 daily passengers were expected to ride the new airport light rail line. (92) More than 100,000 people rode during the first week of service, a slightly higher weekly ridership than when BART light rail service was first introduced in September 1972. (93)

As expansion and infrastructure improvements were taking place with other transit agencies in the Bay Area, so it was with Caltrain. Commuter rail infrastructure projects included building a new primary maintenance facility and constructing a new rail line extension in San Francisco. The previously suspended 1997 Caltrain San Francisco Downtown Extension (DTX) included the design and construction of a new DTX/Transbay Terminal as part of a downtown joint development project. The main purpose of the $450 million extension was to bring commuter rail to a more central location serving downtown. (94)

The $888 million Transbay Terminal was a 600,000 square foot intermodal transit facility, designed to have six through-tracks underground and two bus transit levels above ground that would accommodate 50 bus bays. Daily train and bus passenger capacity through the terminal was not to exceed 300,000 people based on design specifications. Retail, hotel and office space would also be incorporated into the massive structure as part of a mixed-use development plan for the Transbay Terminal area. The multi-use facility would have about 3,000 residential units along with its 225,000 square feet of retail. The project was part of a Transit Oriented Development (TOD) effort to encourage the use of public transportation instead of driving. Extending Caltrain service beyond its Fourth and Townsend Street terminus to the developing Financial District/South of Market Area was expected to reduce downtown driving by moving the Caltrain terminal and other transit services to a more central location. With 4,700 new residential units planned for the Transbay Terminal area, people were expected to go shopping, seek entertainment, and commute to work without the use of an automobile to get there. Construction of the Transbay Terminal was set to begin in December 2003, with the permanent station completed in 2007. An estimated 80,000 train and bus passengers were expected opening day. The entire facility would be completed in 2012. (95)

Of the terminal's railroad passengers, some might someday be able to ride Caltrain or Amtrak over the Peninsula Corridor to as far south as Monterey by rail. Caltrain passengers could already transfer to one of three daily buses to Salinas and Monterey at the Caltrain station in Gilroy, a service which began on September 9, 2003. The buses had to traverse the heavily congested U.S. Highway 101, therefore, a faster rail alternative was preferred. Studies conducted by Monterey County estimated that 8,500 county residents commuted to and from work in the Silicon Valley every weekday. Between Salinas and San Jose, daily vehicle use on Highway 101 had reached 61,000. "More people are moving down here. We don't think that trend will change," said Alan Forrest, transportation planner for Monterey/Salinas Transit. "These people are working in Silicon Valley. There really isn't any alternative to 101 right now." (96)

The California Department of Transportation's Caltrans Rail Program envisioned reintroducing a modern version of Southern Pacific's old commuter and intercity passenger train, the "Del Monte." According to Caltrans, establishing intercity passenger rail service between San Francisco and Monterey was estimated to require $62.3 million for track and signal improvements and other infrastructure expenditures. (97) Monterey County hoped to extend Caltrain commuter service to Salinas by 2005. County officials were able to raise $28 million to upgrade track and add station stops along Union Pacific's 38-mile former Southern Pacific line between Gilroy and Salinas. Negotiating with freight carrier Union Pacific for use of the rail line, however, was proving difficult. Passenger trains would inevitably interfere with the normal operations of freight trains, Union Pacific's primary source of revenue. "Union Pacific is the 9,000-pound gorilla in all this," said Caltrain deputy executive director Jim Gallagher. "That is a significant hurtle to leap." (98)

Despite the social benefits, freight railroads have usually been apprehensive about handling passenger trains, their own or anybody else's. Since the glory days of railroading, railroad executives have worked hard to reduce the infrastructure and physical plant of their rail systems to the least necessary required to operate existent levels of freight traffic. Further, the business of hauling rail freight in the U.S. has improved since the 1980s, meaning more trains and more time sensitive freights operating at capacity on many lines. Caltrain's trackage rights over the former Southern Pacific between San Jose and Gilroy meant that freight trains were not supposed to be dispatched during peak commuter travel periods. Slower and longer freight trains would bottleneck the line, potentially delaying rush hour commuter trains. Consequently, freight trains were often delayed, waiting to be dispatched during brief daytime operating windows or at night. Such delays could anger shippers or even cause some to switch to trucks. These same operating conditions would exist if Caltrain were permitted to use Union Pacific trackage from Gilroy to Salinas or Monterey.

"Relieving traffic congestion is central to the quality of life here," said Laura Stuchinsky, the Director of Transportation and Land Use for the 191 companies represented by the Silicon Valley Manufacturing Group. "It is critical for Silicon Valley to be able to attract and keep people here. There is a very real concern that employees are spending way too much time in their cars rather than with their families or at work." (99)

Monterey County expected a weekday ridership of 550 passengers the first year if Caltrain service were extended to Salinas. An additional 100 daily commuters would board in Castroville and 250 in Pajaro. If commuters from Santa Cruz County drove to the Pajaro station to ride Caltrain, passenger boardings in this small village could eventually exceed Salinas. Farebox revenue was expected to cover only about 40 percent of operating expenses. Federal, state and local funding would have to be secured before trains would begin operating to Salinas or Monterey. In the meantime, Caltrain was making significant improvements to its existing service. (100)

"Caltrain is in the process of bringing this railroad into the 21st century. That means an upgrade to everything from tracks to equipment," said Mike Scanlon, executive director for Caltrain. "Caltrain's new equipment looks and feels different, representing a new era in peninsula rail service." (101) In May 1999, the Joint Powers Board authorized an $836 million Rapid Rail Plan. The plan's main objective was to electrify the Peninsula Corridor. (102)

To upgrade the railroad for high-speed electrified passenger service, modifications to everything from station platforms to the purchase of new electric locomotives would have to take place. Initially, infrastructure upgrades would improve diesel-powered commute service. Actual electrification between San Francisco and Gilroy would occur during the final phase of the project. Immediate improvements to the track included more than eight miles of new passing tracks installed in strategic locations in Sunnyvale, Redwood City, and between Bayshore and San Francisco.

Continuous welded rail would replace jointed rail on existing track. The track would be supported by sturdier concrete ties installed at various locations in place of standard wooden ties. Centralized Traffic Control (CTC) would be installed over the entire corridor to improve the dispatching of trains and upgrade the signaling system. Twelve new signal bridges and 110 stand-alone signals would be required. High-speed crossovers (from one track to another) would further enhance train operations in CTC territory. Approximately 40 miles of railroad was not yet operating under central control. The addition of CTC between Bayshore and Santa Clara would improve safety, system reliability, and train speed and frequency. The $110 million CTX Construction Project, which began during the summer of 2002, was in part in anticipation of Caltrain Baby Bullet service. (103)

"Baby Bullet" was Caltrain's name for a speedy express train. The railroad infrastructure work was being done to enable faster trains to operate safely and be given operational priority over slower local trains. No longer would all trains fall under the general heading of Caltrain commute train. "We've taken the 1950s technology that Caltrain inherited and have updated it to allow for Baby Bullet service tomorrow and for high-speed operations a few years later," said Dave Obedoza, Caltrain's manager of signals and communications. "The installation of CTC will establish a good signal foundation for the migration to future signal systems that will be needed when train operations require an increase in the number of trains and higher speeds." (104)

Additional passing tracks installed between San Francisco and San Jose were to enable 79 mile-per-hour limited-stop Baby Bullet trains to overtake other trains in slower local service. Five new diesel-powered trainsets would be purchased, specifically for use as Baby Bullets. A $14 million order for six 3,600 horsepower MP36PH-3C diesel locomotives was contracted to Motive Power Industries of Boise, Idaho. Caltrain envisioned the average one hour and 45 minute commute between San Francisco and San Jose to be reduced to approximately 50 minutes. (105) Initially, Baby Bullet trains would make intermediate stops at Millbrae, Hillsdale, Palo Alto and Mountain View. The development of this service was funded, at least in part, by Governor Gray Davis's transportation initiative projects for the San Francisco Bay Area. Governor Davis's year 2000 Traffic Congestion Relief Plan included $336 million toward the improvement and expansion of light rail, commuter rail and intercity passenger rail serving the city of San Francisco and surrounding areas. (106)

Finally, the long standing zone fare system was restructured, effective September 22, 2003. Some of the changes included reducing the number of zones from nine to six, replacing weekend passes and round trip tickets with a day pass, and initiating a zone fare upgrade. The zone upgrade option enabled ticket holders, especially those with day or monthly passes, to travel outside of their normal zone without having to pay the base fare a second time. Also, tickets would no longer be sold aboard the trains as it was since the days of Southern Pacific. Instead, tickets would be purchased in advance and would serve as proof of payment during periodic inspection by fare inspectors or by the onboard conductor. Changes to the fare structure and other operations were in anticipation of faster and improved rail service and eventual electrification.

If the Peninsula Corridor is electrified, San Francisco commute service may be integrated into the California High-Speed Rail Authority's 200 mile-per-hour electrified intercity rail network. "A San Francisco alignment would directly serve the region's most important travel destination as well as its most prominent airport at SFO," stated the High-Speed Rail Summary Report & 20-Year Action Plan. (107)

Almost 10 million commuters a year were expected to ride the new high-speed trains within the metropolitan areas of San Francisco, San Jose, Los Angeles and San Diego by the year 2020. During the three-hour peak travel periods, on weekday mornings and evenings, a projected four trains per hour would serve high-speed corridor stations within the designated commuter rail territories. One train per hour would serve each station during off-peak hours. Train speed would be restricted to 125 miles-per-hour within densely populated urban areas. Nearly 38,000 weekday commuters were expected to make up about 23 percent of the annual systemwide high-speed rail ridership total. "Providing high-speed train service for commuters would utilize the high-speed infrastructure more efficiently and greatly improve mobility in highly congested commute corridors, increasing the public benefits of and broadening the base of support for the system," stated the Final High-Speed Train Plan. (108)

Given that Caltrain was financed by federal, state and local tax dollars, these rehabilitation and improvement projects were happening on a massive scale. Ticket sales typically do not recover the cost of day-to-day operations. For a commuter railroad to expect to receive the kind of public funding required for such elaborate improvement projects was unprecedented. Yet, in the state of California, such projects were taking place as exemplified by

Caltrans' Rapid Rail Plan and its relationship to the Intercity High-Speed Rail project. As of January 2002, Caltrain reported that, on average, about 34,400 people were riding commute trains each weekday. An average of 10,700 were riding on Saturdays, 6,400 on Sundays. (109)

Back in the days of Southern Pacific after World War II, when rail transport was largely viewed as uninteresting and outmoded, no effort was made to build a network of commuter rail lines during this time when California led the nation in roadway expansion. As a result, the Peninsula Corridor remained limited in its reach to serve as a transportation alternative during the age of severe roadway gridlock. Increased connectivity with light rail and bus transit helped Caltrain extend its reach. But there was more to be done. Caltrans would sponsor a program that would make a personal automobile a direct extension of Caltrain.

A CarLink to Caltrain

A significant reason why people hesitate to use mass transit systems, unless they absolutely have to, has been they do not want to give up the convenience of having a personal automobile at their disposal. When they can, people use the most popular roads at the most popular times, driving alone. With this problem in mind, a pilot project was initiated in Palo Alto, California, to offer people the convenience of having an automobile available when using commuter rail. Caltrain was part of a "carsharing" program which enabled people to drive out from and back to the California Avenue station without having to own an automobile.

Car Sharing Organizations, or CSOs, began during the late 1980s in Europe. The idea was to coordinate the schedules of several people who "shared" the use of only a handful of automobiles. A fleet of vehicles was owned by a CSO, which scheduled its cars for use by its members. Customers paid a membership fee to belong to the program. Often usage fees were collected depending on what kind of car was reserved, where it was based and how many miles the vehicle was driven. Carsharing was inspired by difficult parking problems in European cities and the price of gasoline being almost three times higher than that in the United States. One of the most successful and influential of Europe's carsharing organizations began during the late 1980s as a public-private cooperative. By 2003, Mobility CarSharing Switzerland had at least 55,000 members. Its successful business-oriented approach served as a model for North American CSOs. In the United States, carsharing programs were proving their usefulness in densely populated areas. (110)

Classical European carsharing programs did not typically link with transit. Automobiles loaned to members would originate and be returned to a base parking lot. Neighborhood carsharing lots were most practical in high-density housing areas where a modest number of people could conveniently walk to the cars they would be driving. In contrast, linking "station cars" with public transportation was developed in the United States to provide an on-demand flexible extension to fixed-route rail transit.

An experimental carsharing research project was initiated in San Francisco in January 1999. "CarLink" was a ten-month commuter oriented program, based at the Dublin/Pleasanton light rail station served by Bay Area Rapid Transit (BART). One of the goals was to determine if carsharing could help attract people to use rail mass transit. Primary advantages included potential declines in air pollution and automobile traffic congestion by having fewer cars on the road. CarLink researchers concluded that the test program resulted in an average driving reduction of 20 miles per commuter each workday. (111) "The one-person, one-car approach to transportation is not sustainable," said University of California Professor Daniel Sperling, director of the Institute of Transportation Studies. "Smart carsharing is an innovative step in the right direction toward transportation that is more economic, equitable and environmental." (112)

Caltrain agreed to participate in "CarLink II," based at the California Avenue commute station in Palo Alto. The expanded carsharing project was launched during a ceremony held at the Caltrain depot on August 23, 2001. It was backed by the Caltrans New Technology and Research Program and American Honda's Intelligent Community Vehicle System (ICVS) program. Caltrans agreed to fund CarLink II through June 2002, at a cost of about $750,000. Unlike CarLink I, CarLink II was expected to phase into a self-sustaining CSO. Partners in research included the University of California's Institute of Transportation Studies and Partners for Advanced Transit and Highways. (113)

American Honda provided new ultra low emission vehicles, 25 to be used by customers and two set aside as back-up. The vehicle fleet of 27 four-door 2001 Honda Civics was stored at the California Avenue station in 27 dedicated parking spaces provided by Caltrain. The Palo Alto depot was the eighth busiest for passenger boardings on the Peninsula Corridor. Approximately 1,400 commuters passed through each weekday, according to

Caltrain. CarLink II was expected to be able to accommodate as many as 300 customers per day, if necessary. "This program could radically change the way employees travel to and from their jobs," said Randell Iwasaki, the deputy director of maintenance and traffic operations for Caltrans. (114)

There were three types of CarLink II customers: home-based users, work-based commuters and work-based day users. (115) Home-based users, who lived in the Palo Alto area but worked elsewhere, could take a reserved Honda home at night after arriving at the train station. These members enjoyed full use of the vehicles during the evenings and weekends. They returned the vehicles to the Caltrain station at the beginning of each workday.

Work-based commuters rode Caltrain to the California Avenue station, then transferred to a reserved Honda Civic to drive to work. Members who were work based were required to be employed at participating businesses, initially located at the Stanford Research Park. Dedicated parking was provided for CarLink II members who worked at SAP, Genencor or Motorola. Other companies at or near the Stanford Research Park joined the CarLink program over time. During the workday, the Hondas were then available to employees of those member companies who wished to reserve a vehicle for business or personal use. A Honda Civic was to be available instantaneously to work-based day users through an Internet advance reservation system. A standing reservation schedule properly coordinated the use of the vehicles so that members could expect their cars to be available as anticipated. After the workday was over, work-based commuters were required to return the vehicles to the California Avenue station for their train ride home. Home-based users would pick up their reserved vehicles in the evening and the cycle would begin again. "Personal vehicles sit an average of 23 hours per day," said Susan Shaheen, head director of the CarLink II project. "When we do use them, they usually carry only one person. With carsharing, individuals have access to a car when they need it, but when it's not in use others have access to it." (116)

To enroll in the CarLink II program, home-based users were required to reside in the Palo Alto metro area. Membership was available only to those individuals who possessed a valid California drivers license and had a good driving record. An introductory monthly fee of 300 dollars was required. The cost covered, among other things, gasoline charges for up to 1,000 miles of driving per month. Each vehicle was equipped with a gas card which drivers could use to purchase fuel as necessary. More significantly, the cost of registration, insurance, maintenance and cleaning of the vehicles was also the responsibility of the carsharing organization. (117) Runzheimer International consultants estimated that these costs, plus the depreciating value of the average automobile, made car ownership cost between $6,400 to $9,200 a year, depending on location. (118)

A valid in-state drivers license and clean driving history was also required of work-based commuters and day users, although membership fees were not required. A monthly per-vehicle subscription fee was paid by participating businesses which offered carsharing as an employee benefit.

Vehicle use and location was monitored by CarLink II, using "smart technology" through cellular and Global Positioning Satellite (GPS) communications systems. Such things as fuel level, trip mileage, usage time beginning and ending, and member identification could be reliably transmitted. A radio frequency-based system tried during the limited CarLink I program proved far less reliable and adaptable than originally anticipated. The much more dependable GPS system was also available to CarLink II members for personal navigation.

To access the vehicles, members received a "smart key fob" which, when held over a transponder mounted inside the designated vehicle's back window, activated the door lock release. A personal identification number had to be entered into a computer access panel before an ignition key could be used to start the vehicle. If a car broke down or was not available, a toll-free call to CarLink II would guarantee a ride day or night. Smoking was not allowed in the vehicles and cleanliness was appreciated. "When we get the technology developed that can provide a highly professional product and keep the costs down, then the revenues are only likely to increase as people value the service more and are more willing to pay for it," said CarLink II director Shaheen. (119)

More than 65 participants signed up with CarLink II during the first few months of operation. Most were work-based users employed at the Stanford Research Park. Carsharing programs differed from rent-a-car companies by the fact that multiple drivers used the same vehicle throughout the day, daily, on a long-term basis. Other experimental carsharing programs were being established elsewhere in the United States, including CarSharing Portland Inc., in Portland, Oregon; Zipcar in Boston, Massachusetts; and CarSharing Traverse Inc., in Traverse City, Michigan. "I'm trying in as many ways as possible to differentiate ourselves from a car-rental company," said Robin Chase, chief executive officer and co-founder of Zipcar. "If you had to go to the airport to get the car, and stand in line, and fill out forms each time, then it's not an interesting idea." (120)

According to a University of California U.S. Shared-Use Vehicle Survey, there were three primary obstacles impeding the development of more than a handful of carsharing programs in the United States. The purchase or leasing of a fleet of automobiles and equipping them with expensive technology such as GPS were two major factors that significantly increased start-up costs. The increased cost of insurance was a third major factor. Shared-use automobile insurance premiums ranged between $1,200 and $2,100 per vehicle annually during the 1998 through 2001 development, testing and analysis period for CarLink I. By July 2002, according to the study, a carsharing organization could have to pay up to $6,000 per vehicle each year, if coverage was offered. With carsharing in the United States viewed as highly experimental, many insurance companies refused coverage to carsharing organizations or offered only limited coverage. The only major exception was insurance for carsharing vehicles which could be included as part of a company or public agency's existing vehicle fleet policy. Pooling insurance policies or sharing vehicle ownership were some of the ways private and public partnerships with carsharing organizations could mitigate the difficulties of starting and operating a carsharing program. (121)

In Palo Alto, California, Caltrain commuters had a new option for connectivity between roadway and railroad. A means for using commuter rail while also having the convenience of a personal automobile available was finally possible. Through Caltrain and carsharing, commuters could help mitigate automobile traffic congestion, reduce parking problems at stations and improve air quality without giving up the luxury of driving a car. Integrating automobile use with fixed-rail transit could make for an important transportation link in car-saturated California.

CHAPTER SIX

Chicagoland Commuter Rail Network

The city of Chicago and its metropolitan area enjoyed continuous commuter rail service, because here commuter lines were not abandoned on such a wide scale as they were in other cities during the lean years of rail transportation. The height of the automobile era did cost Chicago, Illinois, two of its three major interurban lines and its streetcar service, but the Second City continued to maintain its status as a rail-oriented industrial society. Further, the automobile could not overcome the high density of Chicago's core city and the advantage rail had over real-estate-hungry automobiles. There simply was no room to build wider roads or provide vast amounts of parking. Chicagoland commuter railroads tell a story about the durability of local passenger rail, even through railroading's most difficult period.

As was the case elsewhere in the United States, the independent railroads which provided commuter rail service to Chicago were increasingly in need of government subsidy to cover capital and operating costs not covered by ticket fare revenue. The railroad's demands for subsidy increased as ridership and service levels dropped due to competition from expanding roadway use. In 1974, the Regional Transportation Authority (RTA) was established to oversee Chicago's entire bus and rail transit network. Included under RTA jurisdiction was the Chicago Transit Authority (CTA), which maintained control over inner city bus and rail rapid transit operations, specifically Chicago's elevated "L."

Not until the RTA Amendatory Act of 1983 were commuter rail, inner city transit and suburban bus service decentralized into three separate components under RTA. Inner city Chicago transit remained under the control of CTA. Suburban bus service came under the control of "Pace," a division of RTA created specifically to provide bus transit to Chicago's outlaying suburbs. Finally, the Northeast Illinois Railroad Corporation was established to transition Chicago's many commuter rail lines into a fully functional unified commuter rail agency. Chicago Metropolitan Rail, marketed as "Metra," officially gained control over Chicago commuter rail operations from several independent railroads in 1984. The 495-mile Metra commuter rail network served six counties in Illinois and the city of Kenosha in Wisconsin.

Starting in 1995, according to Metra, ridership on Chicago-area commuter trains began to increase. In 1999, Metra passengers took more than 79.5 million trips, an increase of 2.9 percent over 1998. (122) For the year 2000, ridership increased another 2.9 percent, topping out at almost 81.9 million passenger trips. These figures included travel on the South Shore Line between Chicago and Hegewisch, Illinois, which the Regional Transportation Authority helped to support. RTA was responsible for subsidizing about 20 percent of the Chicago South Shore & South Bend Railroad, which operated commuter trains east from Chicago across northern Indiana to South Bend, Indiana. Overall, Chicago commuter ridership was up 38 percent since 1983 when Metropolitan Rail was created. (123) "We keep growing because we provide safe, reliable service as an alternative to road travel," said Metra chairman Jeffrey R. Ladd. "Apparently, more people are becoming tired of slow, congested highways. The traveling public has also become more aware that riding the train is considerably cheaper and faster than commuting by car." (124)

Factors other than automobile traffic congestion which effected commuter rail ridership, according to Metra, included strong downtown Chicago employment, a steady increase in suburban population growth, and more parking spaces available at Metra stations. Metra also experienced strong ticket sales on weekends. Commuter trains traversed twelve routes serving 224 city and suburban stations outside of downtown Chicago. By 2003, about 700 weekday Metra trains were needed to handle approximately 292,000 daily passenger trips. (125)

RTA provided Metra with financial support to cover capital and operating costs through a six county transit-dedicated sales tax. A preliminary capital budget of $371 million was approved by Metra directors for 2002. (126) Between 1984 and the year 2001, Metra's capital improvement expenditures totaled more than $3.6 billion. However, capital costs were expected to significantly increase, according to Metra, to nearly $2 billion over just four years. A major portion was to be spent on the purchase of 26 new diesel locomotives and 325 new commuter cars. (127) Other infrastructure programs included the rehabilitation of older rolling stock, the rebuilding of bridges, improvements to wayside signals, upgrades in communication devices, and the largest station improvement effort in Metra's history. Systemwide station and parking facility projects were estimated to cost more than $178 million. (128)

The cost of success meant further investing in infrastructure improvements for Metra. For example, in population-expanding McHenry County, the Metra station in downtown Crystal Lake went from 900 daily passenger boardings in 1983 to 1,600 daily boardings by 2003. Crystal Lake was located more than 40 miles from downtown Chicago on Metra's Union Pacific Northwest Line to Harvard, Illinois. To accommodate existing riders and attract new ones, construction of a new 2,000 square-foot Crystal Lake depot began with a ground breaking ceremony on June 9, 2003. The $7.6 million station project was located at the eastern edge of town and would serve as a supplement to the downtown station. (129)

"In recent years, it has become increasingly difficult to meet parking demand in southeastern McHenry County," said Metra deputy executive director Rick Tidwell. "With the county's population growing at a fast clip and commuter parking in downtown Crystal Lake becoming scarce very early each morning, it's necessary for increased access to our system. We feel we can become a transportation alternative for many more people." (130) Up to 80 percent of Metra's capital project costs were eligible, through various provisions, to be covered by the federal government's Transportation Equity Act for the 21st Century, or TEA-21.

Commuter rail ridership climbed again for the sixth year in a row in 2001, according to Metra. The annual volume of passengers was the highest the commuter railroad had experienced so far. Passenger trips taken during the year 2001 totaled more than 82.3 million. Gains in patronage were highest on Metra's Heritage Corridor to Joliet, Illinois. Passenger trips increased there by 26 percent in 2001. This compared to a four percent increase on Metra's SouthWest Service to Orland Park, Illinois, and a three percent ridership increase on the Union Pacific North Line to Kenosha, Wisconsin. (131)

Metra directors approved a preliminary operating budget of $450 million for 2002. "The cost of providing safe, reliable, convenient and comfortable commuter rail service has steadily increased," said Ladd. "Thus, our proposed 2002 operating budget envisions our first fare increase in six years, which will likely take effect June 1. It will be a five percent increase. State law requires that 55 percent of our total operating budget must be paid with fares. Therefore, to avoid cutting service, a fare increase will be needed to reach the required level." (132)

A fare increase was not expected to significantly discourage commuters from riding Metra. More and more people were choosing to ride commuter rail as an alternative to driving. In Chicago, as in other major metropolitan areas throughout the nation, severe automobile traffic congestion was outpacing road building as roads filled beyond their designed capacity. The amount of money designated to be spent on commuter rail reflected this trend. Rail transit would not have received such investment if it were not a priority for elected officials and the majority of impacted voters.

Each of Chicago's commuter rail lines has its own history and a different story to tell about the transition from private railroad operation to a unified public agency. Some of these railroads established many of the modern standards for 21st century commuter rail in the United States. Developed on Chicago area rail lines were the templates on which the modern and efficient operation of commuter railroads such as Metra and others are based.

Innovations to Maximize Service, Minimize Loss

The Chicago, Burlington & Quincy was the first U.S. commuter railroad to modernize its 38-mile Chicago-Aurora suburban corridor with Budd-built stainless steel bi-level coaches. Introduced in 1950, these cars replaced standard passenger coaches in commuter service. More new Gallery cars were purchased from the Budd Company during the early 1960s. Some cars were specially designed to have control cabs for push-pull capability. The CB&Q merged to become part of the Burlington Northern Railroad in March 1970.

Prior to the voter-approved formation of the Regional Transportation Authority in 1974, smaller suburban mass transit agencies were being created on a case-by-case basis. In 1967, the South Suburban Mass Transit District was established to finance the purchase and maintenance of rolling stock for Illinois Central. In 1971, other transit agencies were created including the West Suburban Mass Transit District for Burlington Northern. The West Suburban district purchased 25 used CB&Q streamlined passenger diesels and 94 Burlington bi-level commuter cars, then leased them back to Burlington Northern. Between 1973 and 1978, 47 more Budd push-pull Gallery cars were purchased and leased to Burlington Northern and eventually RTA.

Infrastructure improvements also were subsidized, including work on various commuter rail stations in conjunction with the Illinois Department of

Transportation. Track and signal improvements on Burlington Northern's triple-track raceway made freight, Amtrak passenger and Metra commuter service Chicago's most flexible coexistent relationship. Centralized Traffic Control (CTC) and 14 crossovers (from one track to another) allowed trains to easily pass other trains at a multiplicity of times and places.

Former Chicago, Burlington & Quincy passenger diesels pulled suburban trains well into the Burlington Northern and Metra eras. Twenty-five E8 and E9 units, as they were designated, were rebuilt to E9 specifications by locomotive builder Morrison-Knudsen between 1973 and 1978. They were originally built between 1949 and 1956 by EMD, the Electro-Motive Division of General Motors. Metra intended for these units to last in Chicago-Aurora commuter service through 1996. Their systematic retirement actually began, however, in October 1992.

To replace all 25 heritage locomotives on a one-for-one basis were 30 new diesels built by EMD for use anywhere on Metra's expanding rail network. Purchased at a cost of $59.9 million for the entire order, the new F40PH-2M diesels were equipped with miniature video cameras and monitors designed to improve the engine crew's ability to view station platforms. The idea was to help ensure that passengers were fully boarded before departure. (133)

The Burlington Northern Railroad and the Atchison, Topeka & Santa Fe Railway merged to create the Burlington Northern & Santa Fe Railway (BNSF) on September 22, 1995. Some of Metra's busiest stations were located on the old Burlington. They included the Downers Grove Main Street station, Lisle, Naperville, and the Route 59 station west of Naperville. Also in 1995, another predominant Chicago commuter railroad, the Chicago & North Western, was absorbed into the massive Union Pacific Railroad.

Commuter rail service on the former Chicago & North Western made the Union Pacific Metra's largest host railroad. The lines were named for the directions in which they fanned out from the C&NW terminal in downtown Chicago. They were the North Line, the Northwest Line and the West Line. Between Chicago and Harvard, Illinois, the Northwest Line went a distance of 63 miles, the longest stretch of continuous track on Metra's system. Off the Northwest Line at Crystal Lake, a 7.4-mile branch went north to McHenry. The only Metra line that left the state of Illinois was the North Line to Kenosha, Wisconsin. The West Line went to Geneva on Union Pacific's transcontinental freight route to the West Coast.

One of the busiest freight corridors on Metra's commuter rail system was the Union Pacific West Line. It was to be part of a commuter rail expansion program which also included two other major Metra lines, the North Central Service to Antioch and the SouthWest Service to Orland Park. The West Line was to extend nine miles west of Geneva to LaFox and Elburn, Illinois. Although the Union Pacific Railroad already had a double track main line through Elburn, a third track needed to be added to accommodate 59 weekday commuter trains on a heavy freight railroad. Further, the signaling system needed to be improved, and two new stations and a new passenger train storage yard needed to be built.

The cost to improve and expand Metra commuter rail on all three lines was to be shared by the federal government, the state of Illinois, effected local communities, and Metra. Sixty percent, or $81 million of the estimated $135 million necessary to extend the Union Pacific West Line, was to be covered by the Federal Transit Administration (FTA) as part of "New Start" transit funding, according to Metra. The state would cover 20 percent of the remaining 40 percent local match. Metra and local municipalities would cover the rest. On November 5, 2001, the FTA agreed to pay the federal share of an estimated $558 million necessary to complete the three major commuter rail expansion projects, all scheduled to be completed in 2005. "We're delighted that the U.S. Department of Transportation has recognized the importance of our program to a region where there is serious gridlock," said Metra chairman Jeffrey Ladd. (134) "We also see this as recognition of the commitment contained in the local share of the funding, which is much higher than the national average." (135)

Smooth-sided bi-level cars were introduced on the Chicago & North Western in 1955. In 1959, the first push-pull operation of any Chicago commuter railroad was inaugurated. Control cab cars enabled an engine crew to operate a train in either direction with the locomotive either pulling or pushing the train. The Chicago, Milwaukee, St. Paul & Pacific began purchasing Gallery cars for push-pull service on its North and West lines in 1961. By this time, all Chicago & North Western commuter trains were operating in push-pull fashion. By 1969, the Milwaukee Road had followed suit with 20 of its 62 Budd-built stainless steel Gallery cars purchased with control cabs. Further modernization of the Milwaukee Road took place when new six-axle passenger diesels were purchased in 1974, designed and built for the Milwaukee Road by EMD. Instead of being added to the railroad's regular pool of locomotives, new F40C units, as they were designated, were dedicated to Chicago commuter service.

The Regional Transportation Authority developed a "purchase-of-service" agreement which it negotiated with the railroads. The agency wanted to manage commuter service, including fares and schedules, while leaving the responsibility of day-to-day operations in the hands of railroad management. As the trains, stations and personnel became more the responsibility of RTA, a different kind of relationship between RTA and the rail line providers developed. The first railroad to sign a purchase-of-service contract was the Milwaukee Road in 1976. Effectively, RTA was purchasing the service of providing commuter rail from the Milwaukee Road. The Milwaukee Road maintained ownership of the right-of-way and tracks and was responsible for dispatching the trains.

December 19, 1977, marked the beginning of the end of the Milwaukee Road due to bankruptcy. The railroad's progressive demise was emphasized by the elimination of 61 percent of its roughly 10,000 miles of track. When the purchase-of-service contract ran out on June 30, 1981, the Milwaukee Road chose not to renew. For a short while the railroad took complete control of all its Chicago commuter rail services.

Commuter trains operated over two rail routes, the North Line to Fox Lake, Illinois, and the West Line to just beyond Elgin, Illinois. The North Line utilized track that originally went from Chicago to Madison, Wisconsin. The railroad beyond Fox Lake eventually became the property of the Wisconsin & Southern Railroad. Much of the West Line, which went through Iowa to Omaha, Nebraska, was eventually abandoned. On October 1, 1982, the Northeast Illinois Railroad Corporation leased the North and West lines from the Milwaukee Road for RTA commuter operations. In bankruptcy, but encouraged by a possible merger with Canadian National subsidiary Grand Trunk Western, the Milwaukee Road sold part of its right-of-way, its commuter cars and its passenger related facilities to RTA. Metra paid $67.9 million to acquire what would become the commuter railroad's Milwaukee District in 1985. (136)

When the merger agreement with Grand Trunk Western fell through and as annual freight revenues continued to decline, Milwaukee Road executives made the decision to fold. In 1985, Canadian Pacific subsidiary Soo Line acquired the Milwaukee Road for $575 million. Virtually overnight the Soo Line expanded from a 4,400-mile railroad to 7,500 miles. The Soo Line used trackage rights to operate freight trains over Metra-owned former Milwaukee Road lines. Despite Metra ownership, the dispatching of commuter trains became the responsibility of the Canadian Pacific Railway. (137) By the year 2001, average weekday ridership in and out of Chicago Union Station on the Milwaukee District North and West lines totaled about 44,500 passenger trips. This was substantially higher than the 31,000 weekday trips taken in 1984. (138)

As a result of the need for additional motive power to handle more and longer trains, the Federal Transit Administration agreed to pay 80 percent of the cost to purchase more locomotives for Metra. The state of Illinois agreed to pay the remaining 20 percent local match required by federal law. On January 12, 2001, Metra's board of directors approved the purchase of 26 new diesel locomotives for $79.4 million. They would be built by Motive Power Industries of Boise, Idaho, and delivered to the commuter railroad by 2005. Of these 26 more powerful and more efficient Metra passenger engines, designated MP36PH-3C units, 22 were to replace older units, 15 on the Milwaukee District North and West lines. The other four locomotives would cover service expansion throughout Metra's commuter rail network. The locomotives to be replaced on the Milwaukee District were those 1974-built F40C units. After having been rebuilt twice, Metra decided they were ready for retirement. (139)

Also among Metra's new rolling stock purchases were 250 stainless steel bi-level cars from the Sumitomo Corporation of America. The $2 billion contract, with an option to purchase 50 more cars, would enable Metra to retire 258 Gallery cars built during the 1950s and 1960s. Ten new cars were to be delivered to Metra per month, beginning in 2003. Japan-built shells were to be shipped to Milwaukee for assembly at Super Steel. Larger windows and more comfortable seats were promised. Delivery was expected to be completed by 2006.

With Chicago's first Gallery cars on the Burlington, push-pull service on the Chicago & North Western and the first purchase-of-service agreement signed by the Milwaukee Road, Chicago commuter railroads developed innovations in equipment and policies. Cost savings were realized during difficult times by putting more people on fewer passenger cars using the design of a double deck. Push-pull service made for efficient use of employees and equipment since trains no longer had to be turned. Finally, landmark agreements such as the purchase-of-service contract established how a commuter rail agency, independent from the host railroad, was going to provide rail service over tracks it did not own.

Metra adopted the practices, efficient operations and specialized rolling stock developed by its predecessor railroads. Adding to that was the purchase of energy efficient locomotives and modern Gallery cars. Service expansion, by adding track, lengthening lines and building more stations, made better use of Metra's infrastructure and provided more and better access to the trains. These investments served to maximize service, increase farebox revenue and raise the value of each subsidy dollar to minimize loss.

Despite these efforts toward uniformity and efficiency, however, each railroad had its nuances which were often determined by corporate history and management style. In stark contrast to 21st century Metra, the Rock Island was one Chicago commuter railroad which offered surely the strangest rail service, at one time, to Chicagoland commuters.

The Rock Island District

Made famous by its Chicago-Colorado "Rocky Mountain Rocket" and other Rocket luxury passenger trains, the Chicago, Rock Island & Pacific also hauled Chicago area commuters by rail. Passenger and freight trains operated to Joliet, Illinois, 40 miles southwest of Chicago, where Rock Island commuter service terminated. Express trains operated over the main line, making only two stops each way. A 16.4 mile suburban line began at Gresham, then swung back to the main line at Blue Island. Trains on the suburban branch typically stopped every four blocks.

General Motors designer Chuck Jordon led a design team that created a long-distance passenger train, which found an unlikely place in Rock Island commuter service. Introduced in 1955, the "Aerotrain," of which there were two prototype trainsets, toured the United States for promotional purposes until 1957. Railroads which tested the Aerotrains were the Santa Fe, Union Pacific, New York Central, and the Pennsylvania.

In an effort to better integrate rail travel into the automobile era, General Motors specifically designed the ten-car Aerotrains to look much like automobiles. However, the trainsets had ultra-lightweight coaches, an air suspension system, and other new technology designed to best compete against the automobile. Its streamlined design features included the locomotive's front end, which was shaped like the grill of a car. The roof line was made to resemble a mid-1950s GM hardtop convertible. The 1955 Chevrolet Nomad station wagon inspired the design of the Aerotrain's rear car.

The truest embrace of the automobile era was in the design of its coaches. General Motors intercity buses were redesigned to be passenger cars for the trainsets. The idea was to have GM's Truck & Coach Division handle the rail car orders while Electro-Motive built the engines. However, it was the use of buses as passenger cars that doomed the Aerotrains to fail. Although the locomotives could handle speeds of 100 miles per hour, the ride was exceedingly uncomfortable for passengers riding in bus bodies at such a high velocity. Therefore, the Aerotrains were unable to function as the highly competitive, high-speed, long-distance trains that they were intended to be.

In 1957, both trainsets were sold to the Rock Island for use as commuter trains. At slower stop-and-go commuter train speeds, the ride was much more comfortable. By 1969, the Rock Island was operating an unusual variety of passenger commuter equipment. Of its 117 cars, 77 were Pullman steam-era coaches from the 1920s. There were 20 air-conditioned streamlined coaches and 20 Budd-built bi-level cars which arrived on the Rock Island in 1965. Of the Gallery cars, five were equipped with control cabs for push-pull service.

Ten new smooth-sided bi-level cars from car builder Pullman-Standard were added to the commuter fleet in 1970. This would be the last effort by the Rock Island to modernize its commuter rail service. Tight on finances, the railroad began to go into a serious state of decay. Commuter trains were progressively running late. Track speeds were reduced due to deferred maintenance and a progressively deteriorating right-of-way. Freight trains became the priority of Rock Island management, which lacked the money to further invest in the railroad's passenger service.

During the mid-1970s, negotiations with Amtrak began regarding the future of Rock Island long-distance passenger trains. By 1970, the famous Rocky Mountain Rocket between Chicago and Colorado's Front Range had been discontinued, but other Rocket trains were still operating. After negotiations, Amtrak finally refused to take over passenger operations. Within the defining legal statutes which formed Amtrak in 1971, the words "modern and efficient" appeared. Decidedly, no such service was possible on the Rock Island in its condition.

Through a purchase-of-service agreement, Chicago's RTA took control of Rock Island commuter service in October 1976. Between 1978 and 1979, the aged Pullman-built coaches and some older Gallery cars were replaced with newer bi-level equipment. Initially, former Chicago & North Western and Amtrak Gallery cars were purchased. Later, new Budd-built versions were added.

Several years after bankruptcy, the Rock Island finally discontinued all rail service on March 23, 1980, and began liquidating its assets. RTA assigned the Chicago & North Western operational control over the Rock Island's Chicago commuter line. An administrative dispute, however, ended with the C&NW returning Rock Island operating responsibilities back to RTA.

For former Rock Island employees, the transition in work rules to RTA expectations was difficult. In response, the Interstate Commerce Commission imposed a directed-service order in accordance with the short-lived Rock Island Transition and Employee Assistance Act. The assistance program expired in 1982, after which RTA purchased the entire Rock Island commuter route for $35 million. During the 1980s, rehabilitation of the 50 trains-a-day, 21,000 daily-passenger commuter rail service took place. (140)

By the turn of the 21st century, Metra's commuter railroad to Joliet was nothing like what the Rock Island had operated before 1980. Its delapidated track and rolling stock were upgraded to Metra's standards for commuter rail operation. In 1999, ridership was up almost five percent over 1998. For the year 2000, ridership was up another 4.5 percent, to more than 9.4 million passenger trips annually taken on the Rock Island District. (141)

Illinois Central and Metra Electric

The Illinois Central Railroad was the first rail provider to introduce commuter service to the city of Chicago. Local commuters began the tradition of riding the train to and from work beginning in June 1856. Trains could be boarded at Randolph Street Station on Michigan Avenue or at the more prominent Great Central Station, built a mile to the south.

Pollution concerns regarding the extreme amount of smoke produced by steam locomotives convinced the Illinois Central to electrify its suburban line in 1926. The suburban line utilized its own track, rolling stock, stations and maintenance facilities, operated separately from the railroad's non-electrified mainline. This was unusual since most railroads in Chicago and elsewhere typically built one railroad for all services, including commuter rail. The subterranean stub-end Randolph Street Station was renovated during electrification for $2.6 million. (142)

In 1963, the Illinois Central came under the control of a holding company, IC Industries (officially not "Illinois Central Industries," but simply IC). The railroad eventually became one of ICI's smaller investments. The corporation gained controlling ownership of Midas (mufflers and brakes), Hussman (freezers), Pet (milk), and several Pepsi-Cola bottling companies.

With the intent to reduce competition and acquire new rail lines, the Illinois Central signed a merger agreement on August 10, 1972, with the Gulf,

Mobile & Ohio Railroad. The newly formed Illinois Central Gulf was created to reduce railroad-against-railroad competition in an effort to better compete against trucks and Mississippi River barge traffic.

Major cutbacks to the railroad's physical plant were made after the merger. The 9,568 miles of original pre-merger ICG trackage was reduced to 7,196 miles by 1982. Track miles were reduced again in 1983 through the elimination of many low-density branch lines. Freight-haul density increased to 6.8 million tons per mile in 1983, from 6.5 million in 1982. Annual revenues for the railroad, however, dropped by three percent in 1983 to $907 million. The railroad was in its sixth straight year of revenue declines. Money from the sale of secondary lines was necessary to pay off accumulated debt. This "streamlining" of the Illinois Central Gulf started to pay off in 1984, due in part to the sale of real estate in downtown Chicago. Annual revenues increased 12 percent to $1.01 billion. With the elimination of 3,650 miles of ICG trackage, the company dropped the word "Gulf" from its official name. This move was appropriate since nearly all of the old Gulf, Mobile & Ohio had been sold or abandoned. (143)

The last major Illinois Central rail line to be put up for sale was its Chicago suburban route. The electrified commuter line operated south from Randolph Street Station to University Park. Two branch lines went to South Chicago and Blue Island off the mainline. The 2.2 mile extension of the mainline from Richton to Park Forest South, later University Park, was built in 1977.

On May 1, 1987, Metra purchased Illinois Central's electrified suburban system at a cost of $28 million. Not included in the sale was a former Gulf, Mobile & Ohio non-electrified commuter route between Chicago and Joliet. Named the "Heritage Corridor" for the parallel Illinois & Michigan Canal Heritage Corridor, Metra purchased the service as part of the $28 million, but not the line itself. (144)

Annual revenues on what became Metra Electric totaled $21.8 million in 1987. Approximately 800 employees, 41 miles of track, 51 stations, and 1,100 trains a week served Chicago commuters, who were taking an average 43,000 trips per weekday. Included in the purchase were 165 multiple-unit bi-level "Highliner" cars. (145) A total of 130 Highliners were originally purchased by the Illinois Central between 1971 and 1972. They replaced all 274 of the railroad's 1925-1926 multiple-unit electrics. One of the 154-seat Highliners was wrecked and scrapped before RTA could add 36 more cars in 1978. By the year 2006, 25 new bi-level electrics were to be delivered, purchased by Metra for its expanding electrified suburban service.

Typically, when railroads trim down their physical plant, passenger service is the first thing to be eliminated. The Illinois Central was unusual for making the electrified suburban line its last rather than its first disacquisition. Once all transactions were completed, eight significant segments of old ICG railroad had been sold. IC Industries made $446.5 million from track, equipment and real estate sales. Systemwide track mileage was down to 2,981 on the Illinois Central by 1988. (146)

On January 1, 1989, IC Industries divested its interest in the railroad by transferring all common stock to the Illinois Central Transportation Company, a company created specifically for relieving the parent company of its railroad. IC Industries changed its name to the Whitman Corporation as a result of its ownership in chocolate candy manufacturing.

The dispatching of some Metra commuter routes was consolidated during the mid-1990s. A new Metra Central Control Center in Chicago dispatched commuter trains on Metra Electric, the Rock Island District, and the SouthWest Service route, leased to Metra by Norfolk Southern. Metra Electric ridership was up 2.2 percent for the year 2000. Annual passenger trips totaled more than 12.1 million. (147)

On February 15, 2002, Metra announced plans to renovate its underground Randolph Street Station. The $15 million four-phase construction project was designed to add an additional 14,000 square feet to the terminal. New amenities included better lighting, modern train information signs, and air conditioning. Approximately 15,000 Metra Electric commuters used Randolph Street Station each weekday, according to Metra, which also served 13,000 daily commuters on Indiana's South Shore Line. (148) More than 45,000 weekday trips were taken on more than 170 Metra Electric trains. (149)

The Illinois Central Railroad, which was absorbed by the Canadian National Railway in 1998, was no longer in the commuter or passenger train business. Through Metra, however, IC's original 1856 suburban rail system was expected to grow. The largest station improvement program on Metra's commuter rail network was to take place on the suburban line between 2002 and 2006. Also under consideration for Metra Electric expansion was a rail line extension from University Park, south along the old IC freight route, to Peotone. "It's interesting to note," said Metra chairman Jeffrey Ladd, "that Metra's busiest lines keep getting busier." (150)

The bankruptcies of the Milwaukee Road and the Rock Island, and the severe rail line reduction program of the Illinois Central, reflected the difficulties the railroads were enduring in Chicago and elsewhere. All of Chicago's commuter railroads endured fluctuations in the economy and competition from the automobile. Metra and other commuter agencies nationwide were built up from the remains of failing railroads and unprofitable commuter trains. With the aid of public money, commuter railroads like Chicago's Metra took the pieces that were left and made them into viable, unified and even successful commuter rail networks.

At twilight on December 27, 1995, a Metra Electric Highliner arrives at University Park, Illinois, the last station on Illinois Central's former electric suburban line. The suburban line is seperate from the two tracks in the background, Illinois Central's non-electrified mainline to New Orleans, Louisiana.

Metra Improves Stations and Expands Service

Making passenger rail an attractive transportation alternative depended on rolling stock, track and other infrastructure improvements. Commuter and intercity train stations were a key part of that infrastructure. The station was the first and last place where most people had contact with the rail system when going to ride a train.

Chicago's major downtown railroad stations were Union Station, Randolph Street Station, LaSalle Street Station, and the Ogilvie Transportation Center. Union Station served the Burlington Northern Santa Fe route, the Milwaukee District, North Central Service, SouthWest Service, and the Heritage Corridor. Randolph Street Station served Metra Electric and the South Shore Line. The Rock Island District was served by LaSalle Street Station. Finally, the former Chicago & NorthWestern Chicago Passenger Terminal, which was redeveloped to become the Ogilvie Transportation Center, served Metra's Union Pacific lines.

The success of any railroad station, refurbished or not, depended on three things: design, function and location. During the booming years of passenger rail service in the United States, the function of a station was obvious. It was to serve railroad passengers. In an age when stations were being revitalized, for a station to once again be viable, more than the function of being a point for transit was often required. Diversifying a station's uses, by offering retail, hotel or office space, or by allowing for professional, institutional or government uses, had the potential to make a railroad station more practical than simply as a place to buy tickets and board a train. Cities such as Nashville, Tennessee; and St. Louis and Kansas City, Missouri, succeeded at such ventures.

Location could be a blessing or a liability for a train station, depending on the economic fortunes or decline of the surrounding neighborhood. Revitalized train stations had the potential to contribute positively toward the economic redevelopment of depressed neighborhoods and business districts, as those areas tried to recover in the inner cities of North America.

In an effort to recentralize some of Chicago's suburban and downtown business communities, the Northeastern Illinois Planning Commission and Metra co-authored a feasibility study entitled "Land Use in Commuter Rail Station Areas." Central to the report were nine commuter rail stations on six different routes. Seven were suburban stations and two were in Chicago. The idea was to have Metra trains, Pace suburban buses, and station areas oriented toward reviving struggling business districts. Local communities were encouraged to embrace Chicago's transit networks. (151)

On April 20, 2001, the board of directors for Metra approved the development of 200,000 square feet of the Ogilvie Transportation Center. Metra and U.S. Equities, which renovated Chicago Union Station in 1992, were to collaborate on the revitalization of underutilized street level space at the former North Western station. The transportation center served about 95,000 weekday passengers, who rode 184 weekday trains over the Union Pacific North, Northwest and West lines. "When Metra acquired the train station in 1991, we had two goals," said Metra chairman Jeffrey Ladd. "The first was to improve it for our passengers, which we did with a massive renovation costing $141 million. Our other goal was to create new revenue streams to offset operating costs. With this development, we will further improve our recovery of costs from revenues, which already is one of the highest among U.S. transit systems." (152)

"MetraMarket," within the Ogilvie Transportation Center, had 90,000 square feet set aside for a specialty food market and retail stores. Another 36,000 square feet would be available for restaurants. As in airports, space would be rented to businesses which could benefit from the heavily concentrated flow of daily passengers. The development would also be another addition to the revival of downtown Chicago. To the east was a renovated theater district and to the west a growing restaurant district. There were 39,000 residents living within one mile of the transportation center, with more growth expected. Construction began in 2002. "MetraMarket will make a welcome addition to Chicago's fastest growing office and residential district," said U.S. Equities chairman Robert Winslow. "We envision this marketplace as an exciting, attractive new restaurant and shopping destination for commuters, city workers, residents and visitors." (153)

U.S. Equities was to oversee the development of MetraMarket, which would function under a 90-year lease. Leasing, tenant construction, and property management would be the responsibility of U.S. Equities. Within the first 25 years, Metra expected a return on capital investment and rental income to be more than $29 million. The redevelopment of the Ogilvie Transportation Center with MetraMarket was an example of how a commuter railroad could utilize real estate within and around commuter rail stations. (154)

Chicago Union Station, completed in 1925, grew to accommodate an average of more than 110,000 rail passengers per weekday by the end of the

20th century. Metra commuters typically made up 95 percent of those who used the station, while the rest rode intercity trains operated by Amtrak. Throughout passenger railroading's lean years, Union Station functioned adequately. In 1992, it was modernized at a cost of $32 million. Utilizing an architectural style from the days of private passenger railroading, the station was remodeled in Art Deco, emphasized by flowing streamlined lines and Egyptian flourishes. Metra contributed $7.7 million toward the station's restoration. Under the terms of the Americans with Disabilities Act, the station was made more spacious with easier access. This included wheelchair ramps, automatic doors, spacious walkways, and more convenient water fountains and restroom facilities. Commercial retailers located in the terminal generated income for Union Station and Metra. (155)

A $1 million study was initiated in January 2001, to make Chicago Union Station even larger. With expanded Metra and Amtrak service planned for the 21st century, capacity at the station needed to increase. The 16-month study was to determine how to enlarge a station that was already handling 306 arriving and departing weekday trains. "Amtrak sees growth, and we see growth in terms of more passengers and more trains," said Metra spokesman Frank Malone. "We hope the study will tell us there are ways to accommodate more trains. Six of Metra's routes use Union Station. We see growth on all of them." (156)

A redevelopment plan for Union Station was presented to the Chicago Landmarks Commission on February 7, 2002. The "mixed-use" redevelopment proposal described a place which offered space for offices, retail outlets, condominiums, and a hotel and conference center. Involved in the proposed 26 story, 1.1 million square-foot urban renewal project were Prime Group Realty Trust and Amtrak. They were working with the city's Department of Planning and Development to gain approval for construction. "The plan will revitalize this great building and create a vibrant mixed-use center for the West Loop," said Richard Curto, chief executive officer of Prime Group Realty Trust. (157)

Modernized and beautified train stations with restaurants and retail stores had the potential to bring in extra income for the transit agency and encourage people to use commuter rail. As businesses and residents located in or near train stations, the more accessible and convenient commuter rail became. A major concern of Metra management was to provide a convenient, easy-access rail mass transit system.

In order to go more places for more people, commuter rail expansion was required, whether it be adding capacity to stations, extending rail lines, or adding new routes to the transportation network. Expanding service did not come without its challenges, however, especially when some suburban residents opposed any increase of rail traffic through their neighborhoods. Such was the case regarding a proposed shuttle route between Barrington, on Metra's Union Pacific Northwest Line, and a new Route 59 station between Naperville and Aurora on the Burlington Northern Santa Fe.

Metra wanted to put diesel powered push-pull commuter trains in service on a lightly used Elgin, Joliet & Eastern freight route. Barrington-area residents who lived in proximity to the EJ&E refused to allow their quiet neighboring railroad to become active. "If they keep it in there (plans for the EJ&E), we'll go to the Regional Transportation Authority and the General Assembly and we'll try to cut their money off," said Gregory Furda, a citizen's representative for the Barrington Area Council of Governments. (158)

So intense was the controversy that any passenger train on the EJ&E was viewed as threatening. As a result, an unrelated September 12, 1992, excursion train was canceled. Studies continued, however, as plans were made to eventually connect Waukegan, Illinois, to Joliet via Barrington using Metra commuter trains on the EJ&E. In the meantime, Metra expansion continued elsewhere.

A major breakthrough in Chicago area regional transit was accomplished when the first downtown-bound commuter train left Antioch, Illinois, at 4:37AM, on Monday, August 19, 1996. Approximately 1,000 passengers rode the new 53-mile North Central Service during its first day of operation. Ten new suburban communities and O'Hare International Airport were connected to the Chicago Loop by Metra commuter rail. "We didn't know what to expect," said Metra executive director Philip Pagano. "If this new line is successful, it will make plans for the next project more believable.... Credibility is the name of the game." (159)

From Chicago Union Station, Metra trains dispatched by rail line-owner Wisconsin Central ran down the former Milwaukee Road West Line, 12.7 miles, to a junction in Franklin Park. A double track connection was built to put Metra trains on the Wisconsin Central for the 40-mile run to Antioch. Following ten years of planning and three years to construct, the total cost to implement commuter rail service to Antioch was $131.4 million. Federal subsidy provided 60 percent of the total cost, the state of Illinois contributed 16 percent, another 16 percent came from Metra, and eight percent came from the communities served. (160)

Passenger rail upgrades to this otherwise single-track freight corridor, which cost less than $1 million per mile, were a real benefit to the freight railroad. Before the Wisconsin Central bought the right-of-way from the Soo Line in 1987, the Soo operated only two freight trains a day. Under new ownership, freight traffic boomed to at least 20 trains a day by the time Metra service began. A new Centralized Traffic Control (CTC) signaling system, additional wayside signals, two improved junctions, four extended passing sidings, and improvements to 69 road/railroad grade crossings provided the Wisconsin Central, and its successor Canadian National, with the opportunity to improve and increase service hauling freight. The Wisconsin Central paid for none of these improvements, but rather agreed to allow Metra trains priority access to a greatly enhanced rail line which the Wisconsin Central would continue to operate and maintain.

"This isn't a public agency make-work project," said chairman Ladd. "It's a shining example of how state, local and federal officials can work together." (161) North Central Service was the first major rail mass transit line to open in the Chicago area since the Chicago North Shore & Milwaukee Railroad opened its Skokie Valley Route in 1926.

By February 1997, Metra North Central Service was hauling, on average, 2,300 weekday riders. There were 1.6 million more people riding Metra trains in 1997 than in 1996. The $558 million infrastructure expansion program, to be completed in 2005, was to be an upgrade rather than an extension of North Central Service. Two other rail lines included in the program were to be upgraded and extended, the Union Pacific West Line nine miles west from Geneva to Elburn, and Metra's SouthWest Service eleven miles south from Orland Park to Manhattan. The frequency of commuter trains on this former Wabash line would almost double from 16 weekday Metra trains to 30. (162)

Upgrades to North Central Service included more double track in places where the railroad was still single track. Wayside signals would also be improved between Franklin Park and Antioch. Finally, five new commuter stations were to be built. More than twice as many Metra trains were expected to operate over the improved rail line, from ten to 22 weekday trains. Ridership gains were high on Metra's North Central Service. In 1999, ridership increased 6.4 percent compared to 1998, the highest gain of any Metra commuter route that year. (163)

From improved stations to rail line expansion, Metra was proving to be one of North America's best examples of a commuter rail operation within a heavily populated metropolitan area. More than just a handful of reorganized commuter rail lines, Metra was a railroad with a determination to do better than survive. It meant to flourish. As the population within Chicago and its outlying suburbs increased, the potential problem of severe automobile traffic congestion increased even more so. While working to improve Metra's commuter rail network, railroad management and government officials anticipated that more people would depend on rail mass transit to get around. The improvement and expansion of Metra could not be justified if increases in ridership were not expected.

Almost a year after Metra service to Antioch, Illinois, was introduced, a northbound North Central Service train crossed the Milwaukee District North Line in Grayslake, on May 20, 1997. Slant nosed F40PH-2M 214 is lettered for Operation Lifesaver, a railroad-based awareness group created to reduce grade crossing accidents between automobiles and trains.

CHAPTER SEVEN

Trinity Railway Express

The first modern commuter rail line in the southwestern United States began serving the northern Texas metropolises of Dallas and Fort Worth on December 3, 2001. From Union Station in downtown Dallas to the reopened Texas & Pacific depot in downtown Fort Worth, the 34-mile Trinity Railway Express hurried commuters between its end points in approximately an hour. This was at least twice as fast as driving the Airport Freeway or along Interstate 30 during peak travel periods. "The completion of the Trinity Railway Express to Fort Worth unites our region, bringing us together like never before," said Dallas Area Rapid Transit board chairman Robert Pope. "This seamless connection between east and west is a tremendous resource for North Texas as we work together to improve mobility and enhance our quality of life." (164)

The Dallas-Fort Worth corridor, known locally as the Metroplex, lost its rail interurban service in 1934. Texas had a web of electric interurban lines which were largely in place by 1913. Nearly 500 miles of interurban railroad put Texas only behind California as the state with the most interurban trackage west of the Mississippi River. Of that, about 70 percent was constructed in the Dallas/Fort Worth area. The 35-mile Northern Texas Traction Company was the second Texas interurban constructed. It was completed and began operating on June 18, 1902. The first opened for service in 1901 and operated 11 miles between Sherman and Denison. The much larger interurban to Dallas grew out of the Fort Worth Street Railway, later Tarrant County Traction, which the Northern Texas Traction Company operated as a subsidiary. (165)

The importance of the line was reflected in the high standards of track construction and rolling stock and that almost half the railroad was double tracked. Electric motor cars were built with arched windows and a similarly designed roof, resembling those operated by the Texas Electric Railway, another prominent Dallas area interurban. Victorian in their appearance, the classy Northern Texas Traction cars ran fast and frequently between Fort Worth and Dallas, a service competing steam railroads did not provide. Express interurbans, or "limiteds," departed Dallas or Fort Worth on the hour, local trains on the half hour. Cars acquired after 1910 could operate in multiple-unit sets, which added passenger capacity by lengthening trains. Limiteds could traverse the route in about an hour, which was speedy for an interurban.

The failure of the Northern Texas Traction Company resulted from its inability or unwillingness to develop carload freight traffic. The interurban was therefore left vulnerable to competition from the automobile and susceptible to the effects of the Great Depression beginning in 1929. Passenger rail operations ceased on Christmas Eve, December 24, 1934. The demise of Texas interurbans and interurban railways throughout the nation was underway. The last to provide passenger rail service in northern Texas was the Texas Electric Railway, abandoned in December 1948.

Years later, however, the Northern Texas Traction Company was not to be the last local passenger rail provider between Dallas and Fort Worth. Dallas Area Rapid Transit (DART) and the Fort Worth Transportation Authority (the "T") coordinated their efforts to rebuild and upgrade a former Chicago, Rock Island & Pacific line, purchased in 1984, with the intent to someday operate commuter trains. Named for the West Fork of the Trinity River, which also connected Dallas and Fort Worth, the first ten mile leg of the Trinity Railway Express (TRE) opened for service on December 30, 1996. Commuters could park their automobiles without charge at South Irving, the farthest station west of Dallas, to ride the train into downtown. The commute by rail cost a dollar one way from any one of three Dallas suburban stations.

Initial ridership projections were exceeded. In early 1998, approximately 1,700 people were riding each day on a railroad that was projected to carry only a thousand daily commuters. Ridership was up 30 percent since opening day. All tolled, $70 million was spent on this initial first segment, including the purchase of 13 rail diesel cars from Via Rail, the national passenger railroad of Canada. (166)

Bi-directional stainless steel rail diesel cars were built by a U.S. manufacturer, the Budd Company, circa 1950. Following an extensive career hauling passengers in Canada, 13 Budd cars were brought down to Texas to be refurbished during the late 1990s. With a seating capacity for 88 to 96 passengers, the self-propelled commuter cars were modernized at a cost of

$1.8 million each. Capable of operating at speeds of up to 79 miles per hour, these cars had passenger amenities that included non-skid rubber flooring, overhead luggage racks and climate control. In compliance with the Americans with Disabilities Act of 1990, up to four wheelchairs could be accommodated per car. (167)

The federal government's contribution toward implementing commuter rail service to Dallas was delivered through the Congestion Mitigation and Air Quality (CMAQ) Improvement program. The Metroplex was located in an air quality non-attainment area and was therefore eligible for this grant. Money also came from DART's one percent sales-and-use tax. Income beyond farebox revenue came from the sale of trackage rights to the freight railroads, so they could run freight trains over the old Rock Island between commuter travel peaks.

The largest ballot proposition of its kind in Texas passed with the largest percentage of voter approval on August 12, 2000. The citizens of DART's 13 member cities voted three-to-one in favor of a $2.9 billion bond initiative for public transit improvements. The proposition was mainly to accelerate the construction of future Dallas light rail extensions, advance improvements to bus service with cleaner running vehicles, and accelerate the construction of 110 miles of permanent High Occupancy Vehicle (HOV) lanes. Nonetheless, the construction schedule for building the Trinity Railway Express directly to the Dallas/Fort Worth (DFW) International Airport was advanced by about eight years, thanks to voter-approved long-term bonds. If DFW Airport were accessed by commuter rail as planned, it would become a very diversified car-bus-train-plane intermodal facility. (168)

In September of 2000, four new Trinity Railway Express stations beyond South Irving opened. Commuter trains began operating as far west as Richland Hills, a suburb of Fort Worth. Opening day ridership totaled more than 5,000 passengers. This more than doubled the commuter railroad's average daily ridership at the time. Increased patronage was due, in part, to the opening of the CentrePort/DFW Airport station. Free shuttle buses carried TRE airport passengers four miles to the nation's second busiest airport. (169)

More trains were necessary to accommodate expanded commuter rail service. Four diesel locomotives, ten bi-level commuter coaches and four bi-level control cab cars were purchased. The 3,000 horsepower four-axle F59PH diesel locomotives were built by General Motors and could operate up to a speed of 63 miles per hour. Aluminum and steel-built control cab cars were manufactured in 1977 by Bombardier. With a seating capacity for 142 passengers, ADA-compliant cab cars had wheelchair accessible restrooms. Similar Bombardier passenger coaches, also built in 1977, were wheelchair accessible and had a seating capacity of 148. Refurbished during the year 2000, fully air conditioned control cab cars and regular coaches offered passengers such amenities as bicycle racks, luggage racks, cup holders and work station tables.

As construction of the joint rail project moved closer toward Fort Worth, contributions for phases two through four came in large part from the Fort Worth Transportation Authority's one-half percent sales-and-use tax. Other contributions came from the Federal Transit Administration, the Federal Highway Administration, the Texas Department of Transportation, Tarrant County, DART sales tax dollars, and railroad usage fees. Additional subsidies for commuter rail operations came from participating Metroplex communities. The cost to complete construction of the Trinity Railway Express to Fort Worth was $245 million. "This is the finest example of regional cooperation between Dallas and Fort Worth since the opening of DFW International Airport nearly 30 years ago," said acting Dallas Mayor Mary Poss. (170)

"The Trinity Railway Express is an impressive model of regional cooperation between neighboring communities," said Fort Worth Mayor Kenneth Barr. "Our collective efforts will increase mobility, decrease traffic congestion and improve air quality...all attractive elements to promote positive economic development." (171)

Construction of the final 1.6-mile segment, completing the connection between Dallas and Fort Worth with commuter rail, required a tunnel to be bored through the Alarm Supply Building, an historic structure in downtown Fort Worth. Laying the last sections of track to the landmark Texas & Pacific Railroad Station, and adding other infrastructure necessities such as signals, cost $60 million. The entire 34-mile commuter rail line was open for service beginning on Monday, December 3, 2001. Morning commuter trains, departing their respective cities both east and westbound, were scheduled out at 5:30 AM each weekday. A limited Saturday schedule was offered, but no trains operated on Sunday. Six of the ten commuter rail stations offered free parking for park and ride passengers, including Fort Worth's T&P station. (172)

Passengers purchased tickets based on a zone fare system similar to what Caltrain used in San Francisco, California. There were only two zones on the

PASSENGER RAIL

Trinity Railway Express, divided by a zone fare boundary at the Tarrant and Dallas County line. Traveling within a county, or zone, cost one dollar one way, two dollars round trip. Otherwise, the cost to ride between Fort Worth and Dallas, or anywhere from one county to another, cost two dollars one way or four dollars round trip. For example, since the CentrePort/DFW Airport Station was located just west of the zone fare boundary, passengers originating in Fort Worth were charged only a dollar to access the airport stop. Dallas riders en route to the same stop were charged two dollars because they entered Tarrant County.

Prior to commuter trains operating into Fort Worth, daily TRE ridership averaged nearly 6,000 passengers, according to DART. (173) An estimated 9,000 daily ridership count followed the opening of the final section of railroad. The North Central Texas Council of Governments projected that more than 11,000 daily passengers would be riding by the year 2010. (174) "We are thrilled to complete this portion of the TRE, allowing our customers the opportunity to utilize service to and from downtown Fort Worth," said the Fort Worth Transit Authority executive committee chairman, Dave Ragan. "Workers from throughout Tarrant County now have options for an easier commute by rail versus automobile." (175)

Part of the strategy of bringing commuter rail into downtown Fort Worth was to create an integrated mass transit network, which enabled passengers to transfer from one mode or transit provider to another. This was already being accomplished at Dallas Union Station as commuter train passengers could transfer to DART light rail vehicles, buses, taxis or to their own personal vehicles. Amtrak also called at Dallas Union Station. In an effort to have a similar kind of transportation diversity and connectivity that existed in downtown Dallas, an Intermodal Transportation Center (ITC) was built, east of the end-of-the-line Texas & Pacific station in downtown Fort Worth.

A formal grand opening took place on Saturday, January 12, 2002. Commuter trains, local buses and taxis called at the ITC to enable travelers convenient connectivity. Located on the first floor of the Passenger Services Building was a centralized information "kiosk." It was designed to offer "one-stop shopping" for ticketing and other transportation services. (176) "Intermodalism, the ability to transfer easily between modes of transportation, is fundamental to expanding public transportation in North Texas," said Mayor Barr. "It will play a major role in the future of Fort Worth." (177)

Amtrak moved out of the former Santa Fe Union Station on February 27, once construction of its portion of the Intermodal Transportation Center was completed. The old Union Station was located six blocks south of the new ITC. A new ticket and reservation office and baggage handling facility were provided. Retail outlets also were expected to locate within the complex, which would produce a greater return on investment. The building was constructed in an architectural style representative of the 1899 Santa Fe depot. With its 70-foot four-faced clock tower, the total cost to construct the 31,000 square-foot building was estimated to be about $25.5 million. (178)

As in many other major metropolitan areas in the United States, when Dallas and Fort Worth said good-bye to interurban passenger rail service, they believed it was gone for good. People preferred the convenience of driving their own personal automobiles, but that convenience ended when the popularity of the automobile took away mobility. As peak hour traffic increased throughout the Metroplex, commuters lost automobile mobility due to heavy traffic. For many, the convenience of shorter commute times became more important than the convenience of driving a car. The Trinity Railway Express put back what the Northern Texas Traction Company had intended all along—to provide a means for transporting large numbers of people quickly and efficiently between two high-density cities and their suburbs. "I think it's exceeded expectations," said DART executive vice president of commuter rail, Doug Allen. "Our ridership figures are pretty healthy for a 35 mile commuter rail line. It's generated a lot of excitement and demonstrated that commuter rail is a viable option.... There is probably more commuter rail in our future." (179)

Through the success of its own light rail service, Dallas Area Rapid Transit understood the economic growth potential for a suburban community connected by rail. A study conducted by the University of North Texas concluded that office and residential properties increased in value when located near or around suburban DART light rail stations. Businesses which were located within one-quarter mile of the 23 surveyed suburban rail stops showed an enhanced average property value of 53 percent above comparable properties located elsewhere. Residential properties increased in value by 39 percent. (180) A boost in the worth of business and residential real estate along the Trinity Railway Express line was expected. "Rail does more than just move people from point to point," said Gary Thomas, president and executive director for DART. "It stimulates new jobs, opens new destinations, creates economic opportunity, and in all those things, raises the quality of life in the region." (181)

Commuter rail in northern Texas and throughout the country had the potential to improve local economies while offering an alternative to peak hour automobile congestion. By increasing property values and attracting development, a commuter or light rail agency also served itself by attracting more riders who traveled to and from these developments. The condensed and overbuilt Dallas/Fort Worth Metroplex made the Trinity Railway Express an instant success. In San Francisco, Caltrain's Transbay Terminal in the developing Financial District/South of Market Area was expected to draw people to commuter rail, increasing ridership and boosting property values. Much the same success was expected for Metra and downtown Chicago with the completion of "MetraMarket" at the Ogilvie Transportation Center. Further, "intermodalism," or connectivity with other modes such as buses, light rail, and even airports made commuter rail easier to use and extended its reach.

As rail transportation is better integrated into city redevelopment projects, the more rail transit agencies and developers are able to prosper. By working together, the people who build cities and the people who provide rail transit can use one another to better their objectives. Through purchasing the old Rock Island line for future commuter rail, the forward thinking administrators of public transit in Fort Worth and Dallas positioned themselves for potential success operating commuter trains through a densely populated region. In turn, Dallas, Fort Worth and the suburbs located along the old Rock Island had the means to attract more people to their respective communities. This cycle was helping to rebuild central business districts, redevelop suburbs that integrated rail transit, and boost transit ridership. Within densely populated metropolitan areas, commuter rail and rail mass transit were becoming a constructed, operating, and successful part of a regional or city development master plan.

Crossing an old wooden trestle on the former Chicago, Rock Island & Pacific line, two 1950s era Rail Diesel Cars made their way west through South Irving, Texas, on April 8, 1997. Thirteen remanufactured Rail Diesel Cars from Canada introduced Trinity Railway Express service, which terminated in South Irving at the time, a station stop ten miles west of Dallas Union Station.

PART THREE

Adapting to Serve Regional and Commuter Rail

CHAPTER EIGHT

Passenger Rail and the Struggling Interurban

Two opposites in American passenger railroading would be interurban lines and Amtrak. Separated by time and circumstance, very little is similar about the kind of service provided by local independent interurbans and the nation's transcontinental passenger rail corporation. Interurban railroads were small, regional, private ventures which operated light-weight passenger and freight trains on their own right-of-way. Amtrak was created to operate full-sized intercity passenger trains, especially long-distance trains, mostly on tracks owned by private railroads otherwise not associated with Amtrak. The operators of typically small electric interurban lines paid for everything from track construction and maintenance, to purchasing their own rolling stock, to paying taxes. Amtrak acquired its rolling stock from the private railroads at its formation to then operate it over their tracks at taxpayers' expense. Nevertheless, the last operating interurban in the United States and the nation's intercity passenger railroad performed the same vital function at the turn of the 21st century.

Both the Chicago South Shore and South Bend interurban and Amtrak functioned as publicly-subsidized short-haul passenger and commuter railroads. The interurban no longer operated as a for-profit private venture, and Amtrak struggled to make its national long-distance service work. But as retrofit regional and commuter railroads supported by the states, both served regions of the country in local service with an appreciable level of success. Arguably, the northern Indiana interurban failed to make money as originally intended, and Amtrak fell noticeably short of comparable national passenger railroads in other countries. But if success can be measured by the effectiveness in which commuter rail and regional passenger rail can provide a transportation alternative to roadway congestion, then there is a place where a failed interurban and a struggling national passenger railroad can find their niche.

The builders of interurban railroads in the United States intended to create something that was much more than a passenger or commuter railroad by definition. They believed that the properties and practices of an electric streetcar line could be combined with that of an intercity passenger railroad. The hybrid was a speedy, electric intercity passenger and light-weight freight hauler which could go fast out in the countryside but could make frequent stops while street-running within cities.

The mixture was not a successful one. For example, trolley lines could operate simpler, lighter equipment with more frequent service. A local trolley could traverse a line within a metropolitan area several times a day. An interurban car would be gone to provide service to other cities. Trolley lines were not built for speed or distance, but to move masses of people within metro areas where populations were dense. A commuter train, however, could move people quickly between cities, with only one or a few stops per community. Such trains were not slowed down by frequent stops within cities or by mixing with automobile traffic while street-running. The interurban unsuccessfully tried to be both a street railway and a commuter railroad.

The interurban failed in another way. It could not compete against the popular use of automobiles on new roadways. Although street railways, interurbans and full-sized railroads all suffered from the effects of this new competition, the interurbans were at a particular disadvantage. In cities where street railways survived, the density of population was such that rail mass transit remained a practical and viable way to move many people within a limited geographic area. The railroads, on the other hand, turned to freight hauling for their profits. Railroad companies allowed their passenger services to decline as they concentrated on getting bulk-commodity shippers to use the rails. The federal government's response to the railroad's desire to rid themselves of their passenger trains was the creation of Amtrak in 1971.

Interurbans, although larger in size and scale than street railways, were not full-sized railroads. They were light-weight, typically electrified, passenger-based rapid transit services. Often sharp curves and steep grades limited the size of the rolling stock and length of interurban trains. Long and heavy freight trains were not practical to operate on most interurban lines. Restricted to hauling passengers and light freight, little could be done to give the interurban a competitive edge over vehicles using parallel roadways.

The Chicago South Shore & South Bend Railroad, marketed as the South Shore Line, developed into an electrified suburban commuter railroad serving the southeastern Chicago, Illinois, area and northern Indiana. Multiple-unit electric commuter cars traversed 91 miles between Randolph Street Station in Chicago and Gary, Michigan City, and South Bend, Indiana.

It was originally built as an interurban with street-running through many of the communities it served. Ironically, the South Shore Line was not very profitable compared to other interurban railways of the day. In 1914, for example, the railroad was earning below one percent on its investment. (182)

The Lincoln Highway is famous for being one of the first continuous state to state highways built in the United States. In 1921, construction of the highway was completed between South Bend and Chicago. It was built almost exactly parallel to the South Shore Line for virtually the entire length of the railroad. Tax dollars, some of which were provided by the interurban, were used by local Indiana and federal government agencies to build a paved highway, enabling the automobile and bus to take passengers, and the truck to take freight, off the rails. The interurban, which had to build, maintain, and pay taxes on its own right-of-way, suffered greatly from this government subsidized competition. A railroad, which once operated over 50 passenger trains a day, cut back to 35 daily trains when the Lincoln Highway was opened through northern Indiana. Further, annual carloads of freight between Chicago and South Bend dropped from about 6,000 carloads in 1921 to 4,000 carloads in 1924. By this time, the railroad's total annual revenues dropped to less than $800,000 per year. As a result of less income, needed maintenance was deferred, plaguing the interurban with an increase in equipment failures and a decrease in performance and service. (183)

When the bankrupt interurban was purchased by utilities tycoon Samuel Insull in 1925, he barely outbid a metal scrap junk dealer. The first transcontinental U.S. highway, the Lincoln Highway, was finished coast-to-coast in 1927. Its impact on the railroad was slow, however. By 1930, a new and improved Chicago South Shore & South Bend interurban was enjoying a $700,000 annual operating surplus. The railroad was able to pay dividends during the early years of the Great Depression. Success during the depression was not lasting as the South Shore Line had to be rescued from bankruptcy again. Despite its troubles, the South Shore Line was transformed from a street-running failed interurban to a dedicated right-of-way, government subsidized commuter railroad, with the introduction of the Northern Indiana Commuter Transportation District in 1977. (184)

The South Shore Line

The Chicago South Shore & South Bend Railroad inherited the "South Shore Line" nickname from its predecessor, the Chicago Lake Shore & South Bend

Railroad. However, the short lived Chicago & Indiana Air Line Railway stands in history as the official beginnings of the South Shore Line.

Incorporated on December 2, 1901, the Chicago & Indiana Air Line built a 3.4 mile trolley car route between Indiana Harbor and East Chicago, Indiana. It opened for service in September 1903, at a construction cost of about $250,000. The new line operated two 44-seat suburban trolleys built by car builder J.G.Brill of Philadelphia. (185)

Even before the 1903 opening, plans were in the works to build a new interurban mainline from Hammond to South Bend, Indiana. Tracks would be laid through the streets of Michigan City, New Carlisle and South Bend, located in succession east from Chicago, in northern Indiana. The idea was to run a comparatively inexpensive passenger and freight railroad which could attract riders and light-freight shippers away from the already established steam railroads. Convenience and accessability were to be the interurban's hallmark, accomplished by laying rail down major city thoroughfares. The new interurban also hoped for summertime ridership by tourists. It would be the first to provide a direct rail route from Michigan City to the Indiana Dunes recreation area along Lake Michigan.

The Chicago & Indiana Air Line changed its name to the more geographically correct Chicago Lake Shore & South Bend Railroad as plans and surveys were being completed. In 1906, U.S. Steel began constructing one of the largest steel mills in the country. The mill was projected to have enough employees to start its own municipality. The city of Gary, Indiana, was named in honor of a chairman of the board of directors at U.S. Steel, Judge Elburt H.Gary. This company town would eventually become the second largest city in Indiana.

Projections in 1906 put Gary at a population of 100,000 by 1916. With this potential future growth in mind, $6 million in capital was acquired for the South Shore Line to connect to this new city by rail. Responsible for raising the money was financier James B. Hanna of Cleveland, Ohio. He and the railroad were able to acquire enough money to build the new interurban to higher steam railway specifications.

Engineering standards on the South Shore Line were exceptional for an interurban. Grading was mostly level, the right of way was largely straight with few curves, and intersections with other railroads were met with overpasses instead of diamond intersections at grade whenever possible. The railroad was built to handle an unusually high maximum speed of 75 miles per hour over rural sections of track.

The delivery of 24 high-standard interurban cars began in March 1908. Built by Niles Car & Manufacturing of Niles, Ohio, these cars were exceptional in their construction. Unlike cars on most interurbans, those for the South Shore Line were built to steam railroad passenger car standards. Of the 24 manufactured, nine were coach-baggage combine cars and the rest were standard coaches. All cars had separate smoking compartments. People could walk around without going through the closed off smoking section to get to their smoke-prohibited coach seats. This was a true innovation since the health risks of cigar and cigarette smoke were not fully known at the time. Multiple-unit capable and geared for 75 miles per hour maximum speed, South Shore Line interurbans were powerful thanks to their 125-horsepower single-phase motors.

Each car was equipped with a high 6,600 volt single-phase alternating current (A.C.) electrical system, built by the Westinghouse Electric & Manufacturing Company. Because of concerns for safety, the railroad would be obligated to reduce its power to 700 volts A.C. within the city limits of East Chicago, Michigan City, and South Bend, anywhere there was street trackage. Interurban cars were each fitted with a high-voltage center pantograph electric collector, and trolley poles at either end of the car. The trolley poles were specifically for use on the low voltage sections of electrification within those restricted communities. The two original Brill-built wooden trolleys operating on the old Chicago & Indiana Air Line route were re-equipped with 75 horsepower A.C.motors. Two additional steel trolleys, similar to the Brill cars, helped to increase service between East Chicago and Indiana Harbor.

Construction of the 32-mile Michigan City-South Bend line, also named the "Hanna Line" after financier James Hanna, was completed and inaugurated on June 30, 1908, with the operation of a special first train. On the following day, the first revenue interurban left South Bend at 6 AM for Michigan City. Passengers who wanted to continue on to Chicago had to transfer to a Lake Michigan steamship until further rail construction could be completed. Tickets on the Hanna Line were 65 cents one way or one dollar round trip.

The building of the entire South Shore Line took one year longer than expected. Despite an original projection of $2.5 million, construction of the rail route actually cost about $4.5 million. Nevertheless, September 6, 1908, marked the beginning of revenue service on the entire 69 miles of railroad between Hammond and South Bend. Ten daily interurban trains in each direction required three hours to traverse the line. To gain entry into Chicago's downtown Loop, passengers were required to transfer either to steam commuter trains on the Lake Shore & Michigan Southern Railway at Calumet, or to local street trolleys in East Chicago or Hammond. (186)

The Chicago Lake Shore & South Bend continued to power its interurban cars through its alternating current (A.C.) electrical network, despite the increasing popularity of direct current (D.C.) electrical systems on other interurbans. Electricity for what had become the largest A.C. powered interurban in the nation, was provided by 1,500 kilowatt turbogenerators located in Michigan City.

In Chicago, Illinois Central Railroad executives felt that it would be advantageous to attract patrons from northern Indiana by connecting with the South Shore Line interurban. The Illinois Central built the Kensington & Eastern Railroad between its suburban commuter line at Pullman, Illinois, and the South Shore's western terminus at Hammond. Leased to the South Shore Line by the Illinois Central, the new rail connection opened for service on April 4, 1909. South Shore Line schedules were coordinated to meet Illinois Central suburban steam trains.

In October 1910, much of the interurban's single track railroad with passing sidings was expanded through an upgrade program to build double track. The railroad increased the frequency of passenger service to 54 trains daily. Despite operating more trains, the railroad would not consider block signals as a way to better control heavy traffic flow. Two serious head-on collisions and an order from the Railroad Commission of Indiana prompted the installation of automatic semaphore signals in 1913. (187)

South Shore Line interurbans were fast and powerful. In 1913 they were the fastest in the nation, holding a record speed average of almost 36 miles per hour including stops. These interurbans ran the 34 miles between Michigan City and South Bend in 57 minutes. Further, the power of A.C. motors enabled the cars to have a higher than average pulling capacity. A single motor car could pull 20 interurban trailers or steam railroad passenger coaches. But their larger size required more electric power. The communities which previously insisted on low voltage operations on local city streets relented to the growing needs of the interurban. Power to the 700 volt sections of railroad was increased to the 6,600 system-wide volt standard. (188)

Although these changes in passenger rail service were significant, the South Shore Line's most notable development was the addition of freight service in 1916. Anticipation of new "Less-than-Carload Lot," or LCL service, prompted the interurban to purchase two new freight motors and 20 all-steel freight cars. This contrasted with pre-1916 freight service which included milk, packaged freight, and Wells, Fargo & Company express freight carried on regularly scheduled passenger trains. Freight motors were built by Baldwin-Westinghouse and delivered in September 1916. With a maximum tractive ability of 20,800 pounds, each freight motor could pull some 30 to 40 cars. The interurban made a considerable amount of money from special movements and hauling freight. By 1918, annual freight revenue was close to $100,000. (189)

Peak passenger volume was attained during World War I. Annual ridership amounted to more than four million passengers in 1917. Indiana became an alcohol-dry state in 1917. Ridership increased because of the war effort, but also because people could still legally purchase and drink alcohol in Illinois. Police typically boarded trains in Gary looking for contraband liquor. People would sometimes deny ownership of their bags to avoid being arrested. Annual ridership declined sharply a year after the prohibition of alcohol became a nationwide constitutional law in January 1920. More than any other Chicago area interurban, the South Shore Line was losing passengers. (190)

In 1921, almost 50 million patrons rode Chicago's seven interurban rail lines. Of that total, nearly twelve million were riding the Chicago North Shore & Milwaukee, while eight million were riding the Chicago Aurora & Elgin interurban. Less than 2.5 million patrons were riding the South Shore annually. A major reason for the South Shore Line's decline was the building of the parallel Lincoln Highway. Competing trucks, buses and private automobiles removed much of the freight and passenger traffic from the rails. In 1924, the interurban ran a net deficit greater than $1.7 million. The initial $10 million capital investment depreciated to about $6 million. The South Shore Line, faced with equipment failures and decreased performance due to deferred maintenance, went into receivership on February 28, 1925. In its place a new railroad was formally incorporated. June 23, 1925, marked the beginning of the Chicago South Shore & South Bend Railroad under the control of Midland Utilities. Purchased for just under $6.5 million on July 15, 1925, the new South Shore Line began its transformation into one of the nation's most successful interurbans. (191)

By 1923, London, England-born Samuel Insull owned several Chicago and northern Illinois utilities. He then moved into the northern Indiana utilities market. He combined his holdings to form the Public Service

Investment Company. Shortly thereafter, Insull combined this and his Philadelphia-based United Gas Improvement Company to form Midland Utilities. Interested in railroad investments, Insull acquired the old Chicago Lake Shore & South Bend Railroad. His son, Samuel Insull, Jr., a vice president of Midland Utilities, led the negotiations. "Junior" became vice president of the South Shore Line and began directing its reconstruction. One of Insull's lieutenants, Britton I. Budd, became its head.

For the first year of operation under new ownership, revenues exceeded $1 million. Passenger revenues were up by 25 percent due to improvements to the railroad. Freight revenues increased by over 30 percent. Strategies learned from reconstructing the South Shore were also applied to Insull's other railroads. Stations neglected on the Chicago North Shore & Milwaukee interurban, as well as on the South Shore Line, were replaced with ones designed in "Insull Spanish" style. (192)

Back in Chicago, Illinois Central Railroad steam locomotives pulling commuter trains were causing a considerable amount of air pollution within the city's metropolitan area. In the interest of cleaner air, the city of Chicago was prompted to demand electrification of the Illinois Central in 1912. The railroad was required to comply by 1927. Great Central Station on South Water Street in Chicago was renovated in 1925, partly in preparation for electrification. The planned opening of the totally electrified suburban line was set for the summer of 1926.

In an effort to make commuter transfers easier, the new Insull-controlled Chicago South Shore & South Bend Railroad was given trackage rights over the Illinois Central through Central Station to the stub-end underground Randolph Street Station. To make its interurban cars compatible with the Illinois Central's electrical system, the South Shore Line had to convert to a 1,500 volt D.C. system from its original 6,600 volt A.C. electrical standard. Changeover first occurred between South Bend and the interurban's headquarters city, Michigan City. July 13, 1926, marked the beginning of operation for converted South Shore Line interurban cars. Trains could start running under electric power on the Illinois Central suburban line on August 29. The Illinois Central invested $50 million in station renovations, right-of-way improvements and electrification. The South Shore Line spent $2.8 million on electrification transformation, new equipment and other system-wide improvements. A casualty in this massive rehabilitation was the discontinuance of the original Chicago & Indiana Air Line trolley between East Chicago and Indiana Harbor. (193)

Commuter and interurban interchange agreements between the Illinois Central and the South Shore Line came easily. As a freight hauler, the Illinois Central valued its relationship with the Insull-controlled Commonwealth Edison plant. It was the railroad's largest freight customer. The Illinois Central hauled extensive amounts of coal to this Chicago-area electric company. Commonwealth Edison also appreciated its relationship with the Illinois Central because the new electrified suburban railway promised to be the electric company's largest electric power consumer. Major freight interchanges occurred between the Illinois Central and the South Shore Line at Kensington. A total of 56 daily interurbans crowded South Shore Line rails during the day. As a result, freight operations occurred almost entirely at night. By 1930, Samuel Insull had built a public utilities empire that was worth between $2 and $3 billion. His gas, electric and transportation companies served 5,000 communities in 32 states. (194)

Only one electric commuter coach was required during off-peak hours on the South Shore Line, as exemplified by Northern Indiana Commuter Transportation District car 43, on December 28, 1995. Street running, a once common practice on the South Shore Line, was only unique to Michigan City, Indiana, by this time.

Freight on the South Shore Line

Limited rail freight service prospered on Chicago's three major interurbans. They operated seven LCL receiving stations. These stations, built by 1927, were jointly operated in Chicago's principal shopping districts by the Chicago North Shore & Milwaukee, the Chicago South Shore & South Bend, and the Chicago Aurora & Elgin interurbans, all under Insull control.

Insull's success, however, did not last. The collapse of the stock market in October 1929, followed by the Great Depression, brought about the demise of Midland Utilities in 1933. Although all three of Insull's interurbans survived the depression under new and separate ownerships, the glory years of one man's dream had ended.

Despite entering bankruptcy on September 30, 1933, the South Shore Line, a product of Insull's highest standards, was sturdy enough to eventually succeed Chicago's other two "big three" interurbans. The Chicago Aurora & Elgin folded in 1957. In 1963, when the Chicago North Shore & Milwaukee interurban last operated, annual freight revenues on the South Shore Line exceeded $4 million. (195)

Freight hauled by interurban railroads was restricted to short truck trailers loaded on flat cars, LCL and other limited freight services. Sharp curves and steep grades were two major limitations which kept interurban lines from expanding service beyond mostly hauling passengers. When the Chicago Lake Shore & South Bend built its interurban to steam railroad standards, it inadvertently provided for the future survival of the railroad. Freight service would eventually provide the stable income required to help the South Shore Line survive declines in passenger ridership caused by the effects of the depression and the encroachment of the automobile. Standard carload freight trains could operate over this comparatively overbuilt interurban, unobstructed by sharp curves or steep grades.

During the Insull era, hauling coal to Insull's local electric utilities provided business for the South Shore Line, giving freight service a strong beginning. In 1933, freight revenues gradually climbed as the railroad tried to recover from the depression. After the Insull era, the South Shore Line found success in soliciting outside freight contracts. Off-line freight agents were established in the eastern, western, and Midwestern United States. In 1934, hauling coal amounted to 72 percent of the interurban's freight business. By 1937, annual revenues were up to $2.5 million from a 1933 low of less than $1.7 million. Bankruptcy ended for the South Shore Line in 1938. Excellence in railroad performance, hauling both freight and passengers, persisted despite troubled times. (196)

Since the Insull era, the South Shore Line sought to significantly increase its business hauling freight. But more freight trains presented some problems. As early as 1927, Insull's management saw the need to move increasingly longer freight trains off the busy Chicago Avenue thoroughfare in East Chicago, Indiana. Although this problem was not improved upon during the Insull era, property was purchased by the railroad for a five-mile East Chicago bypass. The East Chicago City Council, concerned about the number of planned grade crossings on the bypass, delayed the project until the depression suspended it indefinitely. When the South Shore Line's financial situation stabilized after reorganization, other more immediate projects were undertaken. The East Chicago bypass project was put on hold.

During the late 1940s, the South Shore was one of the first railroads to install a VHF (Very High Frequency) system-wide radio network, which enabled train crews and dispatchers to keep in direct voice contact with one another. An experiment in the use of welded rail, to replace less reliable jointed rail, began in 1937. Normal replacement and regular use of welded rail began in the 1950s.

Large capacity freight cars and powerful electric motors on the South Shore Line were comparable to other Class One railroads since the 1950s. Its three "Little Joes," purchased in 1949, were the interurban's most powerful. General Electric built 20 2-D-D-2 electric Little Joes for the Soviet Union. They were ordered in 1946. Before the order was completed, "strategic shipments" to the U.S.S.R. were banned by the U.S. State Department in late 1948. When the South Shore Line purchased its three bargain-priced Little Joes (named for Soviet leader Joseph Stalin), the railroad modified each engine's power collection from 3,300 volts D.C. to 1,500 volts D.C. Also known as "Molotov" units, these engines were the largest electric locomotives ever built. They ran at a top speed of 68 miles per hour.

The 1950s marked a period when the definition of freight service changed on the South Shore Line. Only 30 percent of freight hauled originated on the interurban. It had become a "bridge" route, bridging traffic from one connecting railroad to another. Utilizing interchange with 14 connecting mainlines, the South Shore Line originated and delivered 70 percent of its freight business off-line. (197)

During this time, concern for train traffic on Chicago Avenue in East Chicago mounted again. A 1952 traffic census found that, during a 16-hour workday period, an automobile, bus, truck, or South Shore Line train traversed Chicago Avenue an average of every four and a half seconds. Trains were required to observe traffic signals, which slowed their progress. Suddenly plans were in the works to build the five-mile bypass after all. At the same time, the Indiana Toll Road Commission was looking for land to build a toll expressway. The South Shore Line's bypass right-of-way seemed to be the answer. (198)

Railroad-owned land was deeded to the commission for the highway. In return, the commission agreed to build the South Shore a new elevated line through East Chicago. Such a line, built on fill dirt connecting twelve steel bridges over city streets, was required to alleviate the problem of grade crossings. As a further incentive, the Indiana Toll Road Commission gave the South Shore an $850,000 cash advance. Actual construction of the new bypass began in 1954. (199)

As was typical on the South Shore Line, construction of the new East Chicago bypass was equal to the standards of any Class One railroad. Welded rail was installed to handle 60 mile-per-hour speeds with curves no greater than 2.5 degrees. A new Indianapolis Avenue station in East Chicago replaced four old stations. After completion, trains ran 15 to 20 minutes faster with on-time performance rising from 92 to 98 percent. To the relief of the community, freight and passenger rail traffic was off Chicago Avenue. The new bypass opened for regular service on September 16, 1956. An inspection train carrying railroad officials and guests traversed the line the previous day. (200)

Moving the South Shore Line off Chicago Avenue was significant because it ended one of the classic failings of the interurban railroad in East Chicago. The railroad running down Chicago Avenue like a trolley line was sorely inappropriate. This was especially true given the South Shore Line's interest in hauling more freight. The interurban became more like a commuter and freight railroad when the East Chicago bypass was completed. Ironically, the new parallel toll road contributed to the loss of freight and passengers that all railroads were suffering.

Freight trains had long since disappeared from the streets of downtown South Bend by this time. A new freight terminal was built in 1931, a mile west of the old downtown terminal. The South Shore spent $350,000 to get freight movements out of South Bend's business center. Later, to avoid problems operating passenger interurbans through nearly two miles of downtown city streets, the old passenger station was closed and the tracks eliminated in 1970. The South Shore Line's new passenger terminal was located near the Bendix plant on South Bend's west side. (201)

Motive power on the South Shore Line made a significant change from electric to diesel-hauled freight beginning in late 1971. Four Chesapeake & Ohio diesel locomotives joined the South Shore electric fleet. When four more diesels were later added, all electric motors were retired, except for two of the South Shore's three Little Joes.

Ten new diesels were built in 1981 by General Motors' Electro-Motive Division and sold to the South Shore for $650,000 each. They replaced the last two Little Joe electrics and South Shore's older diesel fleet. Revenue electric freight service ended on January 31, 1981, in Gary, Indiana. Switching cars at a Georgia-Pacific warehouse, 2-D-D-2 number 803 damaged some brake rigging and had to be rescued by a diesel. (202)

The Chicago South Shore & South Bend Railroad was classified as an interurban, but it operated in a true Class One manner during the 1950s and 1960s. To be a Class One railroad at the time, a railroad had to have an annual income of $5 million or more. In perspective, by the early 1990s, the Interstate Commerce Commission categorized Class One railroads as generating $93.5 million or more annually. Class Two railroads, recategorized as "regionals," were required to generate $40 to $92 million annually and/or operate a minimum of 350 miles of track. This was not so much an indication of inflation as a reflection of the incredible size some railroads had become, usually the result of several corporate mergers. In 1978, the South Shore was asked by the ICC to be officially reclassified as a Class Two railroad. The ICC wanted to retire its "interurban" category. (203)

The South Shore in Transition

Due in large part to the building of the Indiana Toll Road in 1956 and the Dan Ryan Expressway in 1962, annual passenger ridership on the South Shore Line declined to less than 3.14 million patrons by 1965. This was a reduction of almost 30 percent from a 1955 annual ridership level of more than 4.4 million. Long haul passenger service declined rapidly during the mid-1960s. Of the South Shore Line's total ridership, 85 percent was concentrated between Gary and Chicago, the western-most part of the railroad. Determined to keep passenger trains moving, $670,000 was spent in 1967 on the maintenance and refurbishing of the South Shore Line's 64 interurban coaches. The oldest cars, manufactured to steam railroad standards, had been built by Pullman in 1926. (204) In 1969, operating losses cost the interurban about $750,000 annually. The South Shore Line sought financial assistance under the Urban Mass Transit Assistance Act of 1964. Only in 1973 did any actual outside funding begin. Just a few public agencies in Illinois were contributing. The interurban was ready to call it quits. (205)

The Chicago South Shore & South Bend Railroad asked the Interstate Commerce Commission for permission to discontinue all passenger rail service. The South Shore Line had again fallen into disrepair by 1976, due to mounting operating losses and deferred maintenance. Instead, the ICC allowed the state of Indiana the opportunity to continue interurban service as a public entity. A late 1976 ICC ruling stated that interurban-affected local Indiana governments were required to organize funding, within ten months, or lose the interurban. The ICC prepared a statement regarding the environmental impacts incurred if South Shore passenger rail service was discontinued. This was in compliance with the National Environmental Policy Act of 1969.

Cities with industry-dependent economies, such as Hammond, Gary and Michigan City, were greatly effected by the energy crisis during the 1970s. The steel industry was effected by growing competition from imported steel. Northwest Indiana residents suffered as the steel industry became more automated, cutting labor by two-thirds nationwide. People looked to Chicago to provide jobs and the South Shore Line to take them there. Indiana's steel communities were reinventing themselves in this new economy. Less expensive real estate prices made cities along the South Shore Line attractive bedroom communities for people who worked in Chicago.

"In the 1920s, if you asked which (rail lines) would survive, you wouldn't have said the South Shore. It shouldn't have survived ten minutes," said George Smerk, professor of transportation at Indiana University, regarding the interurban's varied history. But survive it would, once again. (206)

In an effort to save "the last interurban," legislation was passed in late 1977 which created Indiana's four-county Northern Indiana Commuter Transportation District, or NICTD. This new local government agency was given subsidy funding from federal, state and local taxes distributed through the Indiana General Assembly. The South Shore Line continued to operate as a private railroad, but capital improvements and system rehabilitation became the responsibility of NICTD. In 1978, 1.48 million passengers used the South Shore Line to commute by rail. (207)

With freight service almost entirely dieselized, the idea of eliminating electrification was considered. Motivated by the ICC Environmental Impact Statement, however, electrification was not abandoned. Choosing electrification over an alternative form of propulsion was a decision made in anticipation of new equipment to replace the old Pullman interurbans.

Three rail car manufacturers were considered by NICTD to build new multiple-unit, electric commuter coaches for the South Shore Line. Prospective manufacturers were Canada's Bombardier, the United States-based Budd Company, and Nippon Sharyo Limited of Japan. Proposed by Bombardier were electric, multiple-unit bi-level cars called "Shoreliners." However, NICTD was more interested in matching its new equipment to the extensively tested Silverliner and Arrow III cars, already in commuter service on southeastern Pennsylvania's SEPTA and New Jersey's NJ Transit. In August 1980, Nippon Sharyo was awarded a contract worth $40 million to build 36 new cars for the South Shore Line. The Budd Company had been underbid by the Japanese car builder by $4 million. The first 97 seat car was built and assembled in Japan for testing. The 35 cars that followed were assembled in the United States by General Electric. The initial contract was written to provide NICTD the option to purchase up to 20 more cars through September 1982. (208)

The order for new commuter equipment came just in time. The old interurban coaches had become unreliable. NICTD leased, from Chicago's Regional Transportation Authority (RTA), two five-car bi-level trainsets powered by diesels. Reserved for winter time emergencies, these trains proved their utility on January 27, 1982, when cold weather rendered many of the Pullman interurbans inoperative. Six Saturday and four Sunday RTA diesel-powered bi-level trains temporarily replaced most electric interurbans operating between Chicago and Gary.

An initial Japan-built and assembled commuter car arrived on the South Shore Line for testing in 1982. The South Shore Line's electrical distribution system was upgraded. Right-of-way and track improvements were made to accommodate the larger cars. Clearance tests were conducted on April 1. The first train of new cars began operating in revenue service in late November 1982. Delivery of the South Shore Line's first 35 General Electric-assembled cars was completed by March 1983. Later that year, eight more cars were delivered. The last regular run of the Pullman interurbans was train number 123 on August 26, 1983. Of the old South Shore Line interurbans, 49 were intended for preservation by 15 organizations.

Between Chicago and Gary, passenger ridership was significantly higher than anywhere else on the South Shore. As a result of an industrial decline in Gary, wives of industrial workers had taken clerical jobs in and around the Chicago Loop. "The South Shore absolutely plays a large role in Gary's economic development, as it has in the past and will in the future," said Ben Clement, director of economic development for the City of Gary. (209)

South Shore Line trains served Cook County in Illinois and the Indiana counties of Lake, Porter, LaPorte and St. Joseph. Electric commuter trains traveled up to 79 miles per hour between cities. The journey from Randolph Street Station in Chicago, around the southern end of Lake Michigan to South Bend, took less than two and a half hours. Capital and operating subsidies came from Chicago's RTA and Indiana's NICTD. The percentage of financial responsibility between RTA and NICTD was determined by the amount of patronage in each respective state. Chicago's RTA contributed about 20 percent of the commuter railroad's total annual subsidy. The Illinois part of the line was short but heavily traveled, stretching from Chicago to Hegewisch, a community just west of the Indiana border. The other 80 percent became the responsibility of NICTD, since the majority of South Shore Line trackage was located in Indiana. Daily ridership averaged 4,400 patrons each way, utilizing 34 scheduled trains. Annual subsidies from NICTD and RTA totaled $4.2 million in 1983. (210)

Additional grant money funded infrastructure improvements throughout the 1980s. Station enhancements included new platforms at Randolph Street Station in downtown Chicago. Entirely new station stops were also built, one in downtown Gary and another named Dune Park Station, located within proximity of the Indiana Dunes State Park. Vacationers used the South Shore Line to access the state park and the Indiana Dunes National Lakeshore. Visits to the beaches, wildflower fields and sand dunes, plus an opportunity to go camping, were within reach from the Ogden Dunes, Dune Park or Beverly Shores stops along Lake Michigan.

South Shore Line commuter and freight trains continued to use Eleventh Street through downtown Michigan City. Thirty-nine passenger trains operated daily in conjunction with five freight trains. "In many ways, the South Shore is a lifeline for us," said Michigan City Mayor Sheila Brillson. "With a sensitivity to traffic and congestion concerns, it's a healthy alternative.... The train ride (down Eleventh Street) has old-fashioned appeal. This is small town living at its best!"(211)

Despite having its commuter rail service subsidized, the South Shore Line failed to make enough money. As directed by a bankruptcy court, commuter rail assets worth $3.9 million were sold to "the District" in December 1989. On January 1, 1990, the South Shore Line itself was sold to a nationwide developer of regional freight railroads. The one-time interurban was purchased by Anacostia & Pacific for $34.5 million. Anacostia & Pacific then sold the railroad right-of-way and track to NICTD for $16.8 million in December 1990. The regional freight railroad retained control of freight service through exclusive trackage rights. Not sold was some remaining freight-only trackage. NICTD was able to make the purchase using state funds and $39 million in federal money presented in regular installments for railroad infrastructure improvements. The first installment of about $18.5 million had been presented to the commuter agency in September of 1990. (212)

Under new ownership, freight service was controlled by an Anacostia & Pacific subsidiary, the Chicago SouthShore (one word) & South Bend Railroad. This subtle name change identified the corporate division of freight and passenger service over the same rail line. To handle freight traffic, 80 employees were retained. The remaining 200 went to NICTD for commuter service. Freight hauled by the SouthShore consisted primarily of coal, coke (coal residue for making steel), and iron ore. As a bridge route carrier, the railroad ran trailer-on-flat-car trains that connected the western railroads to nearby markets in Michigan. SouthShore freight increased by 30 percent in 1990, compared to 1989. The annual number of carloads climbed to 59,000, about 65 percent of which was hauling coal. (213)

Improvements to NICTD's new commuter railroad included the purchase of 17 new electric commuter cars, made up of seven motor cars and ten trailers. Ridership demands required new matching equipment to be added to an operating fleet of 41 multiple-unit electrics. Delivery began during the fall of 1992. Building improvements in 1992 included the opening of a new station facility in Hegewisch in June and a new South Bend Terminal in November. The Bendix depot in South Bend, which the South Shore Line shared with Amtrak, was replaced with a new commuter rail terminal at the Michiana Regional Airport. A new mile-long rail extension and station facility officially opened on November 20, 1992, at a cost of $1.8 million. Convenient passenger connections between air and rail travel were now possible. The multimodal airport also connected people with intercity bus lines and local public bus transit. (214)

By mid-1996, all mainline track had been converted to welded rail. The 1990s also saw improvements to the station stops at Miller, Ogden Dunes, Beverly Shores and Dune Park. An entirely new station was built in Hammond, completed in 1998. New high-level boarding platforms were built, and better sign and audio communication devices were installed, to comply with the Americans with Disabilities Act of 1990. Other key stations without high-level platforms received wheelchair lifts as well as improved signs and audio systems. "We purchased not only the service but the real estate," said NICTD General Manager Gerald Hanas. "The line's greatest asset is the corridor itself. This railroad was ahead of development, and development followed." (215)

Federal funding for extra trains began in 1996, through the Congestion Mitigation and Air Quality Improvement program (CMAQ). These included express trains connecting Chicago to Michigan City and Dune Park. Special trains operated to the sand dunes area for such annual events as the Maple Sugar Time festival in the spring and the Duneland Harvest festival during the fall.

Annual patronage on the District's South Shore Line climbed to 3.5 million by 1999, in contrast to the 1.48 million passengers commuting in 1978. (216) NICTD estimated that rail commuters who earned their paychecks in Chicago pumped $130 million annually back into the northwest Indiana economy. With about 6,500 passengers riding round trip each weekday, the South Shore Line was operating at full capacity. "The South Shore is very important to our economy," said the mayor of Hammond, Duane Dedelow. "They'll locate here. Why? Because it's a great place to live. The South Shore will be a major draw." (217)

The 1982-built cars were undergoing an engineering and mid-life rehabilitation program at the expanded Carroll Avenue Shops in Michigan City. Two of the older fleet of cars were upgraded at a time. Any more than that, and too many cars being unavailable would have a negative impact on commuter service. Refurbishing the cars and upgrades to their motors cost from $725,000 to $750,000 per vehicle. Ten new multiple-unit commuter coaches were purchased to help relieve overcrowding on some morning rush hour trains. The new equipment had an advanced propulsion system, which promised less maintenance costs and offered better acceleration for improved on-time performance. The cost of each new commuter car was $3 million. (218)

Although an increase in ridership on the South Shore Line necessitated the purchase of more rolling stock, NICTD continued to look for ways to bring more people to its trains. South Shore Express Mortgage was established by the District and five partnering Indiana lending companies to increase home ownership in northwest Indiana. The program was in part to attract new residents to live within proximity to the South Shore Line. An incentive for signing up was a one month free rail pass, a rebate intended to encourage commuting by rail. Connected with South Shore Express Mortgage were a variety of community home loan assistance programs provided by the rail-accessible communities of Hammond, East Chicago and Gary.

The Chicago South Shore & South Bend, a railroad interurban, historically was plagued with a roller coaster ride of successes and failures. It should have been abandoned along with the nation's other light-weight, street-running, intercity interurbans. Certainly, it would have been had a government agency not stepped in to provide a tax-based subsidy to help cover capital and operating expenses. With the aid of federal, state and local tax dollars, the South Shore Line was able to make the transition from failed interurban to subsidized electrified suburban commuter railroad. As the District improved the commuter railroad's infrastructure, to provide quality service that was fast, safe, frequent, convenient and economical, the South Shore Line's ability to successfully gain coexistence with the automobile was heightened. In an age of constrained mobility due to severe automobile traffic congestion, the Northern Indiana Commuter Transportation District was not considering rail line abandonment, but instead commuter rail expansion.

South Shore Line GP38-2 number 2003, along with two sisters, await their assignment in front of one of the shop buildings in Michigan City, Indiana. Freight trains were no longer powered by electric motors, but by ten identical diesel locomotives during commuter off-peak hours and at night. Snow covered the landscape on a cold December 28, 1995, winter's day.

The Future of Northern Indiana Commuter Rail Service

At the turn of the 21st century, more than half of the South Shore Line's operating budget came from passenger ticket sales, approximately 58 percent. The federal government contributed 12 percent, while 15 percent came from the state of Indiana through the Indiana Department of Transportation. Tax dollars were not directly collected by NICTD. Thirteen percent of the operating budget came from contract fees, including Chicago's Metra commuter railroad and the District's SouthShore tenant freight railroad. "The South Shore's greatest challenge has been the transition out of its interurban heritage into a full-blown, high-density commuter rail line," said NICTD General Manager Gerald Hanas. (219)

The deterioration of 308 miles of century-old overhead wire caused increased maintenance problems, which became the major cause of disruptions to service, according to NICTD. On-time performance suffered a decline through the 1990s. The District estimated that improvements to the electrical power-supply system, communications system, signals, bridges and rolling stock would come to $166 million. (220) One solution for raising the money, according to NICTD, would be to initiate a local gas, food and beverage, or sales tax, imposed on the four Indiana counties that the commuter railroad served. The District already secured $101 million for its five-year infrastructure improvement program. Contributions came from state grants, Congressional funding, CMAQ, and through the commuter agency's own working capital. But $65 million was still left to be acquired. "A lot of major rail projects owe their success to having a regional sales tax," said John Parsons, the director of marketing and planning for NICTD. "When we meet with elected officials, we tell them we are not unique. This has been done elsewhere, and it has been done successfully elsewhere." (221)

Chicago and northwest Indiana were designated by the Environmental Protection Agency as air quality non-attainment areas. Transportation projects, therefore, must conform to the Clean Air Act requirement that such projects will reduce emission levels produced by combustion-engine driven vehicles. Unless efforts are being made to clean up the air, the EPA can block federal funding for local transportation projects through its Air Quality Conformity Determination legislation. An estimated 61 percent of northwestern Indiana commuters going to all destinations traveled by automobile, according to NICTD. But 39 percent, the majority of those who commuted to and from Chicago, rode the South Shore Line. (222)

In an effort to make the option of commuting by rail available to more people, long-term rail expansion programs were being considered by NICTD. The South Shore Line's 20-year plan included expanding commuter rail service to the Lake County community of Lowell and to Valparaiso in Porter County. NICTD projected the new commuter lines would inject $130 to $140 million annually into the economy of both counties. Access to job opportunities in the Chicago area for Indiana residents were expected to increase by 38 percent. "We would expect the surrounding area to develop even more," said Valparaiso Chamber of Commerce president Bill Oeding. "By putting in a spur here, we'd see property values go up, and an increase in retail commercial value…. The South Shore would add to our community's quality of life." (223)

A Major Investment Study, completed by NICTD in early 2001, revealed plans for a proposed West Lake County Corridor. The former Monon railroad, owned by CSX, would be upgraded for higher speed commuter rail. The initial phase of the project would have CSX trackage rebuilt south from Hammond to 45th Avenue in Munster, Indiana. From there the two intended rail routes would split. The West Lake County Corridor would continue south along the old Monon to Lowell. The other extension would use Canadian National's Grand Trunk Western line east to Valparaiso.

Each new rail alignment upgrade was estimated by the study to cost approximately $250 million, the minimum amount required to properly operate commuter trains along either potential route. Costs included improvements to the railroad right-of-way, specifically to upgrade track, signals, and to build new structures such as stations and maintenance facilities. The Monon corridor would be electrified to Munster. Connecting track and interlocking modifications in Kensington, Illinois, would be required to connect the former Monon to the old South Shore Line. To accommodate an increase in peak-hour train traffic into Randolph Street Station in Chicago, track capacity and signaling improvements would be made to Metra Electric's former Illinois Central electrified suburban line between Chicago and Kensington. (224)

Dual-mode commuter trains would be purchased, which could operate in electric mode between Chicago and Munster, then switch to diesel mode when traveling between Munster and the outlying communities. Trains would operate on both lines daily, according to the study, including weekends and holidays. Three Chicago-bound trains would initially operate during the morning peak travel period, with two off-peak trains running at midday, followed by three returning peak-hour evening trains.

Ridership on the CSX line to Lowell was expected to grow to approximately 3,330 round-trip passengers per day by the year 2020. The Canadian National line between Chicago and Valparaiso was expected to attract about 3,775 daily round-trip riders by 2020. An estimated 57 percent of northwestern Indiana commuters were expected, by this time, to be using the South Shore rail transit network to get to and from the downtown Chicago area. The criteria used to evaluate new route alternatives for commuter rail expansion were, according to the report, "ridership, capital and operating costs, levels of highway congestion, access to jobs, land use development/redevelopment, economic development, environmental impacts, community impacts, and low-income areas served." (225)

Of the two proposed new rail line extensions, NICTD's Major Investment Study preferred the Canadian National line to alleviate area automobile traffic congestion and to reduce train rider congestion on the overburdened original South Bend rail corridor. Further, northern Indiana's low-income population would have greater access to the Chicago area using the CN line from Valparaiso than the CSX line up from Lowell. Once the South Bend corridor was properly modernized, work could begin on the line to Valparaiso followed by construction of the Lowell line. New Start transportation project grants would be sought from the Federal Transit Administration, which could require a local match of anywhere from 25 to 75 percent of the total estimated construction costs, according to the report. (226) "What it comes down to is that this is a 1908 railroad that's being rebuilt piecemeal. No one has the pocketbook to do it all," said Chicago lawyer and NICTD board member Sam Melnick. (227)

Financial discord was nothing new to the South Shore Line interurban, given its history of bankruptcies and tribulation. Nonetheless, the Chicago South Shore & South Bend Railroad endured and survived the most difficult period in interurban history. Through government subsidy and a need to transport large numbers of people quickly during peak-hour travel periods, the South Shore Line was able to find its niche. As infrastructure improvements on the South Bend rail corridor improved service levels, and with the promise of future expansion, residents in northern Indiana were able to rely on this rail transportation alternative for their routine daily commute.

CHAPTER NINE

Amtrak: The Intercity Commuter Railroad

The National Railroad Passenger Corporation, marketed as Amtrak, operated regional commuter-like intercity passenger trains throughout the contiguous United States. Similar to the South Shore Line, a commuter railroad retrofit from a one-time interurban, Amtrak was having to retrofit its passenger rail service as well. Although originally chartered to operate long-distance cross country passenger trains, changes in the government subsidies which Amtrak received to cover capital and operating costs had Amtrak catering more and more to commuters.

In the absence of adequate federal subsidy to maintain a national passenger rail network, Amtrak depended on the investments made by individual states to sustain viability within those states. State governments which poorly funded Amtrak received inadequate service or lost passenger rail service entirely on certain routes. Where Amtrak was properly funded by the states, the national passenger railroad prospered. Since some state governments poured money into Amtrak while others did not, this forced Amtrak to become regionalized. During the 1990s, over 70 million passenger trips annually were taken on trains serving the Northeast Corridor between Boston, Massachusetts, and Washington, D.C., most of which were commuters. "Five of the 44 (Amtrak) routes, the ones in the Northeast and Southern California, account for over 50 percent of all riders, 56 percent of revenues, and 40 percent of cost," said Ken Mead of the U.S. General Accounting Office during the mid-1990s. (228)

At the turn of the 21st century, the state of Illinois was the primary financial supporter of regional Amtrak service between Chicago, and Carbondale, Quincy and Springfield, Illinois. With only $521 million in federal grant money for fiscal year 2001, according to Amtrak, and $279 million designated for capital investment, the passenger railroad's operating subsidy could not cover the cost to run these trains without state support. (229) "An annual federal investment in passenger rail of approximately $1.5

billion for the next 20 years, combined with leveraged state and private investment, will modernize the current rail system and advance high-speed rail corridor development throughout the United States," said Paul Nissenbaum, senior director of business planning for Amtrak. (230)

Insufficient financial support for Amtrak by the federal government put state and local governments in the position to decide the future of intercity passenger rail for the nation. The U.S. Department of Transportation's Inspector General and the federal government's General Accounting Office conducted studies which revealed Amtrak's operating budget shortfall at the turn of the 21st century. Amtrak was behind by $737 million, despite record levels of passenger ridership and ticket sales. (231) According to Amtrak, over 22.5 million passengers rode the company's intercity trains in fiscal year 2000, which brought in about $2.1 billion in revenue. (232)

The federal government created the National Railroad Passenger Corporation in October 1970 through legislation called "Railpax." Private intercity passenger trains officially came under government control when Amtrak began offering rail service on May 1, 1971. A total of 184 trains were to serve 314 destinations, according to Amtrak, beginning with train number 235, the "Clocker." It departed New York Penn Station at 12:05 AM en route to Philadelphia, Pennsylvania. (233)

During the early 21st century, Amtrak claimed to serve over 500 stations in 45 states. States without Amtrak service were South Dakota, Wyoming, Alaska and Hawaii, although Cheyenne, Wyoming, was served by Amtrak Thruway Motorcoaches. Of the more than 22,000 route miles over which Amtrak operated, it owned a mere 730 miles of actual railroad. The majority of Amtrak-owned track was located on the Northeast Corridor and in Michigan. (234)

The nation's passenger railroad was the largest contract commuter rail provider in the United States. According to Amtrak, it hauled an additional 54 million people per year through its contract commuter agencies. Commuter railroads which hired Amtrak as operator included San Francisco's Caltrain, San Diego's Coaster, Los Angeles Metrolink, Maryland Area Rail Commuter, Virginia Railway Express, and Shoreline East in Connecticut. By definition, the Rail Passenger Service Act of 1970 prohibited Amtrak from operating as a commuter railroad. As a result of operating several short-haul intercity connections, however, such as New York to Philadelphia and Los Angeles to San Diego, Amtrak itself became the most extensive commuter railroad in the nation. (235)

When the Nixon Administration approved the creation of Amtrak in 1970, then-Southern Pacific president Benjamin Biaggini said, "I think Amtrak's function should be to preside over the orderly shrinkage of rail passenger service." The Rail Passenger Service Act, however, defined Amtrak's purpose differently. Amtrak was officially given the responsibility to provide a modern and efficient intercity passenger rail service and to develop fully, through innovative operating and marketing concepts, the potential of such a service. A prime example of how Amtrak operated as a viable regional intercity commuter railroad could be found on the Northeast Corridor. Between Boston and Washington, Amtrak made substantial investments in infrastructure improvements and new dedicated trainsets to better serve one of the nation's most densely populated regions. (236)

Amtrak's regional commuter rail service began on the Northeast Corridor with the acquisition of the Metroliner, introduced by Penn Central back in the days before Amtrak. Metroliners were intended to provide regular fast and frequent passenger rail service alongside Penn Central's specified named trains. In 1967, a class of multiple-unit electrics were built by the Budd Company especially for use as Metroliners. Penn Central began operating its new trains between New York and Washington in 1968. Ideal travel time was less than three hours, provided proper care was taken to maintain track, structures, electrical systems and rolling stock. During its first year of operation, Metroliners increased rail passenger ridership by eight percent. Metroliner service had reversed a decline in patronage that began at the end of World War II. In 1972, 2.5 million people rode Amtrak's Metroliners, the trains' best year. (237)

The Railroad Revitalization and Regulatory Reform Act of 1976 enabled Amtrak to purchase the majority of the Northeast Corridor. This legislation also authorized Amtrak to spend $2.5 billion on corridor infrastructure improvements, referred to as the Northeast Corridor Improvement Project. The corridor was Amtrak's first railroad right-of-way purchase. (238)

As former Pennsylvania Railroad premier trains such as the Clocker, the Congressional and the Keystone lost their uniqueness during the Amtrak era, the original Metroliners remained recognizably separate. The service, however, prospered beyond the longevity of the electric commuter cars which had helped enhance high-speed regional rail service on the Northeast Corridor. In their final years, some Metroliner trainsets operated between Philadelphia and Harrisburg, the Pennsylvania state capital, as "Capitoliners." The successors to the 110 mile-per-hour multiple-unit Metroliners were 125 mile-per-hour electric engine-pulled Amfleet trains.

Following the refurbishment of 148 Amfleet passenger cars, "NortheastDirect" was launched by Amtrak in 1995. Northeast Direct was an intensive marketing campaign to boost ridership on conventional trains, offering improved service and half-price "try the train day" incentives. Other service improvements included en route cleaning of coaches and washrooms, better food quality and selection, and reserved Custom Class seating. Custom Class offered reserved seating on some otherwise unreserved peak hour runs at prices lower than premium Metroliner seating. Commuter-like ticketing was introduced to the Northeast Corridor through Amtrak's "Smart Pass" on January 28, 1997. A passenger who purchased a Smart Pass was permitted to travel between two specific cities an unlimited number of times, on designated trains, for an entire month. A less expensive but more limiting ten-ride option was also available. (239)

To further cater to commuters and regional intercity passengers, Amtrak wanted to operate its trains at faster speeds. Complete electrification of the Northeast Corridor, specifically between Boston and New Haven, Connecticut, was required to significantly reduce travel times between stations. New York to New Haven, only 72 miles of the Northeast Corridor, was originally electrified by the New Haven Railroad in 1914. Electrification into New York's Penn Station was completed in 1917. The Pennsylvania Railroad, predecessor to Penn Central, electrified its 226 miles between New York and Washington in 1935. Diesel-powered passenger trains traversed the remaining 157-mile former New Haven "Shore Line" between New Haven and Boston. Although plans to electrify this portion of the Northeast Corridor came and went over the years, serious consideration did not begin until the early 1990s.

Electrification between New Haven and Boston was expected to cost $321 million. Construction began ceremoniously on July 3, 1996, in Providence, Rhode Island. This was part of $1.7 billion authorized to Amtrak for capital improvements and modernization of the entire Northeast Corridor. Further, federal and state grants partially funded major renovation projects designed to enhance several Northeast Corridor stations. (240)

New technologically-advanced trainsets were sought by Amtrak to keep passenger comfort and track/equipment wear at normal levels while increasing Amtrak's Northeast Corridor optimum speed limit. Tested were the Swedish X2000, built by ABB Traction, and the German Inter-City Express "ICE" train, built by the Siemens Corporation. The significant advantages of these 150 mile-per-hour tilt-technology trainsets were due to their ability to increase speeds through the difficult sharp curves characteristic of the Northeast Corridor. "The difference in ride quality between 80 and 120 miles per hour is just enormous," said Amtrak President W. Graham Claytor Jr., of the Northeast Corridor in 1985. "Some of the curves ride rough because there are short spirals. You just go along and suddenly you're in the full arc of the curve. We don't have enough real estate to do proper spirals, either. So on some of these two and three degree curves, we run more slowly than safety would dictate, for comfort." (241)

The Swedish X2000, in particular, utilized an "active" hydraulic tilt system which depended on sensors and microprocessors located throughout the train to activate the mechanism. The system would engage once the train reached 45 miles per hour. Just as significant were its self-steering radial trucks which could sense when the track was bending around a curve. Each axle was designed to turn toward the direction of the curve to reduce friction. Its builder claimed that this technology alone could improve speeds around curves by 40 percent. (242)

Despite the innovation and advanced technology of both the X2000 and the Inter-City Express trains, Amtrak ordered 18 high-speed trains from a builder other than ABB or Siemens. Amtrak chose Canadian car builder Bombardier and Alstom Transport, a British-French company, to design and construct its dual-locomotive (one at each end), six car, 304 passenger, tilt technology electric trainsets. The trains were manufactured and assembled by Montreal-based Bombardier. Consortium partner Alstom, of Paris, France, provided the electric propulsion units. Alstom built the famed 186 mile-per-hour French TGV (Train of Great Velocity). Because it operated on relatively straight dedicated right-of-way, the TGV did not need to employ any kind of tilt mechanism.

Despite the successful tests of the tilt-equipped X2000 and the Inter-City Express trains, Amtrak chose a consortium which had no such prototype, but which offered to build the trainsets for $100 million less than ABB or Siemens. The "American Flyer" trainsets, as they were originally to be called, were part of a major $710 million March 1996 contract, which also included 15 electric 125 mile-per-hour HHP-8 locomotives to pull conventional trains. Interior amenities for American Flyer passengers were to include phone and fax services, electrical outlets for laptop computers, and provisions for audio and video entertainment. (243)

On the Northeast Corridor, 150 mile-per-hour trainsets were introduced as the new "Acela Express," which would gradually replace Metroliner service and extend premium high-speed service to Boston. The new name was given by Amtrak as an abbreviation for the words "acceleration" and "excellence." In July 1998, Amtrak ordered two more trainsets from Bombardier and Alstom for a total of 20. New maintenance facilities were designed and constructed by the consortium in Boston, New York and Washington to accommodate the new locomotives and trains.

Premium Acela Express trains were scheduled to connect Boston and New York in three hours and 15 minutes, compared to a non-electric four and a half hours. Reconditioned Amfleet trains in "Acela Regional" service were expected to need just over three and a half hours. Travel times between New York and Washington were scheduled to decrease to two and a half hours for Acela Express trains, from the three hours and 15 minutes required by 125 mile-per-hour conventional trains. (244)

Until further infrastructure upgrades could be made between New York and Washington, the Acela Express would be restricted to 135 miles-per-hour maximum speed. Nonetheless, time savings were expected to increase patronage 30 percent above Amtrak's corridor ridership of 10 million passengers per year. Concern for the Northeast Corridor's overall condition, however, and improvements to high-speed rail service and the amount of subsidy funding Amtrak received to maintain and operate the Northeast Corridor, were reflected in a report released by Amtrak in January 2000. It stated that the New York-Washington segment, in particular, "has been and is facing a period of under-investment that threatens the quality and reliability of all service providers on the South End." (245)

The report estimated that a 25-year investment of $12 billion would be required to properly improve the former Pennsylvania Railroad between New York and Washington for increased 150 miles-per-hour high-speed service and to counter a backlog of deferred maintenance. Despite the slow progress in Amtrak's ability to properly maintain and upgrade the Northeast Corridor, the Acela Express was nonetheless introduced to top officials and rail advocates with fanfare. A Washington to Boston demonstration run took place on November 16, 2000. (246)

The Acela Express was scheduled to reduce the eight and a half hour run between Boston and Washington to six and a half hours. Between Paris and Avignon, France, about the same distance by rail as the Northeast Corridor, the TGV clobbered those miles in just over two and a half hours. Only during eight miles between Kingston and Davisville, Rhode Island, could the Acela reach 150 miles per hour. The geography and physical condition of the

Northeast Corridor limited the high-speed train's potential operating ability. The first revenue Acela Express left Union Station in Washington, D.C., at 5 AM on Monday, December 11, 2000. It arrived six hours and 43 minutes later in Boston, twelve minutes late.

In roughly the first six months of service, through June 1, 2001, Acela Express trains attracted 130,486 passengers, according to Amtrak. Revenue from ticket sales was approximately $15.3 million. "The success of Acela Express in its first six months is particularly significant in light of the lackluster trends in the business travel segment as a whole," said Amtrak president George D. Warrington. "Travelers want a comfortable, efficient mode of travel between the major business hubs of the Northeast." (247)

If given proper financial support, according to Amtrak, there would be an increase in Acela Express service to 27 weekday round trips between New York and Washington, by fiscal year 2005. The new trains were projected by Amtrak to attract 3 million more passengers and bring in $180 million in new revenue a year. (248) "The Acela Express is a response to the stress calls of travelers," said Wisconsin Governor and Amtrak board member Tommy Thompson. "And this high-speed passenger rail service should not be just for Eastern Seaboard residents. America must invest in a national rail network." (249)

According to the Amtrak 2001 Strategic Business Plan, the 1997 Taxpayer Relief Act provided Amtrak with $2.2 billion to invest in qualified capital infrastructure projects. This enabled Amtrak to significantly contribute toward the development efforts of high-speed rail projects in California, the Pacific Northwest, the Midwest and elsewhere, while also improving high-speed rail service on the Northeast Corridor. (250)

True high-speed rail was defined by the Railroad Revitalization and Regulatory Reform Act of 1976, and since then by the U.S. General Accounting Office, as trains which were capable of sustaining speeds greater than 125 miles per hour. According to Amtrak, over 30 states were involved in formal high-speed rail initiatives at the turn of the 21st century. Local and state governments were learning the benefits of regional intercity passenger rail, especially where roadway and airport expansion were deemed impractical to stimulate mobility. If people on the Eastern Seaboard expected viable regional rail service, then effected local and state governments would have to make investments where federal funding proved inadequate. States which enjoyed having the Northeast Corridor paid for by the nation as part of a national network, would have to make some financial sacrifices to preserve or improve existing high-speed rail service within their region.

On-time performance decreased in 2002 for Amtrak's Acela Express. According to Amtrak, Acela trains traveling between Boston, New York and Washington achieved an 85 percent on-time performance rating for the month of January. In July, however, only 74 percent maintained their schedules. Amtrak president David L. Gunn was considering cutting back Acela Express service to operate only between Boston and New York due to reliability problems based on equipment failures, the primary cause of delayed trains. (251)

The financial requirements necessary to repair and maintain the Acela Express, as well as cover other Northeast Corridor infrastructure and operating costs, were going to require investment through government subsidy. With proper financial support, Amtrak could live up to its congressional mandate to provide modern and efficient train service. As a retrofit commuter and regional passenger carrier, however, Amtrak served those parts of the country where local investments were being made.

Regional Passenger Rail in California

Southern Pacific's "San Joaquin Daylight," a once-proud streamliner, served California's Central Valley between Oakland and Los Angeles. Before the creation of Amtrak in 1971, the San Joaquin Daylight had been reduced to a coach-baggage combine car and a regular coach. At one time, dining car service was provided, later replaced by an "Automatic Buffet" vending machine.

Three years following the formation of Amtrak, Congress mandated the implementation of an Oakland-Bakersfield regional intercity passenger train. Amtrak's new "San Joaquin" began as an "experimental operation." State support did not begin until 1980. At that time, Amtrak was able to cover only 29.5 percent of its operating expenses over this route with passenger fares. In 1992, more than 1,200 passengers a day were riding three trains each way, which enabled Amtrak to cover 75 percent of its expenses operating the San Joaquins. A significant change in the way the state of California viewed rail mass transit brought the importance of regional intercity passenger rail to the forefront. (252)

The congressional legislation that created Amtrak included Section 403b of the Rail Passenger Service Act of 1970. Section 403b outlined how federal funds for state-supported Amtrak passenger trains would be available to match state subsidies provided for those trains. Despite the prospect of federal grant money offered by Section 403b, state governments continued to treat passenger rail service marginally. In 1981, however, the federal government reaffirmed its commitment to Section 403b. This underscored a desire to expand financial partnerships with states in an effort to improve passenger rail service outside of the heavily traveled Northeast Corridor.

A breakthrough in public intercity rail travel in California began with the December 11, 1991, inaugural run of Amtrak's six car "Capitol" from San Jose to Roseville and return. The train ran via the state capital of Sacramento and paralleled the Interstate 80 Corridor, an area populated by more than five million people. California Proposition 116: "The Clean Air and Transportation Improvement Bond Act of 1990" provided $1.99 billion to be spent in part on rail. It gave the California Department of Transportation (Caltrans) the money necessary to properly support intercity passenger rail service and the local match required to gain federal funding. Six daily Amtrak trains began serving the Capitol Corridor on December 12, 1991, just in time for the Christmas holiday season. Two round trip trains operated between San Jose and Sacramento, while a third operated round trip between San Jose and Roseville, a growing high-technology center east of Sacramento. Passengers rode three and four car trains of Amtrak Amfleet and Horizon cars. The June 1990 passage of California's Proposition 116 marked the beginning of a new era for Section 403b and regional intercity passenger rail. California was ready to make a greater capital investment in Amtrak passenger trains than any other state. Rolling stock paid for in part by the state would be given "exclusive use by Caltrans." (253)

General obligation bonds from propositions 108 and 116, worth $2.99 billion, were to be used to improve regional passenger rail throughout California. As part of this investment, Amtrak received $658 million from the state to improve routes and services. Infrastructure improvements to passenger rail corridors included new rail and additional trackage, station and parking lot improvements, bridge repairs, grade crossing upgrades, new signals, and the purchase of new locomotives and bi-level cars. (254)

Initially, $42.1 million was invested into the Capitol Corridor to upgrade track, signals, stations and rolling stock. Improvements would help the Capitols to better their 38 mile-per-hour average speed, including stops, in 1992. Capitol Corridor trains were operated under contract with Caltrans, managed by San Francisco's Bay Area Rapid Transit (BART) under the Capitol Corridor Joint Powers Authority. People who lived in the central coast, northern California, and western Nevada areas had access to the

Capitol Corridor via dedicated Amtrak Thruway Motorcoach connections. Amtrak's conservative ridership projections estimated that 226,000 people would ride the new Capitols the first year. In 1992, however, ticket sales would cover only 29.6 percent of Capitol Corridor operating expenses. (255)

As a result of financing regional Amtrak service to cover budget shortfalls, the state of California wanted to distinguish its trains from the nation's otherwise largely underfunded passenger rail network. When Caltrans acquired new locomotives and bi-level cars for exclusive use in California, a new "Amtrak California" was established. Nine 3,200 horsepower passenger diesels were ordered from General Motors' Electro-Motive Division for delivery in 1994. Even though capable of speeds up to 110 miles per hour, the designated F59PHI locomotive was tuned for low emissions. The order was part of a $20.8 million contract with Caltrans. The passenger engine, designed to operate in push-pull service, was the first of its kind to comply with California's strict pollution-control requirements for both emissions and noise. Cab-control cars, food-service cars and intercity coaches were to operate on Amtrak California's three major in-state routes, the San Joaquin, Capitol and San Diegan corridors. The first double-deck "California Cars" were built by Morrison-Knudsen and operated for the first time in Southern California on October 28, 1995. (256)

"Our mission is to make decisions that maximize the three 'C's: Comfort and Convenience at an affordable Cost," said Caltrans spokesman Jim Drago in 1997. "This year, ridership on the San Jose-Sacramento Capitols is up 50 percent. We added more trains and extended the service farther east (35 miles to Colfax, California), so expenses are up 60 percent. But revenue is up 38 percent.... So the real bottom line here is that we've attracted more drivers out of their cars and created a transportation product more people find useful." (257)

The population of California's Central Valley grew significantly during the 1980s. By the 1990s, five metropolitan areas in the 400-mile Central Valley had nearly 500,000 residents each. From Redding near the Cascade Mountain Range to the north to Bakersfield at the foot of the Tehachapi Mountains, Amtrak's buses and trains served the Central Valley.

In 1998, under contract with Caltrans, Amtrak expanded its Oakland-Bakersfield San Joaquin service to also operate between Sacramento and Bakersfield. Sacramento trains switched onto or off of the Oakland route at Stockton. A new 8,000 square-foot Amtrak Passenger Station opened in Bakersfield on July 4, 2000. Most of the $15 million in construction costs was financed through Proposition 116 and other state sources. (258) "These projects are important to the communities they serve," said Rob Krebs, chairman and former chief executive officer of the Burlington Northern & Santa Fe Railway. "Each addresses a community need, whether it's air pollution reduction, traffic congestion mitigation, downtown redevelopment or other community quality of life benefits." (259)

The Los Angeles-San Diego corridor along the Pacific Ocean was an important enough passenger rail route to the Atchison, Topeka & Santa Fe Railway, that a light-weight six-car streamliner trainset was ordered to be built by the Budd Company in 1936. Delivered in early 1938, the Santa Fe's new "San Diegan" consisted of a baggage-mail car, four coaches, one tavern-lunch counter car, and a parlor-coach observation car on the end. The "Surf Line" was finally given significance as a major passenger rail route with the inauguration of the San Diegan on March 27, 1938. Two more coaches were typically added to the San Diegans due to the popularity of the streamliner. Its two daily round trips were on a tight two and a half hour schedule connecting Los Angeles and San Diego. A second trainset went into service on June 8, 1941, which enabled the Santa Fe to offer four streamliner round trips each day.

The San Diegan operated as an express train, stopping only at Oceanside midway between Los Angeles and San Diego, plus a whistlestop at Santa Ana. Additional passenger service was provided as needed. During World War II, up to twelve passenger trains a day were pressed into service on the largely single-track Surf Line, including local trains which stopped at every station. Traffic rose from 16 trains a day in 1941 to 42 in 1943. Freight trains, helper movements, and local and express passenger trains were crowding the train-order-operated single-track mainline between Fullerton and San Diego. During wartime, however, the Santa Fe would be unable to acquire the large quantities of track material necessary to build a second main line. Instead, trains were scheduled to wait in passing sidings to meet opposing trains. Similar problems across the country inspired the development of Centralized Traffic Control to increase track capacity by operating trains more efficiently. (260)

Centralized Traffic Control (CTC) enabled a single switch-tower operator to control signals and switches over an entire district. Trains could be controlled in real time rather than by train order, enabling for shorter dwell times at sidings and better timed meets. On the Surf Line, CTC machines were installed at Fullerton, covering 52 miles including a double-track segment to Los Angeles, and Oceanside covering 76 miles. Still used more than half a century later, CTC was a significant technological advancement in railroad operations for getting people and freight quickly across the landscape.

Amtrak took over San Diegan service from the Santa Fe Railway at the time of Amtrak's formation. Only about 300,000 passengers a year rode over the Santa Fe's "Surf Line" between Los Angeles and San Diego. (261) In January 1989, the San Diegan was extended northwest of Los Angeles to Santa Barbara, up Southern Pacific's "Coast Line." By the turn of the 21st century, the Los Angeles-San Diego corridor was Amtrak's second busiest behind the Northeast Corridor, with an annual ridership of more than 1.5 million. (262) The overall state population was expected to increase by 40 percent over the course of 20 years, according to Amtrak. California would have an additional 15 million more residents using the state's transportation systems by 2020. (263)

Eight new five-car bi-level trainsets were purchased for the Surf Line by Amtrak for $125 million. The state of California purchased a ninth, all to be delivered from France-based Alstom Transport through 2001. New F59PHI 110 mile-per-hour passenger diesels were built by the Electro-Motive Division of General Motors. The 427-passenger trainsets each had a coach-baggage control cab car for push-pull service, a coach-café car, two regular coaches and a Pacific Business Class car. Special amenities included television sets on the seat backs, outlets for laptop computers, and racks for bicycles and surfboards. (264)

The new trainsets were introduced as Amtrak's "Pacific Surfliner" to replace the San Diegan. An inaugural revenue run took place on Friday, May 26, 2000. Revenue break-in runs continued through the Memorial Day weekend. Officially, the Pacific Surfliner went into regular service on Thursday, June 1. The 347-mile Pacific Surfliner corridor connected San Luis Obispo and Santa Barbara to San Diego via Los Angeles. "More than just a brand new name, equipment or stations," said Amtrak president George D. Warrington, "Pacific Surfliner is a significant step in upgrading and expanding rail service throughout the state." (265)

A $10.1 billion "California Passenger Rail System 20-Year Improvement Plan" was announced to the public on March 6, 2001. The objective of the plan, according to Amtrak, was to improve mobility between major metropolitan centers in the state and enable passenger rail ridership to increase by 300 percent. Specific 20-year objectives included hourly Pacific

Surfliner service between Los Angeles and San Diego. Capital improvements to the old Santa Fe Surf Line were expected to reduce travel time from two hours and 45 minutes to less than two hours. (266)

Between Sacramento, Oakland and San Jose, the Capitol would also operate hourly, with the three hour travel time knocked down to two hours and 20 minutes. According to the Caltrans Rail Program, $20.6 million invested in either the San Joaquin or Capitol corridors would enable two daily round trips to extend north of Sacramento to Redding. Amtrak Thruway Motorcoaches connected Redding and other communities to the state's passenger rail network. The Capitol could also be expanded to Reno, Nevada, for $52 million. (267)

Finally, Amtrak's Pacific Coast long-distance train, the "Coast Starlight" from Seattle, Washington, to Los Angeles, offered one daily round trip on the Coast Line between Oakland and Los Angeles. The Caltrans Rail Program estimated that $247.3 million would be required to add local passenger rail service to what Amtrak had designated the "Coast Corridor." (268)

"This is the work of a broad coalition sharing a fundamental belief that paving more highway lanes or building more runways won't meet the transportation challenges of the 21st century in California," said Amtrak vice chairman Michael Dukakis regarding the California Passenger Rail System 20-Year Improvement Plan. "Passenger rail gives people a choice and people are responding. Amtrak ridership in California and across the country is skyrocketing. It offers a safe, comfortable and enjoyable alternative to freeway traffic and airport delays." (269)

The state of California made a determination that to restore mobility to the region and maintain it for the foreseeable future, a diversified transportation network was required. As faster, cleaner and quieter trains helped to improve quality of life, Californians were able to rely on a viable transportation alternative to roadway and airport congestion. But mobility required on-going financial investment. As exemplified by the Caltrans Rail Program and the 20-year rail improvement plan, the state and its citizens were committed to making long-term investments in passenger rail. By dividing Amtrak's national rail network into Amtrak California in the Golden State, Amtrak began passenger rail regionalization based on state support. Regional intercity passenger trains, supported by both Amtrak and the state of California, were developing into an integral and important part of California's transportation infrastructure.

Amtrak, the Freight Railroads, and Positive Train Control

When a new passenger rail service is introduced using existing railroad that once only carried freight trains, significant cost savings are realized by the commuter or intercity passenger rail agency. Avoided are the costs of surveying a new railroad, purchasing irregularly-sized plots of land, removing structures, and laying down new track, signals and other required railroad infrastructure. The basic physical plant is already in place when an established rail line can be used for hauling passengers, even if some work has to be done to improve it. Often the belief is that any railroad has the capacity to operate passenger trains in conjunction with regular freight traffic without significantly imposing on the host railroad. But if a conflict does arise, the social need to transport people would automatically take precedence over a railroad's desire to deliver a customer's load of freight. In contrast, the freight railroads depend on customer shipments for their financial stability. Therefore, railroad management should not be expected to see the operation of a commuter or passenger train as anything but a barrier, keeping a delivery from being delivered.

The Rail Passenger Service Act of 1970 obligated the railroads, those at least that were still operating passenger trains, to either continue to provide passenger service on existing routes or join Amtrak. The 25 year contract, effective May 1, 1971, imposed track standards greater than necessary to haul freight and gave Amtrak priority over freight trains anytime there was limited track capacity. Most railroads signed with Amtrak, deciding that the expense in higher track standards and delays in freight service would cost less than continuing to operate and maintain their own passenger trains. The only major railroads that did not join Amtrak in 1971 were the Southern, the Rock Island, and the Denver & Rio Grande Western. The Southern Railway signed with Amtrak in 1979, the Chicago, Rock Island & Pacific went into bankruptcy in 1980 and therefore never joined, leaving the Rio Grande to be the last Class One railroad to sign with Amtrak in 1983.

The Railroad Revitalization and Regulatory Reform Act of 1976, followed by the Staggers Rail Act of 1980, deregulated the way freight railroads could do business, which began a surge in rail freight traffic during the early 1980s. At the same time, railroads were reducing their physical plant to save money by operating trains over the least amount of trackage necessary. Over the years, such efficiencies made the dispatching of passenger trains ahead of freight trains more difficult. Freight trains were sometimes unable, or dispatchers were unwilling, to clear the line to get Amtrak trains quickly to their destinations.

For example, the Illinois Central Railroad had reduced its Central Corridor, along its Chicago-New Orleans mainline, from double track to single track with passing sidings. This was an effort by the Illinois Central to save money by reducing the on-going expense of track maintenance. As a result, freight trains began to significantly interfere with the operation of higher-priority Amtrak trains. These delays were in direct violation of the Railway Passenger Service Act of 1970. Other railroads were experiencing similar problems. In 1994, Amtrak executives threatened to ask the U.S. Attorney General to prosecute any freight railroad which did not comply with regulations giving passenger trains priority.

On the day of Amtrak's 25th anniversary, May 1, 1996, Amtrak's original contract with the freight railroads expired. Passenger service continued, however, as railroads either renegotiated a new contract or extended Amtrak's old contract until negotiations could take place. But Amtrak service suffered a blow once again as provisions which further limited Amtrak's service were included in the renegotiated contracts.

Negotiations with Conrail, which began in 1995, set a standard of compromise between the freight railroads and Amtrak. Before being phased out at the end of 1995, the Interstate Commerce Commission arbitrated Amtrak's passenger rail operations contract with Conrail. Until this time, Conrail steadfastly refused to compensate Amtrak for passenger trains delayed by fault of the freight railroad. The ICC allowed Amtrak the provision to fine railroads for delayed passenger trains, but gave the freight railroads the ability to charge Amtrak higher tenant rates for track that had to be better maintained for passenger trains. Conrail and Amtrak finally signed a ten-year contract in April 1996.

The Chicago-Washington, D.C.,"Cardinal," and the "Silver Star" between New York and Miami, Florida, suffered a top-speed reduction from 79 to 60 miles per hour on CSX lines. Track maintenance standards were reduced from class four to class three. Amtrak could not cover the cost to have CSX trackage maintained to class four standards. The railroad was being maintained for slower freight train speeds only. Before the speed reductions, the Silver Star already operated two hours slower than its 1969 Seaboard Coast Line Railroad namesake. Between Chicago and Los Angeles, the "Southwest Chief" formerly operated at 90 miles per hour over sections of Burlington Northern Santa Fe trackage. As track maintenance standards were reduced from class five to class four, the Chief was slowed to a top speed of 79. Already burdened by the increasing capital costs of maintaining the infrastructure required to operate freight trains, the railroads were reluctant to spend more to accommodate higher passenger train speeds. "So what are our true incremental costs (for passenger trains)?" asked Al Aftoora, vice president of rail corridor development at CSX. "That's the question we're trying to answer. If we only need the track for 60 miles per hour, and Amtrak wants to go 79, we would expect them to bear the full amount of the difference." (270)

Another significant issue concerning the freight railroads was liability. The freight railroads did not want to bear all of the liability for a passenger train disaster, no matter how negligent the host railroad. The freight railroads wanted a per-passenger liability cap of $250,000, in the event of a derailment ending in passenger injury or death. This was a reasonable amount of money for which the larger railroads could budget. They wanted the days of huge damage settlements to be over. In the final agreement between Amtrak and the freight railroads, Amtrak would self-insure its passengers, crews, and equipment, and the freight railroads were liable for their own employees and equipment.

As Amtrak negotiated with the freight railroads over liability, track capacity, and on-time performance, not all of the railroad's efficiencies spelled disaster for the intercity rail passenger. Although the reconditioned Illinois Central north-south Central Corridor was single track with passing sidings, improved track standards allowed for 60 mile-per-hour freight trains and 79 mile-per-hour passenger trains. On-time performance for passenger trains improved due to higher track speeds, while the implementation of Centralized Traffic Control (CTC) improved dispatching of all trains. The Illinois Central also was the first railroad to sign an operating agreement with Amtrak beyond the April 30, 1996, contract expiration date. "There was a lot of skepticism on Amtrak's part when we took out the double track," said John McPherson, the senior vice president of operations for Illinois Central. "But we've been able to raise Amtrak on-time performance from 40 to 45 percent in the double-track era to the low 80 percent range, because our whole operating plan has evolved (since the early 1990s) to a precision-type operation." (271)

On the Illinois Central, Amtrak operated a long-distance intercity train, the "City of New Orleans" between Chicago and New Orleans, Louisiana, and an Illinois regional train, the "Illini" between Chicago and Carbondale.

The Illini was primarily supported by the state of Illinois. Improvements to rail freight operations on the Central Corridor helped to better Amtrak service, but only as a byproduct. Amtrak wanted to take it one step further, however, by suggesting that improvements to rail freight corridors for passenger trains can have a positive effect on the business of hauling freight. As the transportation departments of various states negotiated with Amtrak to improve or expand passenger rail service throughout their region, Amtrak and state officials negotiated with the freight railroads to be able to provide that service. Negotiations of this type with the Burlington Northern and Southern Pacific railroads led to the successful introduction of a different kind of regional passenger train to serve the Pacific Northwest.

The 466-mile Pacific Northwest Rail Corridor extended from Vancouver, British Columbia, in Canada, through Seattle and Tacoma, Washington, to Portland and Eugene, Oregon. Annual ridership increased by more than 160 percent between 1993 and 1999, according to Amtrak. Regional intercity passenger trains carried more than 226,000 passengers in 1993. In 1999, that number climbed to more than 565,000 passengers. A viable transportation alternative to driving or flying was being developed along the Cascade Mountain Range. (272)

Dedicated Amtrak trains along what was also designated the "Cascadia Corridor" came about as part of a state-funded passenger rail program that was one of the first in a new era for passenger rail. The Washington state legislature subsidized a train station improvement program during the late 1980s, which developed into a high-speed rail initiative.

In 1992, the Federal Railroad Administration designated the Cascadia Corridor as one of only five rail routes in the United States to be significantly upgraded for high-speed passenger rail. The Washington state legislature approved the first $40.2 million in May of 1993, to make significant rail line infrastructure improvements toward that goal. A six year, $266 million high-speed rail strategy was developed by the Washington State Department of Transportation (WSDOT). All transportation modes within the state were considered by Washington's transportation commission for two, six, and 20 years into the future. "It required broad political support, but legislators eventually took the enlightened view that improving the (freight) railroad's competitiveness improved the region's economic development potential," said Gil Mallery, president of Amtrak West. (273)

High-speed passenger rail was in anticipation of a regional population increase from almost 7 million in 1993 to approximately 11 million over the course of 20 years. Within that time, regional intercity travel was expected to increase by 75 percent. Parallel Interstate 5 was not expected to be able to adequately accommodate the resulting growth in automobile traffic. The estimated cost to widen Interstate 5 by one lane each way, 185-miles between Seattle and Portland, was approximately $6.5 million per mile, according to regional transportation studies. Once completed, the total cost of highway expansion was expected to reach $2.4 billion. To upgrade this segment of the Cascadia Corridor for high-speed passenger rail was estimated to cost $2.7 million per mile. "The alternative of a new four lane or six lane highway to cope with the increase in highway traffic is very expensive," said British Columbia Premier Mike Harcourt. "The cost will be in the billions if we don't do something with rail." (274)

Reinstallation of super-elevated track curves and other track upgrades for higher speeds and increased train frequency, plus $23 million to improve signals, bridges and grade crossings along the Cascadia Corridor, began on July 1, 1993. The work was done under contract for the Burlington Northern Railroad, which owned and operated the line north of Portland. The Southern Pacific owned trackage in Oregon between Portland and Eugene. A private-public partnership was being developed that could potentially benefit the railroads for hauling freight while providing a transportation alternative for the daily commuter and intercity passenger. (275)

Technologically advanced safety features were installed for testing along 57 miles of the corridor in Washington, initially costing $6 million. A "Positive Train Control" system, designed to use satellites, was tested to pinpoint trains within about 30 feet of their actual location. Radio signals from Global Positioning System satellites informed train dispatchers of a train's location. Further, radio signals could interface with computers aboard locomotives to automatically slow or stop a train approaching track crews, maintenance equipment or other trains. The satellite system was tested against wayside transponders also designed to pinpoint trains. Either system was intended to reduce catastrophic derailments, often caused by excessive speed or other human error. The Cascadia Corridor was to be a test for Positive Train Control (PTC) implementation nationwide. Other passenger service improvements included upgrading corridor stations at a cost of about $7 million. (276)

New technologically-advanced passenger trains were introduced on the Cascadia Corridor to eventually operate in conjunction with Positive Train Control. A light-weight, high-speed Spanish Talgo tilt train was assigned to

Amtrak's "Mount Baker International" in October 1994, which operated between Vancouver and Seattle. The Talgo TP200 had a scheduled travel time 35 minutes faster than the previous passenger service, Amtrak's "Pacific International," eliminated in 1981. The twelve passive-tilt-suspension articulated passenger cars were designed to automatically tilt around curves, redistributing weight in order to allow higher speeds. Unlike a power-controlled "active" tilt mechanism, a passive or pendulum tilt suspension system allows the low-riding car bodies to tilt freely with respect to their under frames. Centrifugal force causes the cars to tilt as the train speeds around a curve.

By 1995, a public-private cooperative effort by the states of Washington and Oregon and the Burlington Northern Railroad had committed more than $80 million to upgrade Cascadia Corridor passenger rail service. Encouraged by the success of Talgo train operations, Washington State, Amtrak and Renfe Talgo of America leased another Talgo trainset from Spanish railcar manufacturer Patentes Talgo S.A. for use on the Seattle-Portland "Mt.Adams." The twelve-car Talgo replaced bi-level Superliner cars on May 19, 1996. Each trainset seated 250 passengers and contained a baggage car, a café car, a dining car and an electric generator car for head-end power. Of the eight coaches, two offered first class parlor car service. (277)

The Talgo TP200 was so named because its counterparts in Spain could reach speeds around 200 kilometers-per-hour, or 124.3 miles-per-hour. Talgo Inc., involved in the passenger rail market since 1942, developed numerous innovative technologies from its headquarters in Madrid. Initiatives to improve the Cascadia Corridor enabled Talgo to penetrate the U.S. market. "We knew when we started this service that we wanted the equipment to be top of the line, and to be unique enough to attract ridership. This has certainly been the case with Talgo," said Jim Slakey, the director of public transportation and rail division for the Washington State Department of Transportation. (278)

Individual train names were eventually dropped and all Pacific Northwest Rail Corridor trains between Vancouver and Eugene were renamed the "Cascades." The only exception was Amtrak's long-distance train, the "Coast Starlight," between Seattle and Los Angeles. A pool of five 110 mile-per-hour high-efficiency F59PHI diesel locomotives, built by General Motors' Electro-Motive Division, were assigned to the new trainsets for push-pull operation.

Initially, speeds were slow as work was being done to improve a railroad maintained primarily for freight train use. The Talgo pendulum tilt trains were limited to 79 miles-per-hour. Average speed was about 40 miles-per-hour, including stops. In 1996, an automobile took just under three hours to travel between Seattle and Portland on Interstate 5. A passenger train required just under four hours to traverse the same route by rail.

Nonetheless, the proponents of the project envisioned 125 mile-per-hour high-speed rail with a desired frequency of almost one regional passenger train per hour. The project, which Amtrak estimated would exceed $2.6 billion in total cost, was supported by the federal government, the states of Washington and Oregon, Amtrak, the Burlington Northern Santa Fe and Union Pacific railroads, and effected local communities and businesses. (279) "We decided not to try to achieve high-speed service over the entire route, initially. It was just too big and costly a problem to tackle all at once," said Burlington Northern Santa Fe's D.J. Mitchell, the railroad's assistant vice president for passenger rail. "After getting some financial commitments from the state and Amtrak to help us pay for the improvements, we looked at what could be done." (280)

"When we merged with Southern Pacific," said Union Pacific passenger services spokesman Tom Mulligan, "part of their agreement with the state of Oregon was that they would allow the state to put two passenger trains on the line out of Portland, south to Eugene, in exchange for some state-funded capacity improvements." (281)

The Oregon Department of Transportation negotiated with the Union Pacific in 2000 to allow four Talgo trains, up from the initial two, to operate over the former Southern Pacific to Eugene. Washington State owned two custom-built trainsets and Amtrak owned two, worth $10 million apiece. A fifth trainset, leased directly from Talgo by Amtrak but paid for by the state of Oregon, operated between Vancouver and Seattle. (282) A new agreement was made with the Union Pacific to allow two additional trains between Portland and Eugene, which committed the state of Oregon to add new capacity improvements greater than originally promised to the pre-merger Southern Pacific. "If we had more of these trains, we could fill them as well," said Lloyd Flem, executive director of the Washington Association of Rail Passengers. "Weekends find many trains sold out, something we refer to as excess success." (283)

In 1999, railroad infrastructure improvements enabled the Talgo trains to operate 25 minutes faster, connecting Seattle and Portland in three and a half hours. All railroad and equipment upgrades were to be completed by 2018, at which time Amtrak's 110 mile-per-hour Cascades would be able to traverse the line in an aircraft competitive two and a half hours. Talgo trains, traveling in just under four hours between Vancouver and Seattle, were expected to make the same trip in just under three hours, as a result of faster speeds. Although true 125 mile-per-hour high-speed rail was not planned to be accomplished by 2018, infrastructure improvements for 110 mile-per-hour passenger rail service was a significant improvement over Amtrak's usual top speed of 79 miles-per-hour. Frequency of service would increase with the addition of eight more Talgo trainsets by 2018. (284)

Although Union Pacific and Burlington Northern Santa Fe would have to contend with passenger trains interfering with revenue earning freight trains, improved speed and capacity was expected to help these railroads better serve their customers. Dispatching passenger trains over busy rail lines was the consideration required so that government subsidy could be used, even in part, to significantly improve a railroad's mainline freight corridor. Through a collaborative effort and the use of Positive Train Control, passenger trains could operate with freight trains on a congested rail corridor in such a way that the needs of the commuter and the needs of the shipper could be met.

Transformation of the Alton Route

Amtrak's Cascades and the Pacific Northwest Rail Corridor required collaboration and a cooperative effort to bring regional high speed passenger rail to the states of Washington and Oregon. Increases in Amtrak's ridership levels demonstrated that, even with mild improvements, a rail freight corridor can be upgraded to support passenger trains and freight trains operating over the same line. Significant improvements in regional intercity passenger rail and rail freight service were being made nationwide as the public and private sectors worked together toward a specific goal. In contrast to rail initiatives in California supported by only one state, or the Pacific Northwest Rail Corridor supported by two states, a proposed Midwest Regional Rail System was a multi-state effort to introduce world-class passenger rail service to America's heartland. Union Pacific's former Chicago & Alton line, between Chicago, Illinois, and St. Louis, Missouri, was one of three mid-western rail corridors selected to be upgraded for 110 mile-per-hour regional intercity passenger rail.

The eventual goal of the Midwest Regional Rail System was to make Chicago a hub for improved passenger rail service along several existent short-haul freight and passenger rail routes throughout the northern Middle

West of the United States. Michigan, Illinois and Wisconsin led the initiative which would eventually connect Ohio, Indiana, Minnesota, Iowa, Missouri and Nebraska to the completed rail network. The first three lines designated to initiate building the system connected Chicago and Detroit, Michigan; Chicago and Madison, Wisconsin; and Chicago-St. Louis. Passenger trains would be augmented by bus feeder service and community transit networks. Buses would serve those communities located within about an hour's drive of the nearest train station. More than 60 million people lived within proximity to the proposed super railroad of the Midwest.

"Rather than begin with a huge $6 billion Big-Dig-like project, the Midwest Regional Rail Initiative states opted to start small and prove the concept of an integrated, hub-and-spoke regional rail network," said Amtrak vice president of high-speed rail corridors David Carol. "We're looking at existing corridors where investment is already underway. These three corridors give us a great starting point." (285)

Since the 1970s, the Chicago-St. Louis "Alton Route" gradually fell into disrepair under the ownership of the Illinois Central Gulf and Chicago, Missouri & Western railroads. Amtrak struggled to provide viable regional and long-distance passenger service over the dilapidated line. Better days were coming, however, following the purchase of the Chicago-St. Louis corridor by a Class One railroad on November 8, 1989.

The Southern Pacific Railroad bought 246 miles of trackage between Joliet and East St. Louis, Illinois, from the bankrupt regional freight carrier Chicago, Missouri & Western, for $22 million. Most CM&W debt to the state of Illinois was also assumed. With financial backing from the Southern Pacific, subsidiary railroad Southern Pacific-Chicago-St. Louis (SPCSL) invested heavily in the rehabilitation of the old Chicago & Alton line. It was Southern Pacific's new gateway into Chicago. Construction began in earnest during the summer of 1990 to bring track maintenance up to standards. New cross ties and welded rail would enable priority freight trains to operate up to 70 miles per hour. For Amtrak, passenger trains would be able to run comfortably at 79 miles per hour. Financing for the work was aided by federal and state loans worth $36 million. (286)

The Southern Pacific was officially absorbed into the massive Union Pacific rail network on September 11, 1996. The $5.4 billion acquisition included Southern Pacific subsidiary railroads such as SPCSL. The new 36,500-mile Union Pacific had become the largest railroad in North America. At the time, Illinois in-state Amtrak service was supported by the state with piecemeal expenditures that were often federally sponsored. (287)

In 2000, the federal government was asked to contribute up to 80 percent of the capital cost to develop and modernize the proposed 3,000-mile Midwest Regional Rail System through 2010. The local share of investment was hoped to be accomplished, in part, through improvements to stations within each effected community. Private sector contributions from the freight railroads were also expected. Rail freight operations would benefit from the upgrades made to track and right-of-way infrastructure. Local participation through joint public and private development projects was necessary for the success of such a venture. (288)

"Transportation is really about people," said U.S. Department of Transportation secretary Rodney Slater. "It's really a matter of providing all transportation modes in a balanced kind of way that gives people choices. The transportation system of the future will have to include a good intercity rail system." (289)

Separate from Amtrak was the North American Joint Positive Train Control Program. It was a partnership agreement made between the Federal Railroad Administration, the Illinois Department of Transportation and the Association of American Railroads. The North American Joint Positive Train Control Program awarded Lockheed Martin $34 million to begin installing and developing Positive Train Control (PTC) along a 123-mile portion of the Chicago-St.Louis corridor. The pilot project would have PTC installed between Mazonia, Illinois, south of Joliet, and the Illinois capital city of Springfield. In 2000, $6.5 million was given to the Illinois Department of Transportation by the federal government toward this $60 million rail corridor upgrade. (290)

In line with a two-year $50 million Union Pacific track upgrade program, the installation of Positive Train Control would enable Amtrak to increase passenger train speeds from 79 miles-per-hour to 110 over some parts of the line. A 1994 study recommended a maximum velocity of 125 miles-per-hour for passenger trains. That recommendation was reduced to a top speed of 110 due to the high number of public grade crossings along the route, only 30 percent of which were earmarked to be closed. The Illinois Department of Transportation estimated that vehicle and pedestrian accidents would be reduced by 18 percent due to this and other safety measures. (291)

Modern technologies utilized by PTC included the Global Positioning System and other computer systems to help trains operate more safely and closer together. Computer interaction between Union Pacific's Harriman Dispatching Center in Omaha, Nebraska, and PTC-equipped trains would enable UP dispatchers to more closely monitor, and to a certain degree control, train operations. Safety protocols would have the computer stop a train if the train operator failed to obey operating instructions sent from Omaha. In theory, wayside signals could be eliminated if trains were able to run closer together in "flexible block" operation.

Between Mazonia and Bloomington, Illinois, PTC would be integrated as an enhanced overlay into the existent signaling system. Stand-alone PTC would be installed between Bloomington, Illinois, and Springfield. If the technology proved successful, most line side signals in true PTC territory would be turned off and eventually removed. Trains, both freight and passenger, would be completely dependent on Global Positioning System satellites. The dispatchers in Omaha would determine a train's location in relationship to other trains and track crews along the line. Global positioning was accurate to about 30 feet of a train's actual location.

In anticipation of increased passenger rail service on the old Chicago & Alton and other lines, both Chicago and St. Louis made plans to expand the capacity of their downtown stations. In Chicago, Amtrak and Chicago-area commuter railroad Metra commissioned a $1 million study to increase capacity at Chicago Union Station, which began in January 2001.

Train stations were less of a concern for Amtrak during its first 25 years. In many cities Amtrak abandoned its large central or union stations in favor of smaller structures which required less care and maintenance. Sometimes an alternative structure was not available, so Amtrak established "temporary" stations made up of one or more house trailers. These stations became more than just temporary, however, as best exemplified by the four trailers welded together in downtown St. Louis. They served as the city's main terminal beginning on November 1, 1978.

Plans were finally being made to close the four welded trailers, according to St. Louis city officials. A new $29 million intermodal transportation center would be built near the old historic Union Station. The facility was intended to be a hub for Amtrak, light rail, city bus and Greyhound intercity bus service. A new Amtrak maintenance facility would also be built. "I think it could be the symbol of the rebirth of downtown St. Louis," said Citizens for Modern Transit representative Tom Shrout. "Train stations have historically been the center of activity in major cities like St. Louis." (292)

Amtrak trains, which took five and a half hours to travel between Chicago and St.Louis, would be able to make the trip in three and a half hours as a result of significant rail corridor improvements. Higher speeds and an increase from three to eight daily round trips, according to the Illinois Department of Transportation, were projected to boost corridor ridership from 271,000 passengers at the turn of the 21st century, to nearly 1.3 million riders annually, once fully operational. Train tickets would almost double in price, but would be competitive with regional airline fares. (293)

The completed Midwest Regional Rail System was expected to operate 66 push-pull, tilt-technology, 110 mile-per-hour diesel propelled trainsets. Operating and maintenance costs were projected to be about $30 million per year or more. People targeted to use the short-haul rail network would be business people, senior citizens and in some cases tourists. University and college students would also ride the new trains, given the high density of higher education institutions within the proposed service area. By 2010, 9.6 million people were expected to commute or travel utilizing faster and more frequent rail service throughout the Midwest Regional Rail System annually. (294)

As the private railroads upgraded mainline track standards to improve freight service, Amtrak's national passenger rail system had an opportunity to improve and expand in a way that was not possible when the railroads were actively reducing their infrastructure. In 1971, the main purpose of Amtrak was to "save the passenger train." It was an era before crowded airports, severe automobile traffic congestion and the push for cleaner air. Without Amtrak, the nation's intercity passenger trains could very well have disappeared. But Amtrak did save the passenger train by bringing it into a new era. If Amtrak were dismantled sometime during the early 21st century, the passenger train would not disappear. State transportation agencies would likely continue to operate trains over many of Amtrak's former routes.

For example, without the National Railroad Passenger Corporation (Amtrak), the Seattle-Los Angeles Coast Starlight could be taken over by Amtrak California and the departments of transportation in Washington and Oregon. With financial support from the federal government, states such as Wisconsin, Minnesota, North Dakota, Montana and Washington could coordinate continued operation of the Chicago-Seattle/Portland "Empire Builder." Small northern state's communities served by this money-losing long-distance train would become further isolated during severe winter storms if daily passenger rail service was no longer provided. "Take the Empire Builder," said Amtrak President Thomas M. Downs in 1994. "We view it as another entry in a long list of trains that we run. We forget that it's really a rolling hotel with 350 guests." (295)

Without Amtrak at the helm, state agencies could be commissioned to operate the Cascades, the Northeast Corridor or the Midwest Regional Rail System. Coordinated joint-power boards would be created similar to the San Joaquin Regional Rail Commission in California. In an era when the passenger train provided a necessary transportation alternative, Amtrak completed its primary task. The passenger train was saved. The wisdom of federal and state governments to spend billions of dollars a year on highways came into question.

If Positive Train Control worked the way its designers intended, more trains would be able to operate closer together at much faster speeds. Such technology had the potential to revolutionize how North American trains were dispatched and operated in the 21st century. The freight railroads had as much to gain from the technology as Amtrak did. Public-private partnerships between government and the railroads could arguably be the key to developing successful passenger rail lines in America.

As the Northern Indiana Commuter Transportation District transformed a failing interurban into a viable regional commuter railroad, so did Amtrak and the states save the passenger train through the development and modernization of regional intercity passenger rail. With the increasing severity of automobile traffic congestion throughout the nation, automobiles were going slower in an era when passenger trains were going faster.

PASSENGER RAIL

The control cab car of Amtrak's Chicago-Springfield *Loop* passed one of the many grade crossings along the Southern Pacific Chicago-St. Louis line, on October 18, 1995. The former Baltimore & Ohio color position-light signal in Chenoa, Illinois, protected trains separated by signal blocks. Positive Train Control could make wayside signals obsolete.

PART FOUR

Revitalization of Street Railways and
New Light Rail

CHAPTER TEN

Modernization, Tourism, or New Start

The viability of a street railway is its ability to serve a high-density metropolitan area from a centralized location. Automobile gridlock occurs when traffic from several low density suburbs converge on one or a few high density areas such as business districts, shopping malls, or sports arenas, to name a few. It is at this point that a bus or rail mass transit system becomes more advantageous than driving. In places where large numbers of people converge, making parking difficult and automobile travel slow, a circulator or corridor streetcar line with frequent service and convenient stops can serve as an alternative to automobile traffic congestion.

A circulator street railway averages in speed from eight to 15 miles per hour, including stops, integrated with the normal flow of automobile traffic. Corridor electric trolleys on a dedicated transitway can travel much faster. A U.S. General Accounting Office (GAO) study showed that, based on the cities reviewed, the capital cost to build light rail transit (LRT) lines is greater than implementing bus rapid transit (BRT) lines. The cost to start up arterial street-based bus service, according to the GAO study, could be as low as $200,000 per mile. A more expensive, dedicated right-of-way busway system could cost upwards of $55 million per mile. The capital costs to build light rail transit systems ranged between $12.4 million and $118.8 million per mile. Once startup costs are out of the way, however, no clear advantage of one transit system over another could be determined by the study regarding operating costs. The study did determine that buses are more flexible in so much as where they can operate and the service they provide. The permanence of a light rail line, however, can better influence economic development over time. (296)

Modernization was one of the means through which old street railways were able to bounce back, as long as funding was available. A U.S. Department of Transportation study, conducted in 1999, concluded that $17 billion annually should be spent to properly invest in the maintenance and necessary improvements required to adequately sustain the nation's mass transit systems. (297) Federal funding for U.S. transit systems, including bus service, increased for fiscal year 2002. From an appropriated $6.3 billion spent on transit in 2001, $6.7 billion was allocated for 2002. In contrast, however, the aviation industry was allocated $13 billion in appropriation dollars for the same fiscal year. Highways were to receive $32.9 billion. (298) The federal investment for public transit, credited in part to the Transportation Equity Act for the 21st Century (TEA-21), amounted to $7.2 billion for the 2003 fiscal year. (299)

Philadelphia's Southeastern Pennsylvania Transportation Authority (SEPTA) provided an example of an uninterrupted rail mass transit operation. Rail transit in the Philadelphia area continued to operate, albeit with government subsidy, even after automobile use became extremely popular. Following years of deferred maintenance and the operation of obsolete equipment, SEPTA initiated programs to upgrade its service and rebuild or replace its aging rolling stock.

To improve necessary fare box revenue, city transit providers were creative in their initiatives to raise money. Where commuter ridership alone fell short, street railways as tourist attractions offered a means to restore vitality. The idea behind the preservation of an historic streetcar line was to encourage economic development through tourism while continuing to provide a viable transportation alternative. In many cities, streetcars played a significant role in shaping the very communities that subsequently abandoned them. An historic streetcar line served as a rolling museum, providing an accurate representation of street railway and community history. Therefore, some cities preferred an historic electric street railway to a regular bus transit or modern light rail system.

The streetcars on St. Charles Avenue in New Orleans, Louisiana, offered a classic example of a once threatened trolley system that was later preserved. Not only did streetcars continually operate on St. Charles Avenue without interruption, but the refurbished historic trolleys ran as much for the sake of commuter transport as they did to attract tourists.

To be more than just an alternative for commuters, an "interest" in the transit system needed to be developed to bring people to the trolleys for recreation. Through the efforts of the streetcar company and the community, tourists and residents could gain an understanding and appreciation for, not only the history of regional trolley service, but also for the history of the community itself as influenced by long-ago street railways. Further, businesses along the rail line could benefit financially from both commuter and tourist ridership. Although the daily commuter might desire the smoothness of a light rail vehicle, a long-time resident or tourist might prefer the sway and clickity-clack of an old-fashioned trolley.

The implementation of subsidized rail mass transit has often been challenging given that the public must provide much of the funding through taxation. When the Regional Transportation District (RTD) in Denver, Colorado, began constructing a new light rail line to downtown, it was controversial. The normal flow of automobile traffic was disrupted during construction. An experimental and potentially worthless public transit project was getting in the way. Further, overhead electric wires might have a negative impact on urban landscape aesthetics. But more was going on as improvements in lighting, street paving and repairs to area sidewalks were taking place at the same time. Transportation planners could only try to predict whether or not people would ride light rail, or if it would significantly reduce automobile traffic congestion.

Denver's popular light rail line became a success story as a "New Start" rail mass transit system. Its ridership success was not based on financial profitability, or even as a way to necessarily reduce traffic jams, but as an effort to diversify the transportation network of a metropolis. "Every time there is a new piece added to light rail, there is encouragement for future business opportunity for the community," said Denver businesswoman Selena Dunham. "We (downtown businesses) feel very good about our working relationship with RTD." (300)

The rarest kind of New Start street railway was one designed as an historic trolley line. In communities where electric streetcar systems had long since been abandoned, the only way to implement an historic street railway was to build it new. Kenosha Transit Electric Streetcar in Kenosha, Wisconsin, represented one such historic trolley line. A very modern electric street railway was built to accommodate the use of refurbished old trolley cars. By starting fresh, Kenosha Transit was able to build using the most modern technologies, without having to update or retrofit an old trolley system. The use of historic streetcars, however, made this otherwise new light rail line an attraction for residents and tourists alike.

The trolley car returned to America's streets at the turn of the 21st century. In some cases, only the right-of-way was left as evidence of an old street railway, transformed into a modern light rail system. Through preservation efforts, other street railways maintained their rustic charm while providing a contemporary rail transit service. New light rail lines were built as state-of-the-industry technological advancements or as historic street railways for the sake of nostalgia. Regardless if they were meant to be an alternative for the daily commuter, a tourist attraction or both, publicly financed street railways ushered in a new era for rail mass transit.

Southeastern Pennsylvania Transportation Authority

Created in 1963 by the Pennsylvania state legislature, the Southeastern Pennsylvania Transportation Authority, or SEPTA, assumed responsibility for planning, developing and coordinating a regional transportation system for Philadelphia and its Pennsylvania suburbs. Officially organized on February 18, 1964, SEPTA began serving the counties of Bucks, Chester, Delaware, Montgomery and the city of Philadelphia. In an effort to integrate rail and transit services, SEPTA acquired streetcar and bus lines owned by the Philadelphia Transportation Company in 1968 and the Philadelphia Suburban Transportation Company in 1969.

The way people used mass transportation changed gradually after the First World War. The affordable automobile was gaining in popularity, although rail mass transit was still widely used. The automobile was only one major factor which eventually crippled the street railway industry. Economic hard times followed the stock market crash of October 1929. The Great Depression forced many Americans out of work, which greatly effected rail mass transit lines.

Declining ridership significantly impacted the Philadelphia Rapid Transit Company, which filed for bankruptcy reorganization on December 4, 1934. Following a number of court hearings, the Philadelphia City Council and the Pennsylvania Public Utility Commission adopted a "Reorganization Plan" which became effective on January 1, 1940. The privately-held city transit system was renamed the Philadelphia Transportation Company (PTC). System-wide improvements and the rehabilitation of transit services cost over $10 million. (301)

World War II proved the usefulness of upgrading the Philadelphia transit system. Between 1940 and 1943, ridership increased from approximately 2 million daily riders before the war to 3.3 million. Average transit vehicle miles increased from 232,000 to 325,000 miles traveled each day. These numbers marked the company's operational peak. After the war, a significant increase in government-financed road building took place. Americans in

Philadelphia and elsewhere were buying more cars and moving to the suburbs. This move out of the inner cities only further reduced the viability of rail mass transit. Tracks went to places where people no longer wanted to live or work. Like transit companies all over the United States, the Philadelphia Transportation Company experienced a gradual decline in ridership. PTC therefore reduced transit services, until the September 30, 1968, system takeover by SEPTA. (302)

Philadelphia's rail transit network maintained its viability during a very difficult period for mass transit systems nationally. The transit agency operated regional commuter trains, subway and elevated trains, rail rapid transit cars, streetcars, transit buses and electrified trolley buses. By the early 1980s, SEPTA was the nation's third largest transit system, totaling 80 million vehicle miles per year, with over 2,750 routes. According to SEPTA, Philadelphia had the largest fleet of electric trolleys in the United States. (303)

Three major factors kept the city's street railway lines operating. First, Philadelphia was already a large, densely populated metropolitan area. Such density is not automobile friendly since traffic congestion can occur very easily. Further, parking can be limited and costly. Second, local governments in Philadelphia and the surrounding areas were willing to subsidize rail mass transit. Finally, the use of efficient and durable PCC electric streetcars helped to keep maintenance and operating expenses at a tolerable level.

The PCC car was greatly accepted and widely used. For many large cities, PCCs were the last design of streetcar to operate before the abandonment of their street railway systems. The initials "P.C.C." stood for the "Presidents' Conference Committee." To survive the Great Depression and compete with the automobile, the presidents of 25 city electric railways came together to find a solution. The Presidents' Conference Committee was formed in 1929 to study, design, and test a modern electric streetcar. The prototype was to be fast, safe, quiet, roomy and economical. The PCC car, named for the committee which created it, would become the standard electric trolley throughout the street railway industry.

The first fleet of PCC electric streetcars went into production in 1935. New York City's Brooklyn & Queens Transit Lines was the first electric railway to receive and operate PCC trolleys in 1936. Pullman and the St. Louis Car Company were the primary builders. Air-controlled doors, brakes, windshield wipers and track sanders were installed on early production models. Later versions were all-electric, some equipped with air-conditioning. The Philadelphia Rapid Transit Company purchased the city's first PCC cars in 1938. Manufacture of the cars was discontinued in 1952.

The Philadelphia Transportation Company, and later SEPTA through its City Transit Division, continued to purchase PCC cars, albeit used ones, into the mid-1970s. In 1955, 40 all-electric 1946-built PCC cars were purchased from Kansas City, Missouri. Another 30 cars, built in 1946 and 1947, arrived from Toronto, Canada, in 1976. At a time when other U.S. cities were converting to bus service only, Philadelphia had an unusually large fleet of 520 PCC trolleys on its surface rail lines. (304)

Eventually, PCC electric streetcars became obsolete even for SEPTA. In 1979, the first new fleet of trolley cars were purchased from the Nissholwai American Corporation. Brand-new street railway equipment had not been purchased since the 1940s. The old PCC cars shared rails with SEPTA's first 141 technologically-advanced light rail vehicles. Despite the influx of new equipment, SEPTA continued to maintain and operate much of its fleet of electric PCCs for some time. As a result of their excessive age, however, SEPTA progressively retired or sold the majority of its PCC inventory. Other cities, and some railroad and trolley museums, purchased the cars for their historic value.

For so long, SEPTA kept its PCC fleet alive due to limited funds to purchase new equipment. There was also uncertainty about the future of rail mass transit. Light rail vehicles were purchased out of necessity, but also with a renewed commitment to keep Philadelphia's surface rail lines operating. In celebration of 109 years of electrified streetcar service in Philadelphia, SEPTA wrote in the regional Metro newspaper: "From its inception in the latter part of the 19th century, trolleys established a framework for the development of Philadelphia's current mass transit system." (305)

Streetcars had been operating in Philadelphia since the Philadelphia Traction Company opened the city's first electric street rail line on December 15, 1892. Rail transit development continued through the 20th and early 21st centuries. Restored SEPTA PCC trolleys were to operate over a reconstructed Girard Avenue Light Rail Line. Designated Route 15 by SEPTA, the 8.2-mile Girard Avenue line had been converted for bus service back in 1992. The transit agency's PCC fleet had been reduced to 26 serviceable trolleys, stored in North Philadelphia at the old Luzerne depot.

Running east-west from Port Richmond on the Delaware River in North Philadelphia, to Overbrook in West Philadelphia, this important transit segment intersected with 29 diversified bus and rail routes, including the Broad Street and Market-Frankford subway-elevated lines. The total cost to convert Route 15 into a modern light rail line was estimated by SEPTA to require $48 million in local and state funds. Engineering and construction improvements included the renewal and upgrading of the track, overhead wire, and electrical power supply system. Other improvements included the implementation of "Transit First." (306)

Designing a light rail line for "Transit First" meant that rail vehicles would be given right-of-way priority, whenever possible, either while mixing with automobile traffic or by operating over dedicated transit lanes or right-of-way. An exclusive transitway was planned for the Girard Avenue Light Rail Line where feasible. Trolley service and speed would also improve with the implementation of better deterrents to keep people from illegally parking on the streetcar tracks. Safety islands were installed at many of the improved transit stops to facilitate the boarding and alighting process. Trolley cars would operate eight minutes apart, on average, up from twelve minutes apart with bus service.

The estimated cost to restore up to 26 PCC electric streetcars, according to SEPTA, was $45.2 million in local and state dollars. A minimum of 18 1947-built cars were restored for operation on the Girard Avenue line. A complete disassembling and rebuilding was required to convert them into modern light rail vehicles. Remanufactured PCC trolleys were equipped with enhanced safety features and modern passenger amenities. Such amenities included an automatic climate control system, original style Art Deco lighting, and a passenger stop request and public address system. New propulsion and auxiliary power systems would improve operating performance. A rear door wheelchair lift was installed to comply with the Americans with Disabilities Act of 1990. The initial 18 refurbished PCC-2 light rail vehicles, remanufactured by the Brookville Equipment Company in Brookville, Pennsylvania, began arriving in Philadelphia during the summer of 2003. Regular historic electric streetcar service was scheduled to be reintroduced to Route 15 on Monday, June 13, 2004. (307)

Modernization of SEPTA's City Transit Division, including the Girard Avenue Light Rail Line, was more than a specialized project. Investments from local, state and federal sources were making SEPTA's diversified mass transit conglomerate a unified and integral part of Philadelphia's transportation infrastructure. By intersecting with 29 other transit routes, the Girard Avenue project was one example of how SEPTA was improving mobility through connectivity. Such connectivity was imperative if SEPTA was to comply with the Federal Transit Administration's "Access-to-Jobs" program. The transit agency received an FTA Access-to-Jobs grant worth $1.3 million in 1999. Improvements to SEPTA's transit services would enable more low-income workers the opportunity to travel farther to jobs available in Philadelphia's outlying suburbs. Using SEPTA buses, trains and trolleys, more people were expected to be able to transition into jobs from being on welfare. (308)

SEPTA also benefitted from the federal government's Congestion Mitigation and Air Quality Improvement program (CMAQ). Through local, state and federal funding, SEPTA appropriated more than $10 million in flexible highway funds for fiscal year 2002. Up from $790,000 acquired the previous year, part of the money was designated for the CMAQ Regional Park and Ride Program. Rail and bus transit stations were to get new or expanded commuter park and ride lots to accommodate more people using SEPTA's multimodal transit system. Car pool and van pool users would also have access to the park and ride lots. (309)

The CMAQ program was part of the transit agency's station enhancement efforts. For example, the Gulph Mills station on the Norristown High Speed Line was to receive structural improvements, including the construction of a new platform shelter, ramps to the parking area, and new bus shelters. Other station amenities included better lighting, new benches, and ADA-compliant station signs.

These and other improvement programs throughout SEPTA's mass transit network enabled SEPTA to meet the demands of the traveling public within the transit agency's four-county region and the city of Philadelphia. From a one-time scattered array of independently owned and operated rail and bus mass transit systems, SEPTA was able to unify Philadelphia's vast transit network through connectivity and the modernization of its historic transportation services.

PASSENGER RAIL

Originally rebuilt for Germantown historic electric streetcar service in Philadelphia, green and white SEPTA PCC car 2750 awaits its next assignment between two Japan-built light rail vehicles, in August 1996. Painted for SEPTA predecessor Philadelphia Transportation Company, PCC 2750 was not equipped with air conditioning, a distinction that set apart the new PCC-2 light rail vehicles.

Norristown High Speed Line

Philadelphia's wide variety of historic rail transit lines also included an interurban, of a sort, the 13.5-mile Norristown High Speed Line. Built like an interurban on an exclusive dedicated right-of-way (no street running), this electrified third rail rapid transit system provided quick service within a highly populated region. By replacing historic interurban-like rapid transit cars with modern express commuter vehicles, the Southeastern Pennsylvania Transportation Authority brought the Norristown High Speed Line into the 21st century through modernization.

The Philadelphia & Western Railway Company opened the Norristown High Speed Line between the Philadelphia suburbs of Norristown and Upper Darby in 1907. It cost $400,000 per mile to construct. Old wooden-built interurbans required 24 minutes to go from Norristown to the 69th Street Terminal in Upper Darby. People riding to 69th Street could transfer to the Market-Frankford line, an elevated-subway train, to go to downtown Philadelphia. (310)

The Norristown line was famous for operating historic rapid transit cars well into the SEPTA era. Nine were bi-directional "Strafford" cars, built between 1924 and 1929, and ten were double-ended aluminum "Bullet" cars. The streamlined pointed-nosed Bullet cars were built by J. G. Brill in 1931. When the 92 mile-per-hour Brill Bullets arrived on the scene, travel time between Norristown and Upper Darby was cut to 17 minutes. The Bullets served to challenge Pennsylvania Railroad and Reading Company commuter rail competition.

The Philadelphia Suburban Transportation Company acquired the Norristown High Speed Line in 1954. Following the merger, the old Philadelphia & Western was marketed as one of the suburban railway's "Red Arrow Lines." In February 1964, two "Electroliner" trainsets were purchased from the bankrupt Chicago North Shore & Milwaukee interurban. On the Norristown line, the Electroliners were called "Liberty Liners," in honor of Philadelphia's Revolutionary War history and the Liberty Bell.

Before the United States became actively involved in World War II, the 85-mile "North Shore Line" interurban, which operated between Chicago, Illinois, and Milwaukee, Wisconsin, was interested in equipment that would compete against rival steam commuter railroads. The answer came in February 1941 from the St. Louis Car Company. The four-car Electroliner consisted of a coach with a forward train control cab, a tavern lounge car, a coach, and a coach with a reversed train control cab. Designed to operate in either direction, the coaches carried 30 passengers each. The tavern lounge car had space for 26 passengers. (311)

When the only two Electroliners ever built moved to the Norristown High Speed Line, their trolley poles were no longer necessary and therefore removed. Only the third-rail electric power collector shoes remained. Further, extra center doors were added to the mid-train coach of each trainset to increase passenger loading and unloading capacity. The Norristown Line became Route 100 when it was acquired by SEPTA on January 29, 1970. The old North Shore Line Electroliners made their last revenue runs as Liberty Liners in 1976.

During the 1980s, the Strafford and Bullet cars were overhauled for a few more years of service. Each car had traveled well over five million miles in revenue service. SEPTA was also engaged in major upgrades of its Route 100 double track mainline and its single track Schuylkill River Bridge into Norristown. Continuous 115-pound welded rail, new ties, and ballast improved rapid transit operations. The electrical power supply was upgraded with 150-pound third rail. Further, new electrical substations with modern rectifier units were built in place of the old rotary-type units at Villanova and Beechwood. To improve transit operations throughout the former Red Arrow Lines rail network, SEPTA built new 69th Street shop facilities for the Norristown High Speed Line to share with the transit agency's suburban streetcars. "We need to maintain service, maintain speed, and continue to upgrade the property so we'll still have a ridership when the new cars get here," said the superintendent of operations for SEPTA's Suburban Transit Division, Jim Gallagher, in 1986. "It would be so short-sighted to let the line slip." (312)

Gradually all Strafford and Bullet interurbans were replaced by Chicago Transit Authority elevated "L" third-rail electrics and borrowed Philadelphia Market-Frankford line subway-elevated cars. The Chicago and Market-Frankford cars were required because delivery of the first 26 ASEA-Brown Boveri N5 cars were 18 months behind schedule. A prototype of the N5 was tested on July 12, 1991.

When the last five Brill Bullets were still in operation, they were restricted by SEPTA to weekend service only. The "L" and Market-Frankford cars operated during the week only. SEPTA did this because the frames of the Bullet cars differed in height from the frames of the Chicago and Philadelphia elevated cars. Such height differences could greatly increase the severity of a head-on collision. SEPTA got extra use out of its Bullet cars on weekends without endangering passengers.

With expectations for expanded commuter rail service, new N5 rapid transit vehicles were designed larger, longer and more high-tech than their Strafford or Bullet predecessors. Compared to a 55 foot long 52 seat Brill Bullet, an N5 car was built 65 feet long with 64 seats, and was equipped with air conditioning. In anticipation of a worthy successor to the Bullets, SEPTA vehicle engineer Russ Jackson said, "We hope to get a compromise between the Bullet and the breadbox shape of SEPTA's Silverliner MUcars, perhaps something with a three-sided end with rounded corners." (313)

Double-ended and of stainless steel construction, the N5 cars could be hooked up in two to four-car multiple-unit trains like the Bullets. They had a maximum speed of 75 miles per hour. To reduce flange wear by 75 to 80 percent, the cars were equipped with limited steering capability. Flange wear was often caused by steel wheels rubbing against steel rail, especially on curves. A steering mechanism, which could feel a curve and turn the wheels to compensate, was expected to serve well on the curve-dominated Norristown High Speed Line. (314)

Part of line upgrading included the installation of Automatic Train Control, which electronically warns of possible train collisions. The N5 cars were equipped with in-cab signals and designed to operate in conjunction with the Automatic Train Control system. Also unique to the N5, which normally collected electricity from a third rail, was an overhead pantograph for 69th Street yard and shop movements. The N5 cars, which SEPTA purchased to modernize the Norristown High Speed Line in the early 1990s, were due to be overhauled beginning in 2002. They were part of a $552 million system-wide Vehicle Overhaul Program, to be conducted between 2002 and 2013, according to SEPTA. (315)

Uncertain about the future of subsidized rail mass transit, SEPTA made its fleet of Philadelphia & Western interurbans last. Once severe automobile traffic congestion throughout the Philadelphia area made the on-going need for rail mass transit clear, SEPTA began receiving the funding necessary to invest long-term in its varied mass transit infrastructure. The hodgepodge of historic rail transit systems that made up much of SEPTA's mass transportation network were modernized to give the people of Philadelphia and its surrounding areas a viable means to commute within a heavily populated region.

Former Philadelphia & Western Bullet car 208 shows off its unique wind-tunnel shape at the Haverford stop on SEPTA's Philadelphia suburban Route 100. On a hot August day in 1987, the SEPTA-painted Brill Bullet displayed its destination to be the 69th Street Terminal in Upper Darby.

CHAPTER ELEVEN

New Orleans Regional Transit Authority

New Orleans electric streetcars were made famous by the Tennessee Williams play *A Streetcar Named Desire*. By 1951, the New Orleans Public Service, Inc. (NOPSI), eliminated several streetcar routes including the famous "Desire Line." Despite some public opposition, all streetcar lines in New Orleans were abandoned except for one. Preserved and continually operated were the Perley Thomas streetcars on St. Charles Avenue.

The city of New Orleans, Louisiana, was founded in 1718 by Jean Baptiste Le Moyne. He named it for the Duke of Orleans, Regent of France. Nicknamed the Crescent City, New Orleans was originally built on the banks of a crescent-shaped curve in the Mississippi River just south of Lake Pontchartrain. As a result of European wars, France lost New Orleans and most of Louisiana to Spain in 1763, only to reacquire it sometime later. The Louisiana Territory had a population of only 10,000 when the French sold it to the United States. In 1812 Louisiana became a state. Steamboat operation in 1812 signified the beginning of industrial boom times. New York City's seaport was the only U.S. shipping port larger than New Orleans.

The New Orleans and Carrollton Railroad introduced rail mass transit along what later became known as the St. Charles Avenue streetcar line in 1835. Transit cars pulled by steam locomotives connected downtown New Orleans from Canal Street to the "faubourgs," or suburbs. The original five mile rail line was built to the resort community of Carrollton, later annexed by the city. The Crescent City's population reached 100,000 by 1840. Four street railways were in place by 1860. Other transit companies operated horse and mule drawn streetcars called "omnibuses."

New Orleans was captured in 1862 by the Union Army during the American Civil War. Following the war, the decidedly detestable steam locomotives on the New Orleans and Carrollton Railroad were replaced with less efficient but cleaner and quieter horse power. Attempts to replace the obsolete horses led to several, and sometimes unusual, experiments in motive power. Examples included ammonia-powered engines, steam dummy engines (locomotives disguised to look like streetcars), overhead cable cars (an elaborately hung moving cable located above the street rather than under it), and battery operated cars.

Civil War-ravaged New Orleans was in a period of rebuilding at this time. The local Mississippi River channel was deepened in 1877, followed by the establishment of a railroad hub in 1883. In anticipation of street railway electrification, the city's first electric streetcars were put on display during the 1884-1885 New Orleans Cotton Centennial Exposition. More than 20 years would pass before horse cars were finally replaced on the New Orleans & Carrollton Railroad. A silver spike was driven on July 13, 1890, to dedicate the beginning of electric street railway construction.

February 1, 1893, marked the beginning of the Crescent City's first overhead wire electric streetcar service. The first cars purchased for the St. Charles Avenue line were built by the St. Louis Car Company in St. Louis, Missouri. Other local street railways converted to electric power or built new electrified lines. Eventually, New Orleans had over 28 electric streetcar routes, which totaled 225 miles of track.

In 1902, the city's four electric street railways, including the New Orleans & Carrollton Railroad, consolidated to form the New Orleans Railways Company. Each railroad retained its separate ownership until 1922, when they were purchased, along with the city's bus lines, by the newly chartered New Orleans Public Service, Inc. (NOPSI). The city's electric power companies were also reorganized under NOPSI. Perley Thomas electric streetcars were purchased to modernize local streetcar operations.

The new 48-foot long double-trucked electric streetcars were designed and built between 1923 and 1924 by the Perley A. Thomas Car Company in High Point, North Carolina. These 52-seat cars were designed to have a motorman for operations and a conductor to collect fares or offer assistance. Streetcar service reached its peak in 1926 when 148 million people were riding the transit company's 26 streetcar lines. (316)

A severe labor strike in 1929, compounded by the Great Depression, began a decline that cost the street railway 40 million riders a year. Streetcar lines throughout the city were gradually being replaced with buses. During World War II, when the Crescent City's population was 490,000, women played many significant wartime roles. As the men left to fight overseas, the street railway hired women to be "conductorettes." They temporarily replaced male conductors. (317)

NOPSI spent $3.5 million to beautify Canal Street back in 1930. It was one of America's most famous broad boulevards. Wealthy Americans settled in New Orleans outside of the Vieux Carre, the famous French and Spanish-influenced French Quarter, into what became known as the Garden District. Canal Street separated the French Quarter from the Garden District, also known as the "American Quarter." The United States purchased the Louisiana Territory, which included the City of New Orleans, from France in 1803. At that time, Canal Street became the dividing line between the French Quarter's "downtown" Creole culture and the newly-arrived and somewhat unwelcome "uptown" American society. Despite public protests, the Crescent City's next-to-last streetcar route to be phased out was the Canal Street Line in 1964. (318)

With a surplus of electric streetcars, NOPSI sold or donated eleven Perley Thomas cars to various museums throughout the United States. No more cars were to be sold or given away as the only remaining streetcar line in New Orleans, the 13-mile St. Charles Avenue line, gained in historical significance. In the heart of the Garden District, electric streetcars continued to operate. They were reworked and refinished in 1965 to "better than new" condition. Although historically preserved, the Perley Thomas cars lost their conductors to automatic coin machines and operator controlled doors during the mid-1970s. In 1973, the St. Charles Avenue Electric Streetcar Line was listed on the National Register of Historic Places.

New Orleans streetcars were not called trolleys. The term "trolley" is unique to electric streetcars because a trolley is actually the device used to transmit electricity from the overhead wire to the motor. Supposedly, because some form of streetcar operated in New Orleans almost 60 years before the introduction of the electric streetcar, local residents were determined that their streetcars would not be referred to as trolleys.

The oldest continually operated street railway in the world was transporting commuters and tourists alike down the median of St. Charles Avenue. It connected the Garden District and the universities of Tulane and Loyola with downtown New Orleans. From the north end of the Carrollton neighborhood at South Claiborne and South Carrollton avenues, restored bi-directional streetcars traversed St. Charles Avenue on the "neutral ground" in the median. Streetcar stops were located about every two blocks. Patrons knew they were entering the Crescent City's Central Business District when true street running and mixing with automobile traffic began. Operating over only one block of Canal Street, the St. Charles Avenue Electric Streetcar Line terminated at Carondelet and Canal streets.

The Louisiana State Legislature created the Regional Transit Authority (RTA) in 1979. It was controlled by a board of commissioners who were appointed as representatives from participating local parishes (counties). The formation of RTA was to begin the transfer of bus and streetcar operation from the privately owned and operated New Orleans Public Service, Inc. As a private investor-based company, NOPSI was not eligible to request federal grant money to maintain its bus and rail transit systems. Declines in ridership and revenue plagued the transit company following World War II. Only through the city's Office of Transit Administration could a publicly-held mass transit agency apply for federal grants or loans. Without investment from the federal government, the long-term development of New Orleans city transit was not viewed as possible.
   In July 1983, the RTA, NOPSI and the mayor's Office of Transit Administration came together to form Transit Management of Southeast Louisiana, in service to RTA. One of the last private urban mass transit companies in the United States came under the control of a public agency. Increasing its status as a valuable asset to the city, the St. Charles Avenue Electric Streetcar Line was honored again when it was declared a National Historic Mechanical Engineering Landmark in 1984.
   With federal funding available, the Regional Transit Authority could conduct a major street railway overhaul program, which it began in 1988. Major projects included renovating the track, streetcars, and the Carrollton Barn Maintenance Facility. The Federal Transit Administration (FTA) granted RTA $35 million of the $47 million required to cover costs. The overhaul program was completed in 1992. (319)
   The Carrollton carbarn, built in 1893, was renovated with historical accuracy, as were the 35 remaining Perley Thomas streetcars. Both cosmetically and operationally restored, the refurbished cars continued to use a compressed air braking system instead of all-electric. Mechanical restoration was nonetheless conducted under the guidelines of the FTA for operating efficiency and safety. Each Perley Thomas vintage streetcar was powered by a 65-horsepower motor, which collected electricity from a 600-volt power supply. They could operate up to 28 miles per hour.
   The city of New Orleans maintained its status as the second largest shipping port in the United States. It also maintained its attractiveness as a destination for tourists. Known for being the birthplace of Jazz and for its other cultural amenities, notably the annual Marti Gras celebration, New Orleans capitalized on its ability to draw people to it. Some 20,000 daily

commuters and visitors were riding the St. Charles Avenue Electric Streetcar Line. It was an integral part of not only the Crescent City's public mass transit network but its culture and heritage as well. (320)

Original Perley Thomas electric streetcar 945, built between 1923 and 1924, turns onto St. Charles Avenue in the Garden District, on April 10, 1997. The 13-mile St. Charles Avenue Line in New Orleans, Louisiana, had the distinction of being the oldest continually operated street railway in the world.

Riverfront Streetcar Line

The success of the St. Charles Avenue Electric Streetcar Line as a commuter route and tourist attraction convinced RTA and the local business community to consider building a new streetcar line in a very obvious place. If streetcars could attract visitors to St. Charles Avenue, how much more would people ride the cars up and down the river bank of the great Mississippi? As a commuter route also, the idea was to offer residents and tourists easier access to riverfront businesses and attractions.

The idea to build the Riverfront Streetcar Line was developed following the World's Fair in 1984. A way to move large numbers of people quickly and easily during events such as the World's Fair gave credence to the concept of connecting businesses on the riverfront by rail. Riverfront developments and businesses in the French Quarter were to be connected to new commercial developments in the Warehouse District.

The initial 1.5-mile single track riverfront line was to be constructed within an already existing rail corridor. Freight trains served the Crescent City on the New Orleans Public Belt Railroad, a single track regional carrier with an expandable right-of-way. The wide rail corridor would enable streetcar tracks to be laid alongside the freight line. Finally, there was the question of what kind of rolling stock would operate. Many of the people involved wanted something appropriate to complement the Perley Thomas streetcars on St. Charles Avenue.

The "Bring Our Streetcars Home" (BOSH) Committee was formed in 1984 to reclaim the Canal Street cars sold in 1964. All eleven Perley Thomas streetcars were located, but only two returned to New Orleans late the following year. Undaunted, money was being raised to build the city's first new electric streetcar line since 1926.

In 1986, the City of New Orleans, the Regional Transit Authority and the Riverfront Transit Coalition Group, Inc., created a public-private partnership to undertake such a project. Federal funding was sought through a joint application to the Federal Transit Administration. The French Market Corporation and the Downtown Development District also contributed. On August 14, 1988, the Riverfront Streetcar Line was inaugurated.

In contrast to the dark green streetcars on St. Charles, the two reacquired Perley Thomas cars were painted red for use on the riverfront line. They were joined by two Australian cars, purchased by RTA in 1988. Also painted red and converted by RTA for handicap access, the W-2 double-trucked streetcars from Melbourne, Victoria, were built in 1924 and 1925. An additional Melbourne W-2 was purchased in 1989, as was another original Canal Street Perley Thomas car.

Ridership on the riverfront line's six historic streetcars exceeded estimates, which revealed a need to expand service. The federal government's Urban Mass Transportation Administration granted $14 million to be spent on two additional construction phases to extend the line both up the river and down. The second phase included extending the line another half mile, but more significantly a much needed second track was added. More transit shelters were built and two additional wheelchair accessible Perley Thomas cars were assigned to operate the line. A new multi-level transit shelter was constructed at the Aquarium Plaza. Closed for two months during construction, the Riverfront Streetcar Line reopened in August 1990. (321)

"We have had so much new building going on around here in recent years, that I think a lot of people have started to wonder if there is enough room for more," said Janet Speyrer, an economics professor at the University of New Orleans. "But when they see improvements made to non-building structures, such as streetcar lines and road and sewer lines, they are just naturally more supportive." (322)

After almost a decade of use, the Melbourne W-2 cars were retired. They were replaced by five new cars, built by RTA craftsmen at the Carrollton Barn Maintenance Facility, in 1997. The same people who restored the original Perley Thomas cars built five similar-looking modern cars. The new electric streetcars featured state-of-the-industry technology and were wheelchair accessible, in compliance with the Americans with Disabilities Act of 1990.

The third and final phase of the Riverfront Streetcar Line project included rail extensions upriver to the Audubon Park area and down river toward the Industrial Canal. Streetcar system expansion, according to RTA, was meant to alleviate city traffic congestion, provide greater transit access for the disabled, and to comply with the Clean Air Act of 1990. The Clean Air Act was intended by the federal government to encourage communities, such as the City of New Orleans, to reduce air pollution levels caused by combustion-engine vehicle emissions. New Orleans used historic electric streetcars as a means to provide a cleaner and quieter mode of urban mass transit, while also to stimulate tourism.

On April 10, 1997, Australian W2 electric streetcar 452, built between 1924 and 1925, traversed the Riverfront Streetcar Line along the Mississippi River in New Orleans, Louisiana. Soon the Australian cars would be replaced with new Perley Thomas-like cars, built by the transit agency's own shop employees at the Carrollton Barn Maintenance Facility.

Canal Street Line

The Canal Streetcar Project was defined by RTA as an ambitious capital improvement program to return electric streetcar service to one of the Crescent City's most famous major thoroughfares. Feasibility studies began in the early 1990s for what would become an estimated $156.6 million project. By 1997, plans for the construction and operation of the rail route and other Canal Street enhancements were in place. Following the final design phase, construction of special track work began in January 2001. (323)

The double-track Canal Street Line would be built down the median, or "neutral ground," between the east and westbound automobile traffic lanes. An operations proposal by RTA would have Canal Street cars running from Esplanade Avenue, north-south along the Mississippi River on the Riverfront Streetcar Line to Canal Street, before turning onto their namesake boulevard. One half mile of Canal Street already had streetcar tracks built into it. In 1996, a six-block connection between the riverfront line and the St. Charles Avenue line at Carondelet Street was built. This was to enable a more flexible rail system and allow the riverfront streetcars to be serviced at the Carrollton Barn Maintenance Facility on Willow Street.

RTA envisioned the Aquarium of the America's stop on the riverfront line functioning as a transfer point, connecting passengers to the Canal Street Line. Once on Canal Street, streetcars would operate 3.6 miles between the Mississippi River and Greenwood Cemetery at City Park Avenue. The City Park Avenue bus and streetcar terminal would act as a transfer point for riders traveling elsewhere. Express buses would continue to serve the Canal Street service area, while streetcars would operate in local service. Bus lines from Orleans and Jefferson parishes (counties) would also make connections at the City Park Avenue Terminal. A final segment of the Canal Street Line would be a one mile spur built north from Canal Street, up North Carrollton Avenue to Beauregard Circle at Esplanade Avenue. Streetcars would terminate opposite the New Orleans Museum of Art.

New Canal Street Line streetcars were designed by RTA rail superintendent Elmer Von Dullen, based on the design of the Perley Thomas streetcars on St. Charles Avenue. With the Perley A. Thomas Car Company no longer manufacturing electric streetcars, 24 matching New Orleans streetcars would have to be constructed locally by 43 RTA craftsmen working in the city's Carrollton Barn Maintenance Facility. "We are the only transit authority in the country that is building our own cars," said RTA general manager Donald Preau. "And it's going to be a lot of work." (324)

Another renovation of the Carrollton barn and shop facilities was necessary to construct the Canal Street cars. Although some streetcar fabrications would be contracted out, the primary assembly and finishing work would be done at the carbarn. Improvements to the carbarn would be permanent since more streetcars were expected to be built there. RTA had plans to further expand its streetcar system long term. At a cost of $4.5 million, the modernized and upgraded Carrollton barn would continue its role as a major repair facility. Reconstruction was completed in early 2002. (325)

Aluminum and steel-built electric streetcars would feature the latest in European streetcar technology. The double-truck cars would have two 65-horsepower motors (one for each truck), built by CKD of Prague in the Czech Republic. Unlike the air brakes on the original Perley Thomas cars, smoother and faster stopping could be achieved with modern regenerative dynamic brakes. At over 47 feet long, a Canal Street car would be able to seat 40 passengers or carry a maximum of 72 passengers with standees. The mahogany seats would be handmade. In compliance with the Americans with Disabilities Act of 1990, Ricon wheelchair lifts would be installed. Two fold-up benches would make space for wheelchairs. Other amenities which were not fabricated into the original Perley Thomas cars included recessed lighting, window defrosters, windshield wipers and climate control. For safety, the windows would open only partially. The most obvious design variance of these modern historic streetcars was required to accommodate the 12-ton ThermoKing air conditioning system. A decorative cover on the roof was designed to hide the air conditioner. (326)

Each new Perley Thomas-like electric streetcar had an estimated manufacturing cost of more than $1.2 million. "They will look very similar to the St. Charles cars, but they will be a different color, red with white trim, instead of the standard green on the old cars," said general manager Preau in 2001, when construction of the cars began. "And the roofs, which will house the air-conditioning units, will have a slightly different look to them." (327)

The longevity of the new cars was expected to be significantly greater than that of an average city bus, about 60 years with proper maintenance, before needing to be rebuilt. A prototype was unveiled in 1999. The demonstrator car occasionally operated along the six-block Canal Street spur, connecting the riverfront line with the St. Charles Avenue line. The historical ambiance of the 24 new Canal Street cars was expected to increase transit ridership and help generate economic development along the rail route and throughout surrounding areas.

The Canal Street and Riverfront Streetcar Line fleets, and eventually a Desire Line fleet, would be kept and maintained at the A. Philip Randolph Operations Facility at Canal and North Gayoso streets. Built in 1926, this former NOPSI bus garage was listed on the National Register of Historic Places and was located within the Mid-City National Historic District. The cost to historically renovate and further expand the Randolph facility into a Service, Inspection and Storage (SIS) Facility was estimated to be about $13.2 million, according to RTA. The new 29,000 square-foot building would provide a place for general maintenance, cleaning and storage of the cars. All major streetcar repairs would take place at the Carrollton carbarn. (328)

Using a shovel, New Orleans mayor Marc Morial symbolically initiated the first of three phases to begin construction of the Canal Streetcar Project during a July 20, 2001, groundbreaking ceremony. Mayor Morial helped to secure from the Federal Transit Administration 80 percent of the estimated $156.6 million necessary to complete the project. The project's proponents were required to match the remaining 20 percent, which was estimated to be about $31 million. The right-of-way down Canal Street's neutral ground was donated as part of the city's efforts. The local business community donated the steel catenary poles to carry overhead wires, worth a total of about $1 million. A long-suspended one percent city sales tax on occupied hotel rooms was the primary source for funding the local share, which went into effect during the year 2000. (329)

All seemed well for Mayor Morial and the RTA when $54 million of the more than $125 million federal share was sent from Washington, D.C., in 2001. A national economic recession, however, began a debate between Washington officials regarding the long-standing 80/20 split for mass transit. Although $14.8 million was approved in 2001, the money had not been sent to RTA in light of possible changes to the federal financing formula. A proposed 60/40 arrangement would double the financial obligation of RTA to about $62 million. With no federal appropriations coming in since 2001, RTA was paying the entire cost to keep construction of the Canal Street Line moving. "We can't get anyone to tell us why they won't release the money," said RTA board chairman James Reiss, Jr. "What we're talking about is money that was already authorized, appropriated and to some degree spent." (330)

Nonetheless, New Orleans and the RTA were determined to continue building the Canal Street Line on schedule. The Boh Brothers Construction Company secured a $20 million contract to build the first phase of the new street railway, 1.5 miles down Canal Street. Each phase was open for bids. (331)

More than just a streetcar project, it was also a Canal Street beautification and enhancement effort. Over $5 million from RTA and the city was budgeted to reconstruct the roadway, repair sidewalks, and otherwise make Canal Street attractive. (332) "To us, this is another attraction that will bring people to New Orleans.... We know that this is going to be a big boost to business," said the president of the New Orleans Downtown Development District, Zella Tranchina. "And the landscaping that they're planning will make this area so much more beautiful." (333)

Construction of a new Desire Street Line was scheduled to begin after the completion of the Canal Street Line, depending on what kind of federal funding could be secured. The 5.5-mile Canal Street Line began operating electric streetcars in revenue service on Monday, April 18, 2004.

The estimated $115 million Desire Street Line would connect downtown and the French Quarter with the Industrial Canal area to the east. The Desire line would not operate down Desire Street, only cross it. Electric streetcars would operate along North Rampart Street and St. Claude Avenue. (334)

With a population of over 1.3 million in 2001, the City of New Orleans was returning to its residents what they had once lost, a viable commuter and tourist-oriented rail mass transit system. "We have a lot of streetcar-related construction going on right now," said Preau. "It's a pretty exciting time to be in New Orleans." (335)

CHAPTER TWELVE

Denver Regional Transportation District

When the last Denver Tramway trolley made its final run on June 5, 1950, the city of Denver believed it would never again need electrified street railway service. With a more cost effective bus transit service in place since 1925, and the use of automobiles growing ever more popular, the future of regional transportation in Denver, Colorado, seemed obvious. For the next 44 years, rubber-tired vehicles would dominate area commuter travel entirely. But eventually, the city of Denver and its six-county metro area would embrace rail mass transit once again. From a city that was dedicated to operating buses as the only means of mass transit, an ambitious plan to combat severe automobile traffic congestion was developed. Light rail, commuter rail and bus rapid transit were envisioned to operate as a coordinated major mass transit system, to offer metro area commuters a new opportunity for mobility.

Formal mass transit service began in Denver as a result of a Territorial Charter granted to the Denver Horse Railroad Company in 1867. Horse car service was introduced in 1871. In 1886, electric streetcars began operating on 15th Street. It was one of the first electric street railways in the world. In 1914, as automobile use was gaining in popularity, a merger agreement between the Denver City Tramway Company, the Denver & Intermountain Railway, and the Denver Northwestern Railway created the consolidated Denver Tramway Company. The principal provider of rail and bus transit service in the city and county of Denver was Denver Tramway. Rail service ended in 1950.

The Colorado General Assembly created a Regional Transportation District (RTD) for Denver and its suburbs in 1969. Privately-financed bus service was no longer viable. Denver's RTD was created to subsidize money-losing local and regional bus service to six counties and part of a seventh in the Denver metro area. Much like other major cities throughout North America, people were commuting by car from the sprawling suburbs. The result was a significant decline in bus ridership. As automobile traffic congestion developed, the city used tax dollars to widen heavily traveled roadway arterials in an effort to solve the problem. Throughout downtown Denver, buildings were torn down to provide space for pay-to-park parking lots.

Bus transit operations were purchased by the city and county of Denver in 1971. In 1972, a transportation plan for metro Denver was completed. Intercity bus service would extend northwest of Denver to serve the suburban communities of Boulder and Longmont. The city and county of Denver sold its bus transit operations in July 1974, to RTD. Consolidation and service expansion took place thereafter, including the development of a "park-n-ride" system.

During the 1980s, large cities on the West Coast experienced a boom in the construction of new light rail lines. Street and dedicated right-of-way trolley systems were built to deal with the more severe problems of automobile traffic congestion in those areas. San Diego, California, introduced light rail service at a cost of $8.7 million per mile in 1981. The initial 16-mile system cost $139 million. Portland, Oregon, followed in September 1986, with a 15-mile light rail system costing $212 million, or $14.1 million per mile. In March 1987, California's capital city, Sacramento, introduced 18.3 miles of light rail at $176 million, or $9.6 million per mile. Sacramento light rail was built on street trackage, on old railroad right-of-way, and on abandoned future freeway right-of-way. In December 1987, Santa Clara County, California, opened a 21-mile light rail line at a cost of $394 million, or $18.8 million per mile. These and other light rail systems would serve as the examples and inspiration for Denver RTD light rail. As the citizens and politicians of Denver put forth an effort to revitalize the city's downtown central business district, a transportation alternative to the automobile and bus was sought. (336)

The Regional Transportation District reintroduced electrified streetcar service in Denver, on September 17, 1994, with a dedication and inaugural system-wide excursion. The initial 5.3-mile light rail system was officially opened to the public on October 7. A single track loop running along the street served the downtown Denver area. West of downtown, the rail system opened up to a double-track high-speed dedicated transitway parallel to the tracks of the old Denver & Rio Grande Western Railroad. Partially elevated, the line ended south of downtown at Interstate 25 and Broadway at a park-n-ride parking lot. The cost to build the first 5.3 miles was $117 million, or $22 million per mile. All RTD transit services, including buses and the new streetcar line, were marketed as "The Ride." (337)

Light rail vehicles which operated in Denver were just over 80 feet long and could accommodate 125 passengers comfortably, 64 seated and 61 standees. Maximum capacity per vehicle was 200 riders. The bi-directional, 57 mile-per-hour, 750 volt DC powered light rail cars operated at a top cruising speed of 50 miles-per-hour out on the dedicated transitway. (338)

Shortly after the introduction of light rail service, seven new members of the 15-member RTD board were elected by metro area voters in November 1994. Since five members ran unopposed, they did not have to campaign or disclose their views about rail mass transit. When RTD signed a procurement contract worth $11.7 million, to purchase six new streetcars for rush hour service on the downtown loop, the new members of the RTD board surprised light rail supporters by expressing opposition to light rail expansion in equipment or trackage. (339)

The new board opposed plans to extend the light rail line to Littleton, a suburb southwest of Denver. Instead, they said they wanted to test the existing system with existing equipment while considering the idea of abandoning light rail. RTD board chairman Brian Propp said, "I don't think enough attention has been paid to other ways to reduce congestion like telecommuting, bicycling and carpooling. But at least now that we have a real demonstration light rail system to study, let's study it." (340)

Another setback to light rail expansion came during that same November 1994 vote of the people when RTD asked to keep $5.2 million in excess revenue. The majority of voters said no, requiring a $5.50 to $5.75 credit to every metro area Public Service Company utility customer, of which there were 950,000. The money was credited back to the taxpayers due to Amendment One to the Colorado state constitution, which limited the ability of government to tax and spend. Later, in early 1995, auditors recommended RTD return $5.7 million to utility customers for 1993, and another $1.8 million for 1994. (341)

In the first nine months of operation, RTD light rail lost $2.7 million. Fares returned only 19 percent of the cost to operate the rail system. Buses returned 40 percent in fares. But the RTD bus system served more areas, lending itself to a higher return ratio. Denver light rail was only taking advantage of a fraction of its potential business because of its low track mileage. In actuality, light rail ridership targets were met almost exactly during the first year of operation. Weekday ridership averaged almost 13,000. On days when the local Colorado Rockies professional baseball team played, the weekday average rose to more than 14,800. (342)

Originally, Denver RTD light rail was intended to operate in place of regular downtown bus service. Bus passengers were required to transfer to light rail vehicles at the I-25 and Broadway park-n-ride. Citizen complaints about crowded light rail vehicles made RTD restore some bus service to downtown, but light rail ridership continued to grow. By the end of its first year, light rail was removing more than 700 automobiles per day off area roads, according to the Denver Post newspaper. This was out of about 50,000 people a day who were driving to downtown Denver from outlying areas. (343)

"The real problem in downtown ten years ago was lots of cheap, available parking, because it meant nobody was coming here," said the president of the Downtown Denver Partnership, Bill Mosher. "The good thing now is a tougher parking situation, because people have lots of reasons to come downtown." (344)

Curb-side metered parking filled quickly in downtown, compounded by the fact that people who sold parking spaces on private lots were able to charge a premium. To the surprise and delight of RTD, the agency had to more than triple the number of parking spaces at the I-25 and Broadway park-n-ride to 750. Parking at transit stops was attractive because it was free of charge. Increased light rail patronage led to parking shortages at stations, discouraging many late-comers from riding rail transit. All spaces were usually taken by 8 AM. "We could put 2,500 spaces at I-25 and fill them immediately. To me, that is success. It gives credibility to the fact that people will get out of their cars if you give them an alternative," said John Claflin, the director of RTD light rail. (345)

A survey of thousands of light rail passengers, taken in March of 1995, showed that 27 percent of weekday travelers were new to using any form of RTD mass transit. Of people going to see the Rockies play, 70 percent of rail users surveyed were newcomers to the system. (346) Street-running light rail vehicles operated with Transit First priority. A 99.5 percent on-time performance was due in part because traffic signals prioritized rail operations over automobile traffic flow. (347)

By the end of the rail system's first year, October 1995, police investigated 41 accidents between light rail vehicles and automobiles. There also was one pedestrian death, due to an intoxicated man who had ignored traffic signals. In none of these cases was RTD faulted or cited. In contrast, 70 accidents plagued the first year of light rail use in Portland, Oregon. A national safety audit, requested by RTD, showed area mass transit to be very safe, thereby reducing political criticism over the safety of Denver light rail. (348)

Although automobile traffic congestion, parking and safety were good motivators to get people to use mass transit, RTD offered another incentive. Denver businesses were encouraged to join RTD's "Eco Pass" program. The program began in 1991 to encourage more business people to ride the bus. Denver employers purchased discounted annual transit passes for their employees. In July 1995, more than 750 companies, 32 percent located downtown, provided over 30,500 employees with passes. The program was created by the transportation department of nearby Boulder. Other cities copied the Eco Pass idea for mass transit, including San Jose, California, and Dallas, Texas. Also in 1995, Downtown Express/High Occupancy Vehicle (HOV) lanes opened in the Denver area for use by car pool participants and buses. (349)

Expansion of RTD light rail was imperative if Denver intended to take full advantage of the potential rail transit market between downtown and the outlying suburbs. Colorado Governor Roy Romer unveiled an ambitious light rail initiative on November 18, 1997. The purpose was to develop a major rail transit network in an effort to significantly improve metro area mobility.

A majority of Denver area voters had rejected a proposal to build a 73 mile light rail system in 1980. The cost at the time was projected to be $1 billion. By the time Governor Romer unveiled plans to significantly expand rail transit, the population of Denver had grown to 2.1 million. That was an increase of 50 percent since 1980. In 1997, Interstate 25 through Denver averaged 215,000 vehicles a day. "This is not a Denver project," said Governor Romer. "It's a solution to a bottleneck. You can't get from Pueblo to Fort Collins without going down I-25. If we don't solve the problem with light rail, you're going to just block the highway system in this state." (350)

Major Investment Studies (MIS) for the expansion of RTD transit services would be reviewed and considered by RTD, the Colorado Department of Transportation (CDOT), and the Denver Regional Council of Governments (DRCOG). A Major Investment Study was completed in 1997 to determine the best possible transportation solution for commuters between downtown Denver and the outlying suburb of Golden to the west. A total of four possible light rail alignments were investigated by the study. Other transportation solutions considered included roadway widening along 6th Avenue or improved bus and car pool HOV lanes. A light rail line using existent railroad right-of-way was determined as the best alternative to severe automobile traffic congestion, according to the results of the MIS. Following an Environmental Impact Study (EIS), the West Corridor light rail line would be built west from Denver Union Station in downtown, through Lakewood, to the Jefferson County Administration and Courts Facility in Golden, just off U.S. Highway 6. The first light rail extension off the core system would not be the West Corridor, however, but a line southwest of downtown Denver.

The Regional Transportation District asked the U.S. Department of Transportation to direct $41.5 million toward the $177 million needed to continue expansion of Denver light rail. Only $21.4 million was to be granted by Congress in the proposed U.S. DOT budget for fiscal year 1998. This amount was significant compared to the $2.8 million granted of the $8 million requested by RTD for fiscal year 1997. "We are moving forward and being recognized for a major appropriation," said RTD board chairman Ben Klein. "It's a victory for the people of the Front Range and the RTD district, and our long struggle to build and complete the Southwest Corridor." (351)

Construction began on a five station, four park-n-ride Southwest Corridor light rail line, which was scheduled to open in July 2000. It would be built 8.7 miles south from the I-25/Broadway park-n-Ride, along Santa Fe Drive and the railroad tracks, to just south of suburban Littleton. The 1998 subsidy was required to cover the cost of new signals, right-of-way grading, and the relocation of freight railroad track along Santa Fe Drive. A trip into downtown Denver from the end-of-line station at Mineral Avenue would take about 25 minutes.

The town of Littleton was anxious to get RTD light rail into its old downtown area. The neglected central business district was generating only two percent of the community's annual sales tax revenue, which totaled about $10 million. An effort to revive and beautify the downtown area was put forth in anticipation of new light rail. Further, there was a desire to make downtown Littleton a designated historic district. Light rail was expected to help generate interest in the town's central business district. (352)

People also hoped that light rail would reduce non-stop automobile traffic through central Littleton. Commuters often took Santa Fe Drive or Broadway through Littleton from the bedroom community of Highlands Ranch to get to downtown Denver. Developers were planning to just about double the size of Highlands Ranch, which had more than 41,000 people living there by the Summer of 1997. The hope was to get Highlands Ranch residents off area street arterials as much as possible by providing a rail alternative to peak-hour traffic congestion. "Highlands Ranch is having an absolutely tremendous effect on us," said Littleton assistant city manager Kelli Narde. "Everybody who lives in Highlands Ranch and works in downtown (Denver) takes Broadway or Santa Fe to get there. They come right through our town. It can only get worse." (353)

On schedule and under budget, the designated $177 million Southwest Corridor actually cost about $4.5 million less to build than anticipated, according to RTD. (354) A year following the July 14, 2000, rail line opening, average weekday ridership blossomed from a projected 8,400 riders to more than 14,700. (355) This was compared to the approximately 1,900 average weekday riders on RTD express buses which used to serve the same route. Light rail ridership was 43 percent higher than RTD had originally estimated. (356)

There were 15 stations on the original Central Corridor and five on the new Southwest line. The 14-mile light rail system was served by 31 RTD light rail vehicles. The more than 1,200-space parking lot at the Mineral Avenue station was often full on weekdays by as early as 7:30 AM. Six new light rail cars were ordered to be delivered by the end of 2001 to relieve ridership congestion.

During peak travel periods, an automobile averaged 42 minutes driving from the Mineral Avenue park-n-ride to downtown Denver. An RTD light rail vehicle made the trip in 25 minutes. By the year 2015, according to RTD, the average travel time for automobiles was expected to increase to 51 minutes. Light rail trains would still traverse the route in only 25 minutes. (357)

The overall success of the Southwest Corridor light rail line grabbed the attention of other metro Denver high traffic communities. Municipal leaders asked RTD when commuter or light rail could be built out their way. This surge of interest in rail mass transit convinced RTD to develop "FasTracks." Connected with federal and state grants and other local contributions, the $4.7 billion FasTracks transportation expansion program would have a metro area rail network completed in twelve-years time, according to RTD. Effected municipalities and businesses, which stood to benefit from FasTracks, were expected to contribute five percent of the capital cost of construction. These contributions would count as part of the local match for federal funding. (358)

PASSENGER RAIL

Denver, Colorado, motorists are warned that there are *High Speed Trains Approaching* at a grade crossing that, less than a year before, protected only the occasional slow freight. The freight line is still in the background as RTD light rail vehicle 111 leaves downtown, southbound, on June 1, 1995.

Groundbreaking ceremonies took place on January 26, 2001, to begin the construction of more RTD light rail trackage. The estimated total cost to build the Central Platte Valley light rail line on the southeast side of the South Platte River was less than $52 million. The extension was built off the Central Corridor from the Auraria Higher Education Center 1.8 miles to Union Station. Denver Union Station was purchased in July 2001 by RTD, in partnership with the Colorado Department of Transportation, the Denver Regional Council of Governments, and the City and County of Denver. (359)

Several Denver attractions were linked by the new light rail spur. They included Broncos professional football at Invesco Field, the basketball Nuggets and ice hockey Avalanche at the Pepsi Center, Elitch Gardens amusement park, the 16th Street Mall, and Rockies professional baseball at Coors Field. A walkway under Interstate 25 allowed light rail patrons access to Bronco games at Invesco Field. Rockies baseball was accessible from Union Station, a few blocks west of Coors Field. The 16th Street Mall dedicated busway was extended to Union Station to offer convenient access in and out of Lower Downtown.

Intercity rail, light rail and RTD bus patrons were able to use the rail terminal as a transit transfer facility. RTD and its partners envisioned the facility becoming a major intermodal transportation center and office complex. Plans included Greyhound intercity bus, taxi and rental car services to develop alongside existent Amtrak and Winter Park Ski Train service. Bicycle storage would also be made available. The 19.5-acre Union Station site was purchased for $50 million. The shared vision for redevelopment was estimated to cost $560 million. The FasTracks proposal included $200 million to put a light rail terminal underground behind Union Station. (360)

A ceremony marked the opening of the Central Platte Valley light rail line on Friday, April 5, 2002. Limited streetcar rides were offered on the newly designated "C" line. The Central Corridor was designated the "D" line. On Saturday, April 6, all light rail rides were free. Regular service began on Sunday. Twelve more light rail vehicles were purchased to accommodate expanding service. Over the course of the following year, system-wide boardings increased to 36,000 persons every weekday. The operating cost averaged 24 cents per passenger mile, according to RTD. The three starter light rail lines were all constructed on time and within their designated budgets. (361)

As part of a beautification project entitled "art-n-Transit," four separate artists were commissioned to do artwork at all four Central Platte Valley light rail stops. Artwork was to be displayed at several metro area bus and light rail stations. A number of independent artists were commissioned to make archways, sculptures, murals and other artwork in an effort to foster transit-oriented community development. Artwork, intended to enhance aesthetics and add distinction, was also installed at six light rail stations along the Central Corridor and at all five stations on the Southwest Corridor.

"Bringing transit to your community, and community to your transit," was the marketing slogan RTD used to encourage Transit Oriented Development (TOD) around light rail and bus rapid transit stations. (362) According to RTD, the transit agency operated within a service area populated by 2.2 million residents, living in or around 41 cities and towns. (363)

Transit oriented communities, or Transit Villages, were compact mixed-use developments oriented toward mass transit as the primary form of regional transportation. Pedestrian-friendly TOD communities were comprised of residential, neighborhood retail, office space and civic centers. More public areas and open space were to be incorporated into the design. Human-scale "New Urbanism" clusters were to be contained within about a one-fourth mile radius of a transit stop. Metro Denver clusters would not necessarily be built to contain all uses, depending on the orientation of the surrounding area. Discouraging sprawl growth while improving air quality through transit was to be a TOD hallmark.

Two major models of TOD communities existed in Denver at the turn of the 21st century. The 16th Street Mall in Lower Downtown contained residential lofts, entertainment venues, office space and landscaped park-like areas. The region's densest urban village was accessible by light rail from the Central Corridor or the Central Platte Valley line. Electric-hybrid Compressed Natural Gas (CNG) buses served the 16th Street Mall transitway. Eight of a fleet of 976 RTD buses used compressed natural gas, according to RTD, as a clean-burning alternative to traditional diesel fuel. (364)

Transit Villages were dense, complex developments which took years to construct. City Center Englewood, an older first ring suburb on the Southwest Corridor light rail line, was the other significant TOD model in metro Denver. Along with housing, retail and office space, City Center Englewood was oriented toward civic uses such as City Hall, the Englewood Library, the Museum of Outdoor Art and other large outdoor performance spaces. More TOD communities were to develop as RTD transit expanded, including a Transit Village surrounding a remodeled Denver Union Station in Lower Downtown.

Englewood's Cinderella City mall opened in 1968. By 1974, the mall was able to account for 52 percent of Englewood's sales tax revenue. Twenty years later, it claimed only 2.6 percent. Throughout the United States, there were about 400 older malls in a similar depressed condition as Cinderella City. A department store building had been added to the mall during the mid-1980s. It was converted into a civic center. This began the $38 million transformation of Cinderella City and City Center Englewood into a Transit Oriented Development. Englewood Station accommodated 3,400 daily commuters who accessed RTD light rail via automobile, bus, bicycle or on foot. (365)

"Transit is kind of like frosting on the cake, and it gives those places a locational advantage and an identity," said G.B. Arrington, a TOD specialist for Parsons Brinkerhoff. "But it meant that the transit agencies' role in how they did their facilities, where they put things and how the transit infrastructure was designed, all needed to come together in a way that was more development-oriented rather than just traditional transit.... What the light rail does is serve as a catalyst to help bring a bigger vision and other resources to the table that wouldn't be possible otherwise." (366)

New Urbanism Transit Oriented Developments would follow RTD's $4.7 billion FasTracks rail build-out program. As many as six new commuter and light rail lines were to be constructed throughout metro Denver. Commuter rail proposals included establishing passenger service between Denver and Boulder, and eventually extending the line along the Diagonal Highway to the Twin Peaks Mall in Longmont, northwest of Denver. Environmental Impact Studies (EIS) were completed by 2002 for the Denver-Boulder route and for a proposed "Air Train" to connect downtown Union Station to Denver International Airport. The combined cost to conduct the studies was $15 million. (367)

In addition to building the West Corridor light rail line from Denver Union Station to Golden, a $112 million extension of the Southwest Corridor would extend 2.5 miles from the Mineral Avenue terminus in Littleton to the sprawling suburb of Highlands Ranch. According to RTD, the Southwest Extension would be built south along Santa Fe Drive to an 800-space park-n-ride station at highway route C-470. The tracks would then turn east along the south side of C-470 to a new end-of-line station in Highlands Ranch. The 600-space park-n-ride station would be constructed at Lucent Boulevard and C-470. Other light rail lines planned for construction included a line through Arvada northwest to Ward Road, and a line to 160th Avenue in northern Adams County. (368)

Provided a voter-approved one percent sales tax, RTD could begin its design-build initiatives. The Denver metro area was expected to gain an additional one million residents by 2025. Over 60 new transit stops were planned to be built along FasTracks bus and light rail corridors. Thanks to Transit Oriented Development, 320,000 residents were expected to be living within half a mile of RTD transit stations, according to a transportation advocacy group, Environment Colorado. Up to 500,000 people would be working within the same half-mile distance from transit. (369)

Denver city and county commuters who used mass transit in 2002 achieved the state's highest average usage rate of 8.4 percent. Denver also had the lowest average for commuters driving alone in 2002, 68 percent, according to the Denver Post. The highest average for commuters driving alone was in neighboring Douglas County. According to a Douglas County census, lone drivers averaged 81 percent. (370) "A lot of decisions have to be made about whether or not we have relief for congestion in the metro area and what is the future of transit," said RTD director of planning and development Liz Rao. (371)

To reach commuters living in Douglas County, the most ambitious of RTD's light rail projects was already underway. The Southeast Corridor, a 19-mile double-track trunk light rail line, was being built in conjunction with the reconstruction of Interstate highways 25 and 225. This massive rail and roadway Transportation Expansion Project, named "T-REX," was to move southeast from Broadway Boulevard in Denver to Lincoln Avenue in Douglas County. A spur off the Southeast Corridor from Interstate 25 would follow Interstate 225 to Parker Road in Aurora. Almost 17 miles of freeway would be rebuilt as the multimodal light rail and interstate highway improvement project was expected to cost almost $1.67 billion, according to RTD. (372)

Interstate 25 was to be widened to as many as five through lanes in each direction, specifically between Interstate 225 and state highway C-470. Interstate 225 would be widened to three lanes in each direction. Light rail tracks were to be built along the west side of I-25 and within the median between opposing highway lanes along I-225. Higher speeds, increased operational efficiency and better safety were possible as there would be no cross traffic or grade crossings built anywhere along the Southeast Corridor. A new RTD maintenance facility would be built in Englewood to service additional light rail vehicles.

The projected cost to build the light rail portion of the T-REX project was $879 million, which included a federal grant worth $525 million, or almost 60 percent. Roadway expansion was expected to cost $788 million. T-REX became part of FasTracks, but was originally supported by a bond initiative passed by metro Denver voters in November 1999. (373) Almost $400 million of the $1.7 billion in roadway improvement bonds went to the T-REX project. Support also came from the cooperation and participation of the Federal Highway Administration (FHWA), the Federal Transit Administration (FTA), CDOT, and several counties, municipalities and business districts. (374)

To keep FasTracks on track, an additional 0.4 percent sales tax increase was approved by metro area voters in November 2004, to raise about $140 million a year. Millions more could be raised through the sale of bonds using proceeds from the one percent total RTD sales tax. "If we rely only on existing funds, the system will never get built," said executive director Lauren Martens of Transit Alliance, a Denver-area coalition of business and resident groups. "It's part of a smart-growth effort for dealing with a million more people in the metro area in 20 years." (375)

Combining the Interstate highway and light rail projects, to be constructed by a design-build contractor, was expected to cost less than if the two modes had been expanded separately. The advantage of a design-build contractor, operating under the quality-control oversight of RTD and CDOT, was to be a faster and more efficient construction schedule. A Big-Dig project such as T-REX could take 20 years or longer to complete under the design-bid-build approach. The Southeast Corridor was scheduled to be fully operational by June 30, 2008.

The drive during heavy travel periods on I-25, from Lincoln Avenue to downtown Denver, could take an hour or longer. According to RTD, light rail trains averaging 35 to 40 miles per hour between stops, would take about 40 minutes to get to downtown. There were to be 13 light rail stops constructed, with parking at twelve. All 13 Southeast Corridor stations were eventually to have New Urbanism TOD communities developed around them. Express bus service along the same route carried approximately 6,000 commuters each weekday. According to RTD, at least 33,000 people were expected to ride to downtown using light rail on opening day. (376)

To avoid anticipated ridership congestion on the Central Corridor light rail line following the completion of T-REX, a Bus Rapid Transit (BRT) Central Connector was being considered by RTD officials. An estimated $40 million would be spent to introduce high-frequency bus service between the light rail stop at I-25 and Broadway and Union Station. The Central

Connector bus line would serve the State Capitol and Denver's Civic Center, and offer an alternative to the popular 16th Street Mall shuttle. (377)

Based on expected population growth for the Denver metro area, RTD estimated that by 2010 automobile traffic congestion along the Southeast Corridor would double compared to levels at the turn of the 21st century. Although more highway lanes would enable more vehicles to use Interstate highways 25 and 225, Denver transportation planners recognized the limitations of roadway expansion by offering a light rail transit alternative.

Like so many cities in North America during the mid-20th century, the people of Denver believed that automobile use had superceded the need for rail mass transit. Increased population growth combined with an increased dependence on driving through sprawl city planning cost Denver commuters their mobility as they approached the 21st century. Despite a skeptical RTD board during light rail's formative years, once the decision was made to establish a city-wide commuter and light rail transit network, a major build-out program ensued. But FasTracks was more than an effort to provide a transportation alternative to the automobile. Commuter and light rail were to be part of an overall redesign of how the city was to be built and rebuilt. Through Transit Oriented Developments, RTD buses and trains were to be an integral part of a new way of living, beyond simply a new way of commuting. Mass transportation was to play a primary role in a better future for metro Denver.

The station area in Englewood, Colorado, was designed to be part of a bus and light rail Transit Oriented Development. At sunset on July 11, 2002, two RTD buses circle the *art 'n Transit* sculpture, while a light rail vehicle from downtown Denver stops on its way to Mineral Avenue in Littleton.

CHAPTER THIRTEEN

Kenosha Transit Electric Streetcar

Combining practical mass transit with an historic attraction made Kenosha Transit Electric Streetcar more than just a transportation alternative. Progressive in its efforts to explore alternative fuels technology, the suburban community of Kenosha, Wisconsin, introduced five zero-emissions electric trolleys following the procurement of twelve compressed natural gas buses in a fleet of 42. But with historic electric streetcars, Kenosha Transit's new experiment was as unusual as it was environmentally friendly.

The original street railway to lay tracks in the streets of Kenosha began hauling passengers on February 1, 1903. Electric streetcars were replaced by trackless trolley buses on February 15, 1932. Trolley buses used overhead wire electric collection for power, just like a streetcar, but operated on rubber tires. As was the case elsewhere, factors which contributed to the end of street railway service included the Great Depression and the development of the automobile.

An industrial city located just north of the Illinois border, Kenosha was situated within the highly integrated Chicago economic region, populated by some 9.3 million residents. Located on the shore of Lake Michigan, Kenosha was the one-time home of American Motors. An automobile manufacturing company, American Motors employed nearly a third of Kenosha's residents during the 1970s. Its predecessor companies built such famous automobile brands as Nash, Hudson and Jeep. The automobile production facility encompassed 42 acres of Kenosha's 68-acre lakefront area. In 1987, the American Motors lakefront facility was purchased by the Chrysler Corporation. Chrysler closed the majority of its automobile assembly plants in the Kenosha area a year later, including the lakefront plant. Demolition of all plant buildings took place shortly thereafter.

The city of Kenosha did not look at the departure of Chrysler as an economic tragedy but as a significant redevelopment opportunity. In 1989, the city began a process which led to the $22.75 million 1991 Kenosha Downtown Plan. The new HarborPark area between downtown and the lakefront was to employ the mixed-use development approach. Houses, parks, a marina and some commercial development were to be built within just a trolley ride of one another. (378)

The regional economy increased an average 3.5 percent annually between 1985 and 1995, according to the Bureau of Economic Analysis. Kenosha-area economic reform represented 497,000 jobs in 1995, compared to 368,000 in 1985. The primary focus of the HarborPark Development Project was to take advantage of regional economic prosperity through the sale of town homes and garden apartments. Following years of study and planning, the construction of HarborPark began in 1997. Construction was expected to take from five to seven years. A preliminary cost estimate, which included infrastructure development such as streets and utilities, was projected to be about $18.5 million. (379)

In 1999, tracks were laid for a new 1.7-mile "circulator" trolley line, which would connect downtown to HarborPark. A circulator transit service was designed to make frequent stops along a continuous loop within a high-density activity center. A modern trolley barn and maintenance facility was built, which also served as a bus transfer point. A parking lot near the new Transit Center was constructed to enable people to drive into downtown, then use the trolley system to get around. Trolley tracks went by the commuter rail station so that trolley riders could transfer to a Chicago-bound Metra commuter train. "Basically, it will be less than two hours from your front door to downtown Chicago," said the operations supervisor for Kenosha Transit, Dan Cesario. "Just try that driving." (380)

State and federal grants covered the cost to build the streetcar system. The city of Kenosha was given nearly $3.5 million for the construction of the trolley line, improvements to the right-of-way, the Transit Center, and the purchase of five electric streetcars. Part of what made Kenosha eligible for these grants was that it was located in an air quality nonattainment area. In an effort to significantly reduce air pollution levels, electric trolleys were chosen instead of combustion-engine city buses. The five, 46-seat, ADA-compliant (Americans with Disabilities Act) PCC electric streetcars were purchased from Toronto Transit in Canada. Built by Canadian Car and Foundry in 1951, they had formerly operated on the Toronto Lakefront Streetcar Line. Restoration and refurbishment was done by a contractor in Iowa. Kenosha Transit received its first restored PCC streetcar on May 4, 2000. (381)

Only one PCC car retained its Toronto "Wine Red and Cream" color scheme. The other trolleys were painted for transit companies of historical significance which operated PCC cars in the United States. Paint schemes representing Chicago, Illinois; Cincinnati, Ohio; and Pittsburgh, Pennsylvania, were chosen. Almost 5,000 PCC cars were built in North America from 1936 until 1952. The last trolley to arrive on the property was painted for Kenosha. The bright Johnstown Orange of this car resembled the trackless trolley buses which served the city between 1932 and 1952. Former director of transportation for the city of Kenosha, Joe McCarthy, instigated the idea to develop an historic street railway for downtown. "They're working pieces of equipment that people like to ride more than the bus," said city transit commission member Louis Rugani. "It's a desirable way to travel, and it gets people out of their cars." (382)

Maintenance and repair costs of the city-owned PCC trolleys were expected to be the same as city buses. They were to last 15 to 20 years before needing to be rebuilt. Specially trained city bus drivers were to operate the trolleys. The big opening-day celebration took place on Saturday, June 17, 2000. Regular operation of the street railway began the following Monday.

Patrons paid 25 cents each to ride to any point along the two-mile loop. People boarding at the Transit Center could ride through downtown westbound on 54th Street, turn south at the Metra station on 11th Avenue, then go two blocks before turning east on 56th Street toward HarborPark.

One of the most beautified and upgraded downtown streets along the trolley route was 56th Street. The street was widened and a grassy median put in, with the tracks laid down the middle. This was patterned after the design of the St. Charles Line electric railway in New Orleans, Louisiana. Once to HarborPark, Kenosha streetcars passed Celebration Place and the Harborwalk along Lake Michigan and Kenosha Harbor. According to a Public Land Trust Law, established in 1836, the land fill beyond the original shoreline must be rededicated for public use. In the case of HarborPark, this included all land north of 56th Street and east of 2nd Avenue. West from Celebration Place, the trolley line followed 54th Street along Kenosha Harbor before arriving back at the Transit Center. The one-way trolley loop operated in counter-clockwise fashion.

At the time of opening, streetcars operated Monday through Friday from 11:05 AM to 7:05 PM, and Saturday from 10:05 AM to 5:35 PM. There was to be no service on Sundays and only special operations on holidays. Operating days and hours would be reevaluated as HarborPark developed. The 25-cent fare would also increase. The city of Kenosha saw its electric streetcar line as a public service to the community. Patrons could expect a trolley car to pick them up about every 15 minutes.

A year following its inception, Kenosha Transit Electric Streetcar had attracted over 400 weekday riders, on average. Eventually, a daily operating schedule between 5:30 AM and 8 PM was envisioned. Streetcar operations would fluctuate depending on the time of year (tourist season) and city budgetary constraints. (383)

Future rail line expansion could one day have PCC cars operating north of the central business district on 6th Avenue to 50th Street. From there, double track could be built in the center of 7th Avenue to 38th Street, if economically feasible. "It's been our experience that if it's done right, rail transit like our streetcars can work in any setting," said the director of city development, Ray Forgianni. "It fits with the overall design and has raised interest among both tourists and residents alike." (384)

City officials expected HarborPark to generate $60 to $75 million in private investment. Over 700 new residents were expected to move into the new 220 to 300-unit Harborview Residential Neighborhood. Through planning and building what was essentially to be a Transit Oriented Development in an air quality nonattainment area, the city of Kenosha was focusing on the kind of quality of life issues that draw people to live in places like HarborPark. (385)

Cities like Kenosha could look at cities such as Philadelphia to see the benefits of a densely populated region served by rail mass transit over a long period of time. Municipal leaders could also look at Denver to see how to reintroduce light rail into an automobile oriented society. As Denver began to redesign its city and suburbs toward modern transit, other cities could learn from Denver's example. Further, adding historical significance to a rail mass transit system had the potential to do much for the vitality of the region being served. Kenosha Transit was directly influenced by the way 1920s-era streetcars were operated in New Orleans. But even Kenosha was a pioneer city. Only time would tell if its version of mixed-use transit-oriented New Urbanism would attract people to area neighborhoods or riders on its streetcars.

Rail mass transit was a peak-hour transportation alternative to driving through congested automobile traffic. But it also had the potential to be fun like a ride in a theme park. Cleaner and quieter historic streetcars added flavor to newly redeveloped neighborhoods and business districts without significantly contributing to noise and air pollution. Historic electric streetcar lines were finding a niche as part of the nation's 21st century transit boom.

PART FIVE

Planning Commuter Rail on the Front Range

CHAPTER FOURTEEN

The Reluctant Return of Passenger Rail

Proper funding remains a key element in the construction, expansion and potential success of any mass transit system, including commuter and light rail. Budget constraints versus people's demand for better mobility often determine the direction transportation takes in any given city or region. On Colorado's Front Range, stalled commuter rail projects between major metropolitan centers contrasted against Denver's efforts to quickly construct a major rail transportation network within the metro area.

The federal government established trust funds to provide for the construction and expansion of airports, airlines and highways. Financial assistance was provided to the airlines by the Airport and Airway Trust Fund. The same assistance was provided for automobile use and to the trucking industry by the Highway Trust Fund. Although money from the Highway Trust Fund went in part to mass transit, mass transit and passenger rail did not have exclusive access to such a fund. This put highway supporters and mass transit/passenger rail advocates against each other for access to the same trust fund. The Highway Trust Fund was financed with federal tax dollars from the sale of gasoline, diesel fuel and tires.

The motivation behind the establishment of rail mass transit systems nationwide was a desire to develop a balanced transportation network. Underutilizing one form of transportation put a heavy burden on other forms. This limited the ability of different modes to benefit each other. For example, Denver International Airport's (DIA) surface transportation accesses were designed for automobile and bus use only. This was significant considering the distance of the airport from downtown Denver. A rail alternative for downtown-airport commuters was not expected to be necessary when the huge facility was scheduled to open in 1993. About that time, Denver was experiencing a downtown vacancy rate that hit an historic 30 percent. People working on the airport project failed to anticipate the renaissance of downtown Denver and how that would impact travel patterns. Until 1997, the lofts and attractions that rebuilt downtown's Central Platte Valley were nothing but a bare former rail yard. (386)

The Union Pacific Railroad offered to build and operate a commuter rail line to DIA but was turned down. As a freight hauler, the Union Pacific took a supportive role toward commuter rail. "Union Pacific Railroad owns an existing transportation network that has excess capacity, requiring only modest capital improvements to handle commuter rail services. We want to sell that capacity and increase the return on our assets," said the Union Pacific Railroad in a promotional brochure. "We'll not only provide the necessary track, we'll also operate the trains.... Our shareholders will receive an increased return through more intensive use of the railroad's assets." (387)

The idea of building an "Air Train" commuter rail line from downtown Denver to DIA surfaced on August 25, 1997, when DIA bonds were refinanced by Denver City Council. The city set aside at least $20 million in DIA enterprise funds to purchase Union Pacific trackage which was already up for sale. The 25-mile railroad right-of-way went from downtown Denver, east to Interstate 70 and Pena Boulevard. The city already owned the land along Pena Boulevard to the airport. (388)

The bond debt was expected to increase the fees paid by the airlines that served DIA. The Air Transport Association and United Airlines opposed the purchase of the railroad right-of-way. The concern was that the Air Train was an off-airport project that would not exclusively serve the airport. The Air Transport Association was a trade group which represented most U.S. airlines. United Airlines mountain region vice president Roger Gibson expressed his concerns regarding the Air Train. "The train will likely have a benefit for people who are not going to or from DIA to get to and from downtown." In a letter to United Airlines, City Council president Cathy Reynolds justified the use of airport money to build a commuter rail line. She wrote, "Delivering paying customers to DIA efficiently and in an environmentally friendly mode of transportation is a legitimate use of airport revenue." (389)

The Air Train became part of the Regional Transportation District's FasTracks program, a major rail construction initiative for metro Denver. The first rail transit line in the United States to be deliberately built to connect to an airport was constructed in 1968. The Cleveland Rapid Transit in Cleveland, Ohio, extended electric trolley service to a station stop within Hopkins International Airport.

Although the return of local passenger rail to the Denver area was a long time in coming, once rail transit became an important part of city planning and development, other rail line proposals came to the forefront. Colorado Department of Transportation (CDOT) director Tom Norton envisioned two

PASSENGER RAIL

major high-speed passenger rail lines to be built along the Front Range, one of which included the Air Train. In a letter to U.S. Transportation Secretary Norman Mineta in March 2002, Norton proposed a 160-mile east-west high-speed rail line linking Denver International Airport to Union Station via the Air Train route, then continuing west to the ski resort community of Vail and the Eagle County Airport. A second 180-mile north-south rail corridor would link Greeley, Fort Collins, Loveland, Longmont and Boulder to the north of Denver, with Colorado Springs and Pueblo to the south. About 85 percent of Colorado residents lived along this proposed Front Range high-speed rail line. (390)

Rail systems of this size and cost were difficult to build with tax subsidy, especially as a single major project. High-speed rail along Colorado's Front Range would have to be preceded by slower commuter rail lines, built over time as spokes from a hub. The Air Train and a commuter line from Denver Union Station to Boulder, northwest of Denver, would form two of those spokes. A Denver-Boulder train would return commuter rail service to a route that at one time operated electric interurbans.

Burlington Northern SD40-2 7007 and 7940 look northwest from Broomfield, Colorado, toward Longs Peak on the former Denver & Interurban Kite Route line to Boulder. The tracks curve to the right toward Louisville where the north line of the Kite Route went. Remnants of the abandoned south line could still be found near Marshall.

The Kite Route

Built to high standards between Denver and Boulder, Colorado, the Denver & Interurban Railroad Company operated for a short 18 years, 1908 to 1926, before its abandonment. The automobile and bus were able to offer a faster and more convenient transportation alternative for Denver-Boulder commuters. In time, the one-person-one-car approach to transportation would overwhelm the peak period traffic capacity of U.S. Highway 36. Rail transit between Denver and Boulder would be considered viable once again, in an effort to restore transportation efficiency and convenience.

The Denver & Interurban was never truly its own company but a subsidiary of a western steam railroad, the Colorado & Southern Railway Company. The Colorado & Southern was incorporated in December 1898, followed by the Denver & Interurban on September 10, 1904. The intention of the C&S was to have a 110-mile electric interurban connecting Denver to Boulder and then on to Fort Collins, Colorado.

Two routes were built to Boulder. A single line from Denver split at Louisville Junction, where a northerly line went to Boulder via Louisville and a southerly line went via Marshall. At Marshall, a 33-mile southwest line was built to Eldorado Springs, a popular resort town because of its hot spring pools. Interurban cars were to use Denver Tramway street trackage from downtown Denver to Globeville. Once north of Denver, the electric interurban line mainly paralleled the Colorado & Southern to Louisville Junction. Beyond the junction, both lines to Boulder utilized C&S trackage, except for a deviation on the Louisville line near Boulder from Boulder Junction into the city. On a map, this completed rail route resembled a kite with a long tail, hence the D&I advertising slogan: "The Kite Route."

The only rolling stock order went to the St. Louis Car Company in January 1908. The following June, eight motor cars and four trailers arrived on the D&I for service. Resembling heavyweight passenger equipment, motor cars M-151 through M-156 were 59-seat coaches. Numbers M-157 and M-158 were 46-seat coach-baggage combinations. They were purchased for roughly $21,000 each. Built like steam railroad passenger coaches, 58-seat unpowered trailers numbered 201 through 204 cost roughly $6,000 each. Electrical equipment on the motor cars was provided by Westinghouse Electric. Four 125 horsepower AC/DC traction motors enabled a motor car to pull one trailer up a two percent grade or achieve a level speed of 50 miles per hour. (391)

Along the city streets of Denver and Boulder, the D&I operated its interurban cars on 550 volt direct current electricity, collected by a trolley pole. Once on private right-of-way, cars switched to an 11,000 volt single-phase alternating current power system, requiring a change from trolley pole to pantograph electric collection. When the Denver & Interurban opened for service on June 23, 1908, substation equipment for the 550 volt D.C. overhead trolley wire through Boulder had yet to be installed. Minus electric power, a Colorado & Southern steam locomotive towed the first interurban cars to the Boulder depot.

Rail system expansion to Fort Collins was planned for the D&I but never completed. It was mainly blocked by the purchase of the Colorado & Southern by a major long-distance steam railroad. The C&S became a subsidiary itself when it was acquired by the Chicago, Burlington & Quincy in 1908. Interested more in steam railroading than electric interurbans, the Burlington frustrated plans to connect the D&I to the Fort Collins Street Railway, a D&I subsidiary.

The Chicago, Burlington & Quincy Railroad Company officially announced on December 19, 1908, the purchase of 64.3 percent of preferred and common stock of the Colorado & Southern Railway. The Burlington gained controlling interest in a 2,700-mile railroad, including the Colorado & Southern's half interest in the Colorado Midland in Colorado and the Trinity and Brazos Valley in Texas. Strategically, the Burlington's interest in the C&S was to be able to haul cattle, cotton and produce north from Texas and coal and steel north from Colorado. Lumber, fish, fruit, and imports from the Orient would use the C&S in part, moving south from the Pacific Northwest. (392)

Ridership on Colorado & Southern's Denver & Interurban increased until 1911. Except in 1914, patronage declined thereafter. The D&I did not provide carload freight service to offset its passenger losses. The only freight deliveries made were bundles of newspapers to Eldorado Springs. The interurban was not going to compete for freight revenues against its parent company, Colorado & Southern.

Original construction costs of the D&I amounted to $1 million, a debt the interurban was unable to pay off in a timely manner. As operating losses continued to increase, more debt plagued the D&I. It was forced into receivership on June 12, 1918. (393)

A man who had been a part of the interurban's work force since its initial construction, William H. Edmunds, became its receiver. He had worked on the original construction of the Denver & Interurban and was later promoted to electrical engineer and trainmaster in 1912. One of his first major efforts toward bringing the D&I out of debt was through arranging the abandonment and sale of the Fort Collins Street Railway. Edmunds was granted an emergency order to abandon Fort Collins streetcar service by the Colorado Public Utilities Commission on July 9, 1918. Trolley operations ceased the following day. Through the sale of the street railway to the City of Fort Collins, a transaction concluded on May 15, 1919, Edmunds was able to generate $53,000 toward paying off D&I debt. The city-owned Fort Collins Municipal Railway restored electric streetcar service and operated it until 1951. (394)

Streamlining the railroad in 1919, Edmunds cut back the interurban's 16 trains-a-day schedule to 13. In order to do this, Edmunds convinced the city of Boulder to waive its original schedule agreement with the railroad. The idea was to reduce operating costs. Further, Edmunds was able to increase passenger fares and gain a monetary rate reduction for electric power consumption from the Western Light & Power Company.

The First World War, which the United States entered on April 6, 1917, was one of several forces working against Edmund's efforts. Notably, the cost of materials increased significantly. Copper wire went up by 97 percent between 1916 and 1920, railroad ties by 112 percent and steel axles by 208 percent. What Edmunds did not have to contend with yet, however, was a significant increase in labor costs. (395)

Because the D&I was not a freight hauler, and since it followed the route of the Colorado & Southern, it was not taken over by the United States Railroad Administration during the World War. The USRA took over the Colorado & Southern, as it did many railroads for the war effort, and ordered a salary increase for C&S railroad employees. Trainmen who worked for the D&I, but had seniority rights on either railroad, believed a pay increase for D&I employees was also due. The Railway Board of Adjustment acted as arbitrator between the labor unions and the managements of both the D&I and C&S. The board determined, however, that the interurban was a separate entity from the Colorado & Southern, further separated by the fact that the D&I was directed by a bankruptcy court. In fairness, Edmunds was urged by the board to provide the salary increase anyway. In the interest of freeing the D&I from debt, Edmunds denied the request.

The war came to an end on November 11, 1918. By February 20, 1920, Edmunds successfully paid off all debt except for the interurban's overdue bond interest to the Colorado & Southern. Eventually, though, Edmunds was going to have to submit to a salary increase for the trainmen. A 21 percent pay raise was ordered by the United States Labor Board. More financial problems were still ahead for the interurban, especially following a severe head-on collision in Globeville, just outside Denver, on September 6, 1920. (396)

The interurban was exceptionally busy during this particular Labor Day weekend. Extra trains were scheduled to help out regular service trains running at full capacity. The northbound train out of Denver, Extra 158, consisted of combination motor car M-158 and trailer coach 204. It collided head-on with regular train 308 just north of Globeville. Southbound train 308, motor M-153 minus any trailers, came around a blind curve at 60 miles per hour and collided with Extra 158, which was going 35 miles per hour. The two motormen had about four seconds to react after these opposing trains came into view of each other.

Casualties and injuries were highest on 308 from Boulder. Although motor M-153 had seats for 59 passengers, 136 were aboard, more than half standing in the aisle. Further, the baggage compartment on M-158 largely protected the occupants of Extra 158 from severe injury. In all, twelve people lost their lives and 214 were hurt. Damages included $12,500 for each of the two wrecked motor cars, and eventually $144,747 was paid in personal injury claims. Despite the severity of the impact, neither the track, catenary or trailer car 204 were damaged. (397)

An investigation by the Colorado Public Utilities Commission and the Interstate Commerce Commission revealed several factors which contributed to the wreck. One was the line had no signal system. The most significant error, however, was made by the conductor of Extra 158. He expected to meet regular train 308 at 12:30 PM, when actually the meet was scheduled for 11:30 AM. Since regular trains had priority, Extra 158 should have waited on the siding at Globeville, had the conductor known his schedule.

Accumulated overdue bond interest owed to the Colorado & Southern through the Guaranty Trust Company came to $480,155 by June 1921. The trust company dismissed its foreclosure suit following deferment of the bond claim by C&S. On June 28, 1921, Edmunds was discharged as receiver, and the D&I moved out of bankruptcy on July 1. The C&S deferred its claim for five years, with a condition that all accrued interest be paid when the grace period was over. All D&I debt was due on July 1, 1926. The Colorado & Southern promoted Edmunds from electrical engineer and trainmaster to general manager of the Denver & Interurban. (398)

From 1917 to 1922, Edmunds reduced D&I operating costs by relocating the interurban's rail lines off city streets. The heavyweight interurban cars were too heavy for street trackage, requiring heavy maintenance to the track. In Boulder, the D&I moved its passenger service over to the Colorado & Southern and used its station. Steam locomotives pulled the cars into Boulder on the C&S until 11,000 volt A.C. catenary could be put up. The move was urgent since maintenance on the rails in Boulder city streets had been deferred. The old street trackage was not abandoned, however, but donated to a local Western Light & Power streetcar line. The interurban needed to appease the power company so it would not oppose the change over.

In order to stop using Denver Tramway street trackage in downtown Denver, interurban service moved to Denver Union Station on a low density Chicago, Burlington & Quincy line. A platform several tracks distant from the station was built, and the Burlington line electrified for the interurban. The massive weight of the interurban cars helped to justify the move. On the Denver Tramway streetcar line, there was concern regarding the 23rd Street viaduct and its safety. Even after structural reinforcement, D&I cars slowly crossed this insufficiently built trolley bridge, originally designed exclusively for light weight Denver Tramway trolleys. The switch to Union Station was intended to take the interurban cars off the bridge.

Denver Union Station was ready for D&I service by mid-summer 1922. Service in and out of the station was not convenient for the interurban, however, because its cars were not capable of operating in either direction. The equipment had to be turned on a wye a mile from the station and backed to the platform. As a result, interurban cars continued to use the 23rd Street viaduct into downtown during the 1922 summer travel season.

On September 24, 1922, most cars began using the new Union Station access, but some cars continued to use the viaduct. Eager to eliminate street lines not used by Denver Tramway, city officials in Denver ordered the D&I to stop using the viaduct in October 1922. This would have effectively ended D&I street access in Denver. The City wanted to begin a street paving project, a task made easier by the removal of trolley car rails in the street. The D&I ignored the order while it bought its way out of a 20-year contract with Denver Tramway. The Denver & Interurban ceased to be a street railway when interurban cars stopped using Denver Tramway trackage on December 22, 1922.

The problem of turning the interurban cars before they arrived at Denver Union Station continued. Converting the cars for double-ended operation began in 1923. The bulk of the work was performed through 1924, which included removing D.C. electric collection equipment. No longer a street railway, D&I interurban cars could be converted exclusively for 11,000 volt A.C. electric collection. One and a half tons of D.C. electrical equipment was removed from each car.

The emphasis was still on passenger railroading in 1924. Although the D&I only turned a profit in 1921 and 1922, interurban management was determined to resist the encroachment of the automobile, at least for a while. The year 1924 was a turning point for the Denver & Interurban. It was a turn that would lead the interurban to its end.

The Colorado & Southern was able to monopolize mass transit service between Denver and Boulder, for itself and its D&I subsidiary, until December 18, 1924. At this time, C&S asked the Colorado Public Utilities Commission to force potential bus transit lines out of the Denver-Boulder market. This request was based on the use of Common Carrier Certificates required for railroads which the bus lines did not have. But the PUC pointed out that the certificates were required only for railroads, leaving the bus lines exempt from such a limitation. The Boulder Bus & Taxicab Company and the Paradox Land & Transport Company quickly entered into competing service early in 1925.

The intrusion of bus service into the Colorado & Southern's passenger transportation monopoly came when highway construction was quickly expanding. This was a time long before the problem of increased automobile traffic congestion, when public funding could afford to build a network of reasonably sized highways. These highways, built to capacities far larger than their immediate use, were ideal for intercity bus systems. Unencumbered by the delays caused by modern automobile traffic congestion, buses had the advantage of lower maintenance and operating costs. Also, bus lines could change or add routes without cost. There was no cost to build or maintain a right-of-way, and only one employee was required to operate a bus. Not only were railroads responsible for owning and maintaining inflexible rail right-of-ways, but labor agreements required an interurban train to carry three employees—a motorman, a brakeman and a conductor. There were many such rules that the well-established railroads had to contend with which did not effect newly-formed bus companies.

Buses, therefore, became an attractive business venture for the Denver & Interurban. Despite the expense to move its interurban cars off city streets and to double-end its cars for easy access into Denver Union Station, D&I

management understood its losing battle and began to turn away from interurban passenger railroading. An internal memo dated January 10, 1925, stated: "The Denver & Interurban Railroad should be discontinued in a way which would minimize the cost and loss of business to the C&S." (399)

In order for the interurban to effectively replace itself with a bus line under the same management, careful steps needed to be taken to gain PUC approval. Some communities, including Superior, Louisville and Boulder, valued their interurban connection to each other and Denver. The PUC might refuse such a change if it meant the end of the interurban. No moves were taken toward railroad abandonment when the D&I proposed the formation of the Denver & Interurban Motor Company to the PUC. The PUC was led to believe that the D&I intended to operate the D&IMC bus line in conjunction with the interurban.

In the meantime, with two bus companies already operating and two more (including the D&IMC) trying to establish themselves for future service, the PUC became concerned about over-competition. Worried about too many bus companies having a long-term negative effect, the PUC required each company to submit an application for exclusive transit rights to the Denver-Boulder market. On August 4, 1925, the D&IMC was awarded the right to provide bus service, despite protests from the already established Paradox Land & Transport Company. With solid C&S financial backing and its affiliation with the Denver & Interurban, the D&IMC was the PUC's first choice to best provide bus service along this important and growing commuter corridor. The Paradox Land & Transport Company asked the Colorado State Supreme Court to reverse the PUC's decision. Until the appeal was denied, the company continued to operate its competitive bus line between Denver and Boulder. The Denver & Interurban Motor Company opened for service on December 1, 1925, under the leadership of the interurban's president, William H. Edmunds.

The Colorado & Southern established the D&IMC separate from the D&I electric line at a cost of $87,000. By keeping the two subsidiaries separate, the D&IMC was exempt from railroad taxes, railroad labor agreements and the jurisdiction of the Interstate Commerce Commission. Further, abandonment of the electric interurban could be accomplished without directly effecting the bus line. (400)

Interurban abandonment began quietly with a strategy intended to have rail service discontinued by the summer of 1926. A first step was to pay off bonds owed for the electrical system. This was an agreement originally made with the Northern Colorado Power Company, succeeded by the Public Service Company. In order to avoid opposition from the PSC, the bonds were paid off in 1925. The D&I gained clear title to its electrical system through a loan provided by the Colorado & Southern.

Although both the interurban and the bus company operated efficiently under the direction of W.H. Edmunds, his affiliations with the D&I could not allow him to be involved directly with the bus line. This was to avoid any unforeseen problems which might have complicated the abandonment of the Denver & Interurban. In August of 1926, Edmunds resigned as president of the Denver & Interurban Motor Company and took no further interest in its business.

All bond interest owed by the Denver & Interurban was due to the Colorado & Southern on July 1, 1926. However, the C&S allowed payment to be deferred until August 30, when the Guaranty Trust Company, enlisted by the Colorado & Southern as trustee, filed suit against the D&I. The interurban was found in default of $1,079,000, which had accumulated from 1914 to 1926. There was no way the interurban could pay this debt, which was immediately due. Edmunds was once again appointed receiver. (401)

It was not generally known that the Guaranty Trust Company was acting on behalf of the Colorado & Southern, or that C&S and D&I management intended to abandon the interurban. Passenger revenues declined steadily for the Colorado & Southern during the 1920s. The automobile was proving to be a stiff competitor to railroads nationwide, for which the C&S was no exception. Over the years, the losses accrued from operating passenger trains cost the C&S more than $1.5 million. (402)

The towns of Superior, Louisville and Boulder objected to the foreclosure of the Denver & Interurban, believing the railroad served the needs of the public. Town leaders wanted the C&S to continue to support the D&I, as it had been doing since 1914. Being a subsidiary, the towns argued, the D&I should not be considered a separate entity from the C&S. The city of Boulder also noted that the D&I had a franchise agreement with the city to operate until December 14, 1927.

During this time, the Denver & Interurban Motor Company requested permission from the Colorado Public Utilities Commission to operate buses to the intermediate towns served by the interurban. This decision was postponed until a district court judge could rule on the issue of D&I abandonment. That ruling came on December 9, 1926, in favor of the trust company. The district court judge ruled in favor of terminating interurban rail service based on the railroad's checkered past and its inability to function independently. "The line had a long history of insolvency and no means of changing that. Even Boulder did not deny it," stated the judge in making his ruling. "Continued operation would amount to putting Boulder's franchise claim ahead of the claims of all of the other creditors and using up the creditor's property for the convenience of the public." (403)

Operations on the Kite Route were ordered to cease on December 15, 1926. As predicted, the Public Service Company did not oppose the order, and the PUC ultimately gave the D&IMC approval to serve the towns along the former interurban with buses. W. H. Edmunds was once again appointed president of the bus company.

The Colorado & Southern managed its subsidiary bus line until March 1, 1929. More interested in railroading than bus transit, C&S management decided to contract out managing control of the D&IMC to the Rocky Mountain Motor Company. This arrangement continued until the bus line was sold to the Burlington Transportation Company on October 1, 1942. Bus service between Denver and Boulder was eventually taken over by Denver's Regional Transportation District (RTD) as a government subsidy in 1975.

The Denver & Interurban was never as big an interurban as Indiana's Chicago Lake Shore & South Bend Railroad. Nonetheless, both railroads were built to steam railroad standards with large and heavy electric interurban cars. In both cases, the cars were required to switch from pantograph electric power collection to lower-voltage trolley poles while operating in cities during their early years. Further, both railroads phased in and out of bankruptcy, greatly effected by the government-financed construction of competing roadways. The problem of roadway expansion was a problem for most, if not all interurbans, but the D&I and the South Shore Line were similar still.

The years 1924 through 1926 were a critical time for both interurbans concerning their futures. The Chicago Lake Shore & South Bend was suffering from deferred maintenance and a need for intense rehabilitation. It was trapped in receivership. In contrast, the Denver & Interurban was upgrading its fleet, free from bankruptcy and protected under the financial security of the Colorado & Southern. But in 1925, the South Shore Line found a savior in utilities tycoon Samuel Insull. The dilapidated Chicago interurban became the Chicago South Shore & South Bend Railroad, and virtually overnight was rehabilitated into one of the nation's best interurbans.

The Denver & Interurban was in no such dire straits in 1925, but suffering from a severe decline in revenue, needed a savior nonetheless. That savior could have been William Edmunds. The D&I was a costly appendage to the Colorado & Southern, however, which the C&S understandably wanted to eliminate. With a management more interested in steam railroading, the interurban simply did not make sense financially. Only as a public service was the D&I a justified operation. Otherwise, more money was to be made selling the equipment or scrapping it than to keep the operation going. As much could have been said about the South Shore Line, which probably would have ended service had it not been for Samuel Insull.

Even if D&I and South Shore Line management could have seen into the future, the outlook would have been grim. With the Great Depression just a few years away, the continued expansion of highways and the growing popularity of the automobile, Samuel Insull probably would have thought twice before investing so completely into his three Chicago interurbans. Only half a century later were government subsidized, interurban-successor commuter railroads proving to be beneficial in light of too many automobiles on over-burdened roadways.

Unlike most interurbans, which waited until their track was dilapidated, their rolling stock in disrepair and when ridership was severely low, the Denver & Interurban was in first-class operating condition just before management decided to abandon it. The towns of Superior, Louisville and Boulder were demanding its continued operation. Nonetheless, upgraded rail service, removed from street trackage onto Colorado & Southern's private mainline, lasted only a short while. Completely refurbished motor cars, rebuilt for A.C.-only double-ended operation, were scrapped. Only two pieces of rolling stock survived abandonment, trailer coaches 202 and 203. They were sold to a construction company in Michigan and later ended up on Michigan's Toledo & Detroit Railway.

The Front Range at the eastern edge of the Rocky Mountains, specifically between Fort Collins to the north and Pueblo south of Colorado Springs, served as an example of the reluctant return of passenger rail. Although severe automobile traffic congestion brought metro Denver closer to becoming the next Los Angeles or Chicago, the probability of introducing a region-wide Front Range commuter rail system was still far off during the early years of the 21st century. Speculatively, if the D&I had survived another 50 years, it would have been operating at the time of the formation of Denver's Regional Transportation District. As a social necessity, and as a subsidy-dependent transportation alternative, the interurban might have been transformed much the same way as the South Shore Line had been by the

Northern Indiana Commuter Transportation District. Nevertheless, the story of the old Kite Route line was not to come to an end, in so much that the old Denver & Interurban right-of-way was proposed to be reconstructed for commuter rail service by RTD.

Passenger trains occasionally traversed the old Kite Route line through Boulder, Colorado. On June 7, 1997, a Burlington Northern Santa Fe *Employee Appreciation Special* returned to Denver on its round-trip run to Longmont. Freight diesel 9751, an SD70MAC, passed the Boulder station sign with the railroad's business cars in tow.

CHAPTER FIFTEEN

The Kite Route, the Rocket, and Other Lines

The Burlington Northern & Santa Fe Railway owned the former Denver & Interurban "Kite Route" between Denver and Boulder. Freight trains continued to use the north side of the Kite via Louisville. With little need for two lines to Boulder, the pre-BNSF Colorado & Southern Railway ceased rail operations along the southern route. Abandonment between Superior and Boulder via Marshall occurred in 1932. The former Denver & Interurban platform and rails remained intact at Denver Union Station until 1986. As a result of continued freight service preserving the northern right-of-way and keeping the line open, the opportunity to reestablish commuter rail over the old D&I west to Boulder, and the old Colorado & Southern north to Fort Collins, was available for the 21st century.

Plans for the 30-mile Denver-Boulder bus and rail transit route were part of the Denver Regional Transportation District's FasTracks transit build-out program. Burlington Northern Santa Fe trackage would be upgraded for commuter rail, and U.S. Highway 36 reconstructed to include a dedicated bus transitway. Commuter rail was expected to rejuvenate old downtown districts not easily accessible by freeway. Other populous areas, not so easily accessible by rail, would be served by buses. Transit Oriented Developments were expected to sprout around bus and rail transit stations. More than a plan to move people along the U.S. 36 corridor, Transit Oriented Development was an effort to determine where people would live, work or shop based on a master plan.

Buses and trains would call at Denver Union Station. Busway transit stops, in the median of U.S. 36 between the traffic lanes, would serve the intermediate communities of Westminster, Broomfield, and Superior. Additional freeway lanes and a bikeway would also be built. Commuter trains would help revive the older business and residential districts in Westminster, Broomfield, and Louisville.

A sales tax increase would have to be approved by the majority of area voters to cover the cost of construction and to operate both buses and trains.

The city of Boulder was negotiating to purchase eleven acres of land on the city's east side to construct a rail terminal and to initiate the development of a Transit Village. "We're not looking to displace people," said planner Tony Chacon. "We're looking to give them a better habitat." (404)

The vote of the people, and their willingness to pay more in taxes for transportation, may be the single most determining factor in whether or not a transportation alternative is developed. Therefore, even with plans being made and talk of commuter rail along the Front Range, nothing would be forthcoming until the people decided that they have been stuck in traffic long enough to be willing to pay for rail transit.

Thinking ahead, transportation planners were developing transportation strategies larger than RTD's Denver-Boulder corridor or even FasTracks. A separate proposed commuter rail line would connect Denver to Fort Collins via Greeley. Amtrak's tri-weekly "Pioneer" operated over the Denver to Greeley portion of the route during its long journey to and from Portland, Oregon, and Seattle, Washington. On October 12, 1995, the Union Pacific Railroad operated a "City of Portland" excursion to promote commuter rail. The Union Pacific provided its business train to run south from Greeley to Denver Union Station.

Union Pacific's Ed Trandahl explained, "The purpose of this train ride is to give people a better feeling of what it is to go to work on the train rather than on other forms of transportation.... It is friendly to the air, friendly in terms of fuel consumption and friendly compared to building highways.... Once it is up and running, it is very easy to add capacity." The "city of Portland" was named in honor of one of Union Pacific's famous long-distance "Cities" streamliners. It's successor, Amtrak's Pioneer, was discontinued on May 10, 1997, due to Amtrak budget constraints. (405)

A Denver-Boulder-Fort Collins line connected to a Denver-Greeley-Fort Collins line would create a northerly loop commuter rail connection serving major population centers north and west of Denver using existent rail lines. This northerly loop could be complemented by a southerly route linking Denver to Colorado Springs and Pueblo. Burlington Northern Santa Fe and Union Pacific freight trains crossed the mountainous Palmer Divide, south of Denver, on what became known as the "Joint Line."

Expansion of parallel Interstate 25 from four to six lanes was also proposed. This was a "supply-side" tactic for dealing with traffic growth, meaning that the most popular mode of transportation, in this case the automobile, is supplied with more of what it needs, in this case more road.

Mass transportation is a "demand-side" tactic. This means that efforts are put toward establishing a mode of transportation that best serves the demand for mobility in the most viable and economical way. (406)

Mounting mobility problems along Interstate 25 discouraged local municipalities and citizen groups from approving high-density real estate developments. There also was a desire to preserve open space. Opposing concentrated urban development was a way to attempt a limitation on the number of cars on the road. Land north of Castle Rock along I-25 was zoned for agricultural uses only and was otherwise designated non-urban in the master development plan for Douglas County, a large suburban county south of Denver. The area, known as Happy Canyon, was restricted to one dwelling every 35 acres. A developer, Happy Canyon Partners, submitted an application to Douglas County in January 1997 to change the county's master plan.

Over the course of 40 to 50 years, Happy Canyon Partners envisioned two dwellings per acre plus some commercial development. The initial development of 5,587 acres was to be built on the east side of I-25 at the Happy Canyon exit. The nearby communities of Castle Rock, Parker and Lone Tree opposed the development plan. Further, about 20 homeowner associations formed the Douglas County Quality of Life Partnership in an effort to block the plan submitted by Happy Canyon Partners. If the application to change the master plan were to be accepted by Douglas County, another application would then be submitted by Happy Canyon Partners to change the zoning for higher density development.

A member of the Happy Canyon Homeowners Association, Michael Kruger, objected to changing the Douglas County master plan. "It will destroy the last buffer area between Castle Rock and metro Denver…. The quality of life in central Douglas County will be compromised. This is a major project; 12,000 homes. That's about the size of (Denver suburb) Highlands Ranch, and nine million feet of commercial office and retail." (407)

Despite local efforts to control population growth along Colorado's Front Range, growth was inevitable. Over time, the need to find a transportation alternative to the automobile would become increasingly apparent. But to introduce push-pull bi-level commuter trains on the busy BNSF-Union Pacific Joint Line would be challenging.

Through a private-public partnership, rail freight lines could be moved off the Front Range and out onto the Eastern plains, leaving Front Range rail lines available for hauling mostly passengers. The Colorado Transportation Commission allocated $500,000, according to Colorado Department of Transportation director Tom Norton, to determine the benefits of rerouting freight trains away from downtown Denver and other centers of population. Union Pacific and BNSF officials proposed the idea in 2001 to get many of the railroads' freight trains off the hilly and congested Front Range rail routes. "They were looking for alternative plans that would relocate that traffic east of the (Denver) metro area. It would allow them to save time on their shipments, and it would be safer," said Cal Marsella, general manager for Denver's Regional Transportation District. "Burlington's coal comes from Gillette, Wyoming, through the northern part of the state, into the Central Platte Valley, past the Pepsi Center, Invesco Field, along Santa Fe Drive, through Castle Rock, Colorado Springs, Pueblo, and ends up in Texas.... This is larger than just an RTD initiative. This is a whole Front Range mobility plan." (408)

Ninety miles of new track connected to existent rail lines would enable through-freight trains to bypass downtown Denver and other Front Range communities. Freight trains, which often had to creep through downtown Denver at about ten miles per hour, would be able to increase speeds, offering greater efficiency for the railroads. If Denver rail yards were to be reduced or closed, several acres of real estate near downtown could be made available for urban development. Local freight trains serving local industries would continue to operate between Fort Collins, Denver and Pueblo, while through-freights, such as Texas coal trains, would use the bypass route. "Are all the trains ever going to be leaving the central Denver area? No," said Union Pacific's Mike Parras, who handled Denver area rail operations. "But the idea is that it will alleviate the congestion in the central area. But you know, it's pretty dog-gone expensive." (409)

As transportation planners along the Front Range grappled with the problems of severe automobile traffic congestion, in search of a viable transportation alternative, they could look to metro Denver to see how to do it. With Transit Oriented Developments along RTD light rail routes being studied and planned for the suburbs of Denver, a larger scale TOD project could be developed along the proposed commuter rail routes between Fort Collins and Pueblo. Three important questions to ask are: (1) Have people living along the I-25 corridor been as frustrated with automobile congestion as those living in metro Denver? (2) Would they be willing to pay a higher sales or gas tax to have commuter rail as a transportation alternative? Tax increases were a necessary part of the development of rail mass transit in Denver and elsewhere. Finally, (3) would voter-approved tax dollars be more likely forth-coming if more than just commuter rail service was being offered?

The last regular passenger train to serve the Denver-Pueblo corridor was a Denver connection to the Santa Fe's Chicago-Los Angeles *Super Chief*. Two baggage cars and a coach stopped in Colorado Springs, Colorado, about a year prior to the April 30, 1971, termination of the service. The train would continue south through Pueblo, then east to La Junta to meet the Chief.

Commuter Rail and Tourism

For the sake of tourism, commuter trains could be more than for commuter use only. In the same tradition as the streetcars in New Orleans, Louisiana, or Kenosha, Wisconsin, Front Range transportation officials might consider a design of commuter train with an historical interest. Being on the Front Range of the Rocky Mountains, Denver and its surrounding areas have regularly attracted numerous tourists each year. If done properly, commuter trains could be marketed as tourist attractions. A major station or several main station stops could double as museums or have a museum section within them. An accurate representation of railroading and area history could be presented.

In honor of past and present Front Range railroads, historical names and advertising slogans could be used. For example, trains from Denver to Boulder and Longmont or Fort Collins would operate over the "Kite Route Line." Reflecting Union Pacific's many famous Cities trains, commuter trains to Greeley and Fort Collins would operate over the "Cities Line." To Colorado Springs and Pueblo, commuter trains would honor the long gone Chicago, Rock Island & Pacific by being named for the railroad's "Rocky Mountain Rocket" streamliner. The Rocky Mountain Rocket became famous because of its scenic view of Pikes Peak as trains arrived in Colorado Springs from the east. The Rocket did connect to Denver and was therefore considered a Chicago-Denver train. Further, Rock Island trains operated to Pueblo via the Joint Line. Pamphlets would be available to describe the relevant history at appropriate station stops or aboard the commuter trains. Historians might volunteer to ride along to give lectures or answer questions, as has been done on some long-distance Amtrak or private luxury trains.

During the weekends and especially during the summer, commuter trains could make connections with tour buses to bring people to the many tourist attractions around the Front Range area. The Colorado Springs area, for example, had several tourist attractions, including the Garden of the Gods, Seven Falls, the Cave of the Winds, the Air Force Academy, the Olympic Training Center and the Pikes Peak Cog Railroad. When properly marketed and coordinated with the Colorado Springs bus transit system or a private charter bus company, commuter trains could enhance area tourism while also providing a vital commuter rail service. Further, hotel packages could be made available which would include a train ride. The train trip could become an attraction in and of itself as the trains climb the Front Range foothills over the scenic Palmer Divide.

Part of making a commuter rail line function as a tourist railroad would be through the acquisition of historic operating equipment. Ideally the entire train, locomotive and passenger cars, would be historic rolling stock rebuilt accurately to represent railroading's past. The tourist aspect, however, should not interfere with the needs of the daily commuter. Most likely, people commuting on the train would want state-of-the-art equipment. Therefore, new ADA-compliant (Americans with Disabilities Act) bi-level commuter cars should change in paint scheme only.

The locomotives, however, are another matter. For its public relations program and business train fleet, the Union Pacific sent two streamliner-era "E9" cab units and a booster unit to be rebuilt by the VMV Corporation in Paducah, Kentucky. Out-shopped from the former Illinois Central Railroad facility in April 1993, Union Pacific spent $2 million to bring back its 1955-built locomotive set to pull passengers. In the interest of historical accuracy, the exteriors of these General Motors Electro-Motive Division (EMD) E9 diesels were restored to their original prototype image. Beneath the outer shell, the original pair of 567, 12-cylinder motors were replaced with a single 645E, 16-cylinder motor per cab unit. Mechanically, these E9 streamliners were transformed into modern "E38-2" units. (410)

Externally, locomotives like these in Front Range commuter service would look like classic "E"-type diesels for tourists but operate internally as modern "E38PH-2" units in ride and comfort for daily commuters. The added "PH" would indicate Passenger Head-End Power (HEP) necessary to provide electricity for light, heat and air conditioning to the bi-level cars. The 1955 E9 cab units were originally built with steam generators to provide heat and light to the train. They were not rebuilt with HEP capability. A de-engined cabless booster unit was rebuilt to serve this function.

The acquisition of passenger-era diesels for commuter rail service on Colorado's Front Range may seem like a step backwards. Chicago's Metra discontinued its E9 streamliners without rider protest beginning in 1992. But Metra did not try to draw a connection between its trains and railroad history. Without a museum, people and literature to educate and inform, the use of streamliner diesels proved meaningless except as motive power for Metra. As the E9 units were replaced and retired, the historical uniqueness of Chicago-Aurora commuter rail service was lost. The new locomotives matched those operating over the entire Metra system and on lines in other cities.

Several large and small railroad museums were located throughout North America. Many of them owned track and ran trains. Various railroad museums may be willing to have their already restored and often operating streamliner-era locomotives upgraded for commuter rail service. Further, participating museums would be great resources for historical information and guidance during locomotive upgrading in the interest of historical accuracy. The benefits to the museum would be a percentage of ticket revenues and its better-than-new locomotive actually operating again in revenue service.

For example, a Kansas City, Kansas, museum displayed and occasionally operated former Rock Island Rocket streamlined passenger diesels. Southwest of Kansas City, the Midland Railway operated short excursion trains from Baldwin City, Kansas, on a former branch line of the old Santa Fe Railway. Midland Railway was created by the Midland Railway Historical Association and the Santa Fe Trail Historical Society. Part of Midland Railway's collection of operating locomotives included former Rock Island number 630, a 1941 EMD E6, and number 652, a 1953 EMD E8. The E6 was the last of its kind to operate in revenue service.

If upgraded internally with E38PH-2 mechanics, including push-pull and HEP capability, these units could serve actively as museum pieces in revenue commuter service. Two commuter trains could be pulled by authentic Rock Island Rocket diesels along the assigned "Rocky Mountain Rocket Line" between Denver, Colorado Springs, and Pueblo. Freed from static display or slow branch line operation, E6 630 and E8 652 could finally be appreciated doing what they were designed for, hauling passengers at high speeds in revenue service. The museums which provide such historic motive power could also provide literature distributed to passengers so these locomotives could be appreciated to their fullest.

To get modern Metra-style commuter rail service started along Colorado's Front Range would require dealing with much of the same political controversy that Denver light rail had to overcome. But unlike Denver light rail, Front Range commuter rail would require the support of more than just the nearby communities surrounding Denver. The majority of Front Range cities and towns must be supportive of such an idea. A tax increase would have to be approved.

Further, the debate between highway supporters and rail advocates would likely continue, as it had in Denver and throughout many parts of the country. The political success of Denver light rail, however, could be attributed in part to Colorado Governor Bill Owens and his "something for everyone" philosophy toward transportation. The "T-REX" transportation expansion program, for example, was approved by the state legislature and the voters, in part because both a new light rail line to the Denver Tech Center, the Southeast Corridor, and statewide highway improvements were proposed in the same 1999 referendum. With both the implementation of rail transit and interstate highway expansion, the Southeast Corridor illustrated well the benefit of this kind of political compromise. Without compromise, many well-intended public-works projects simply do not get done. The same strategy was also being used in the Denver-Boulder corridor as plans to establish new commuter rail also included a bus transitway for an expanded U.S. Highway 36.

To include the tourism aspect for a proposed commuter rail line invites even more debate. The willingness and political support of individual museums would be required. For streetcar operations in New Orleans, the "Bring Our Streetcars Home" (BOSH) campaign was only able to wrestle three of the eleven Perley Thomas cars away from the museums which had acquired them. Three historic electric streetcars, however, did return to the streets of New Orleans.

Introducing commuter rail at the foot of the Rocky Mountains may be like bringing a little of Chicago to a place that was once the Old West. As "crowded-big-city" as commuter trains may seem, they may help to preserve the West as part of an urban development strategy designed to concentrate human activity and preserve open space. Further, tourist-oriented commuter rail could connect area residents to their regional past while boosting the local economy through tourism. Such multi-use commuter rail service could offer several benefits, beyond regained mobility, to the cities and towns of Colorado's Front Range.

Retired Rock Island Rocket streamliner 652, a six-axle E8, pulled tourist trains for the Midland Railway along a former branch of the Santa Fe in Baldwin City, Kansas. In its glory days, it pulled cross-country trains such as the *Rocky Mountain Rocket* from Chicago to Denver and Colorado Springs.

CHAPTER SIXTEEN

A Public Rail Transportation Revolution

Across the United States and in other parts of the world, the person-per-mile capacity of trolleys and trains was proving its advantage over single-occupant automobile use in and between major cities during peak-hour travel periods. But only when confronted with severe automobile traffic congestion were people in search of a rail transportation alternative in the United States. Even a desire for cleaner air was second to the primary goal of restoring the nation's mobility.

New light rail, commuter rail, and high-speed passenger rail systems did not come easily in a country where major cities were, for the most part, spread out demographically. Sprawl city planning contributed to a spreading within cities that was also anti-transit. Further, people in both government and private enterprise did much to abandon U.S. rail transportation networks during the second half of the 20th century. To have to build or rebuild new rail systems in their entirety was a costly and difficult choice to make. Moreover, this choice was made despite the fact that rail transportation was largely viewed as an antiquated technology. "I think once people in this county ride a train going 200 miles-per-hour, then the old picture of rail will change," said Alstom system division vice president Jean-Marie Aubriot. (411)

The ground-breaking French TGV, introduced in 1981, quickly overtook the market of a once heavy air corridor between Paris and Lyons, France. The dedicated rail service whisked travelers along at a top speed of 167 miles-per-hour. Such trains competed well against air carriers in 300 to 500 mile corridors. The California High-Speed Rail Authority envisioned the same kind of success on its proposed 200 mile-per-hour rail network. People were expected to respond positively to a high-speed rail alternative in a region that was population saturated. Secondly, local officials were concerned enough about quality of life issues and the problems associated with air pollution to see a variety of benefits in having a high-speed electrified rail system.

Light rail and commuter rail lines were springing up in major U.S. cities that were unable to meet air quality standards established by the

Environmental Protection Agency (EPA). According to an independent study conducted to compare the environmental impacts of transit use vs. automobile use, there were 16 major U.S. cities designated as air quality nonattainment areas in 2002. The study, "Conserving Energy and Preserving the Environment: The Role of Transportation," concluded that even small increases in transit use (rail or bus) can have a positive impact on reducing air pollution levels within major metropolitan areas. "If we don't make transit a national priority by increasing investment, America's enduring economic and environmental health will be in jeopardy," said William Millar, president of the American Public Transportation Association, which commissioned the study. "This is our country's greatest opportunity to conserve energy and improve the environment." (412)

An Amtrak California *Pacific Surfliner* bi-level coach blocks a pedestrian crossing, while passengers (out of view) board at the San Juan Capistrano station in March 2002. Passenger service along California's Pacific Coast served as a fine example of a viable clean-air transportation solution to severe automobile traffic congestion.

From a desire to stimulate mobility and improve quality of life, new and innovative ideas were taking shape. San Francisco Caltrain's CarLink program served as one particularly creative example of an effort to make better use of a variety of transportation resources. The experimental carsharing program offered people a new way to get from home to the train station or from the train to work. Connectivity between automobiles, buses, trains and airplanes was giving people transportation options which were rarely if ever before coordinated to work together. Further, developing rail mass transit systems to do more than the singular task of hauling commuters could be found in Philadelphia, New Orleans, and elsewhere. Boosting ridership by attracting residents and tourists to historic streetcar lines was another innovation in the revolution of rail mass transportation.

Great strides were being made all over the contiguous United States to modernize old rail networks or to build new ones. But in many ways, the industry still had a long way to go at the turn of the 21st century. In contrast to the dedicated passenger rail networks overseas, Amtrak outside of the Northeast Corridor largely shared its passenger rail routes with freight trains. "When we put money into highways, airports, and transit systems we call it an investment. When we put it into Amtrak it's a subsidy," said Mark Dysart, president of the High Speed Ground Transportation Association. (413)

Even Acela Express trains, the fastest in the United States operating on a somewhat dedicated right-of-way, were hampered by geographical constraints (sharp curves) and an antiquated rail system as a result of deferred maintenance. On only 18 combined miles of the 452-mile Northeast Corridor were Acela Express trains able to achieve their maximum velocity of 150 miles-per-hour. Despite these setbacks, Acela was capturing about 45 percent of the passenger market between Boston and Washington, D.C., in 2002. (414)

Despite Amtrak's shortcomings as a national passenger railroad, Amtrak was advancing regionally through state support. From Amtrak California and Talgo trains on the Cascadia Corridor to the Midwest Regional Rail System, Amtrak was contributing significantly to the traveling public's mobility and improved quality of life on a regional level. Amtrak also contracted to operate commuter trains for local commuter rail agencies throughout the country.

As the question of quality of life grew more intense throughout major U.S. cities, rail transportation connected with a regional or local master plan came to the forefront. Public rail transportation was becoming as much about community and city planning as it was about moving people across town or between cities. Through New Urbanism and Transit Oriented Developments, trains from local light rail to intercity high-speed rail were becoming more than a way to get there from here, but a new way of living that is planned and structured for a better future.

A restored Chicago & North Western bi-level control cab car was parked on display at the Illinois Railway Museum in Union, Illinois, on June 26, 2003. What was old became new again as city planners, politicians and voters turned toward 19th-century railroad technology to restore mobility in major metropolitan areas throughout North America.

ENDNOTES

(1) "Traffic Congestion Driven By Sprawl," *Surface Transportation Policy Project*, (Nov. 16,1999), http://www.transact.org/Reports/constr99/release.htm.

(2) "Traffic Congestion," http://www.transact.org/Reports/constr99/release.htm.

(3) National Association of Railroad Passengers. "NARP-Hotline #220," *Narprail*, (Dec.7, 2001), http://www.narprail.org/hot220.htm.

(4) Layton, Lyndsey. "Leaving the Driving to Someone Else," *Washington Post National Weekly Edition*, (May 8, 2000), p.29.

(5) Layton, Lyndsey. "And, You Don't Have to Look for Parking," *Washington Post National Weekly Edition*, (Apr. 23-29, 2001), p.34.

(6) "Record Transportation Spending Tilts Toward New Roads," *Surface Transportation Policy Project*, (Mar. 22, 2000), http://www.transact.org/Reports/Cd/pressrel.htm.

(7) Layton, "Leaving the Driving," p.29.

(8) Layton, "And, You Don't," p.34.

(9) Layton, "Leaving the Driving," p.29.

(10) Miniclier, Kit. "City's new light rail service enjoying heavy patronage," *Denver Post*, (Apr. 2, 2000), p.15A.

(11) "Record Transportation," http://www.transact.org/Reports/Cd/pressrel.htm.

(12) Yates, Brock. "An American Love Affair," *Life*, (Winter 1996 Special), pp.11-14.

(13) "Jam nation: Study sees longer commutes," *MSNBC*, (Sept. 30, 2003), http://www.ms-nbc.com/m/pt/printthis_main.asp?storyID=973844.

(14) Kunz, Richard."Toronto: H(arbourfront) + S(padina) = C(ontroversy)," *Passenger Train Journal*, (April 1988), pp.32-35.

(15) Sebree, G. Mac. "GO Transit bulges with riders," *Trains*, (Sept. 2001), p.25.

(16) Meyer, Michael D. and Eric J. Miller. *Urban Transportation Planning: A Decision-Oriented Approach*. (New York, NY: McGraw-Hill Book Company, 1984), p.78.

(17) Sebree, "GO Transit bulges," p.25.

(18) Downs, Anthony. *Stuck In Traffic: Coping With Peak Hour Traffic Congestion*. (Washington, D.C.: The Brookings Institution; and Cambridge, Mass.: The Lincoln Institute of Land Policy, 1992), p.113.

(19) Downs, *Stuck In Traffic*, pp.19, 27, 28, 164.

(20) "Changing Direction: Federal Transportation Spending in the 1990s," *Surface Transportation Policy Project*, (no date), http://www.transact.org/Reports/Cd/exec%20summary.htm.

(21) Doxey, John. "California High-Speed Rail Rolls onto 2004 Ballot," *Environment News Service*, (Sept. 24, 2002), http://www.ens-news.com/ens/sep2002/2002-09-24-03.asp.

(22) Kasindorf, Martin. "The bullet train concept is picking up speed," *USA Today*, (Oct. 11, 2002), p.7A.

(23) Hilton, George W. & John F. Due. *The Electric Interurban Railways In America*. (Stanford, CA: Stanford University Press, 1960), p.406.

(24) Hilton, *The Electric Interurban*, pp.407, 409.

(25) Sterngold, James. "Betting on Rails in the Realm of Cars," *New York Times*, (Jan. 15, 1996), p.A9.

(26) Claiborne, William. "Imagine London Without the Tube – Imagine L.A. With It," *Washington Post National Weekly Edition*, (Mar. 3, 1997), p.31.

(27) Lustig, David. "Commuter rail comes to Los Angeles," *Trains*, (Nov. 1992), pp.34-36.

(28) Lustig, "Commuter rail comes," pp.34-36.

(29) Lustig, "Commuter rail comes," pp.34-36.

(30) Claiborne, "Imagine London Without," p.31.

(31) California High-Speed Rail Authority. "Executive Summary," *Final High-Speed Train Plan*, (no date), http://www.cahighspeedrail.ca.gov/business_plan/index.html.

(32) California High-Speed Rail Authority. "A Comprehensive Approach to Intercity Rail," *Final High-Speed Train Plan*, (no date), http://www.cahighspeedrail.ca.gov/business_plan/index.html.

(33) California High-Speed Rail Authority, "What is a High-Speed Train System?" *Final High-Speed Train Plan*, (no date), http://www.cahighspeedrail.ca.gov/business_plan/index.html.

(34) California High-Speed Rail Authority, "Executive Summary," http://www.cahighspe-edrail.ca.gov/business_plan/index.html.

(35) California High-Speed Rail Authority. "Benefits of High-Speed Trains," *Final High-Speed Train Plan*, (no date), http://www.cahighspeedrail.ca.gov/business_plan/index.html.

(36) Vranich, Joseph. *Derailed: What Went Wrong And What To Do About America's Passenger Trains*. (New York, NY: St. Martin's Press, 1997), p.127.

(37) California Intercity High-Speed Rail Commission. "Executive Summary," *High-Speed Rail Summary Report & 20-Year Action Plan*, (Feb. 24, 1998), http://www.transitin-fo.org/HSR/ex_sum.html.

(38) California High-Speed Rail Authority, "Benefits," http://www.cahighspeedrail.ca.gov/busi-ness_plan/index.html.

(39) California Intercity High-Speed Rail Commission, "Executive Summary," http://www.transitin-fo.org/HSR/ex_sum.html.

(40) Kasindorf, "The bullet train concept," p.7A.

(41) California High-Speed Rail Authority. "Ridership and Revenue," *Final High-Speed Train Plan*, (no date), http://www.cahighspeedrail.ca.gov/business_plan/index.html.

(42) California High-Speed Rail Authority. "Building a High-Speed Train Network," *Final High-Speed Train Plan*, (no date), http://www.cahighspeedrail.ca.gov/business_plan/index.html.

(43) California High-Speed Rail Authority. "Funding and Building the System," *Final High-Speed Train Plan*, (no date), http://www.cahighspeedrail.ca.gov/business_plan/index.html.

(44) California High-Speed Rail Authority. "How Californians View the High-Speed Train Project," *Final High-Speed Train Plan*, (no date), http://www.cahighspeedrail.ca.gov/busi-ness_plan/index.html.

(45) California High-Speed Rail Authority. "A High-Speed Train System Action Plan," *Final High-Speed Train Plan*, (no date), http://www.cahighspeedrail.ca.gov/business_plan/index.html.

(46) Doxey, "California High-Speed Rail Rolls," http://www.ens-news.com/ens/sep2002/2002-09-24-03.asp.

(47) Komarow, Steven. "Magnetic train vows super speed," *USA Today*, (July 6, 2001), http://www.calmaglev.org/documents/usa_today_07062001.html.

(48) Doxey, "California High-Speed Rail Rolls," http://www.ens-news.com/ens/sep2002/2002-09-24-03.asp.

(49) Davis, Leslie. "A Smooth Road Ahead to Reauthorization?," *Metro*, (Feb./Mar. 2003), p.20.

(50) California High-Speed Rail Authority, "Funding," http://www.cahighspeedrail.ca.gov/busi-ness_plan/index.html.
(51) California High-Speed Rail Authority, "Ridership," http://www.cahighspeedrail.ca.gov/busi-ness_plan/index.html.
(52) California Intercity High-Speed Rail Commission, "Executive Summary," http://www.transitin-fo.org/HSR/ex_sum.html.
(53) California High-Speed Rail Authority, "Benefits," http://www.cahighspeedrail.ca.gov/busi-ness_plan/index.html.
(54) Doxey, "California High-Speed Rail Rolls," http://www.ens-news.com/ens/sep2002/2002-09-24-03.asp.
(55) Doxey, "California High-Speed Rail Rolls," http://www.ens-news.com/ens/sep2002/2002-09-24-03.asp.
(56) Stephens, Bill, ed. "Commuter rail ridership hits all-time high in 2000," *Trains NewsWire*, (Apr. 4, 2001), http://www.trains.com/Content/Dynamic/Articles/000/000/000/918pyjxj.asp.
(57) Stephens, "Commuter rail ridership," http://www.trains.com/Content/Dynamic/Arctic-les/000/000/000/918pyjxj.asp.
(58) Millar, William W. "Time to Invest is Now," Rail, (Spring 2001), pp.12-13.
(59) Yenne, Bill, ed. *The Great Railroads Of North America*. (New York:Barnes & Noble Books,1992), p.38.
(60) Dorin, Patrick. *Commuter Railroads:A Pictorial Review Of The Most Traveled Railroads*. (New York:Bonanza Books, 1957, revised 1970), p.94.
(61) Maryland Department of Transportation. *Maryland State Rail Plan*,(version 5,1980), p.II-1.
(62) Maryland Department of Transportation. *Maryland State Rail Plan*,(version 5,1980), p.V-16.
(63) Maryland Department of Transportation. "Commuter Rail Fact Sheet," *State Railroad Administration*, (no date), letter.
(64) Yenne, *The Great Railroads*, p.230.
(65) Maryland Mass Transit Administration. "The Mass Transit Administration Today," *Strategic Plan*, (no date), http://www.mtamaryland.com/aboutmta/strategicplan/strategic_plan_today.htm.
(66) Maryland Mass Transit Administration, "The Mass Transit," http://www.mtamary-land.com/aboutmta/strategicplan/strategic_plan_today.htm.
(67) Maryland Mass Transit Administration. "MARC Frequently Asked Questions," *Marc Train*, (no date), http://www.mtamaryland.com/marc/marc_faq.htm.

(68) Maryland Mass Transit Administration. "Governor Glendening, Lt. Governor Kennedy Townsend Chart New Course For Mass Transit In Maryland," *Strategic Plan*, (Dec. 7, 2000), http://www.mtamaryland.com/news/strategic%20plan/strategic_plan_today.htm.

(69) Maryland Mass Transit Administration. "A Message from Governor Parris N. Glendening," *Marc Train*, (no date), http://www.mtamaryland.com/marc/marc_gov.htm.

(70) Maryland Mass Transit Administration, "The Mass Transit," http://www.mtamary-land.com/aboutmta/strategicplan/strategic_plan_today.htm.

(71) Maryland Mass Transit Administration, "A Message," http://www.mtamaryland.com/ma-rc/marc_gov.htm.

(72) Maryland Mass Transit Administration, "Governor Glendening, Lt. Governor," http://www.mt-amaryland.com/news/strategic%20plan/strategic_plan_today.htm.

(73) Maryland Mass Transit Administration, "Governor Glendening, Lt. Governor," http://www.mt-amaryland.com/news/strategic%20plan/strategic_plan_today.htm.

(74) Zeilinger, Chris. "Record Federal Investment in Passenger Rail," *Rail*, (Fall 2000), pp.52-53.

(75) TransIT Services of Frederick County. "Frederick MARC Shuttle Service," *TransIT*, (no date), http://www.co.frederick.md.us/govt/transit/newmarcshut.htm.

(76) Koontz, Doug. "Frederick, MD., back on the map," *Trains*, (July 2002), pp.28-29.

(77) Maryland Mass Transit Administration, "Governor Glendening, Lt. Governor," http://www.mt-amaryland.com/news/strategic%20plan/strategic_plan_today.htm.

(78) Maryland Mass Transit Administration, "Governor Glendening, Lt. Governor," http://www.mt-amaryland.com/news/strategic%20plan/strategic_plan_today.htm.

(79) Maryland Mass Transit Administration, "Governor Glendening, Lt. Governor," http://www.mt-amaryland.com/news/strategic%20plan/strategic_plan_today.htm.

(80) Dorin, *Commuter Railroads*, pp.155,160.

(81) Dorin, *Commuter Railroads*, pp.155.

(82) Sebree, G. Mac. "Caltrain to build four-track raceway," *Trains*, (Aug. 2002), p.32.

(83) Caltrain. "Staying on Track for the Future: Caltrain Construction Continues," *Caltrain.com - News 2003*, (no date), http://www.caltrain.com/news_2003_construction_continues.html.

(84) Ryerson, Victor D. "California's Capitol idea," *Trains*, (Mar.1992), pp.24-25.

(85) Vranich, *Derailed*, p.120.

(86) Caltrain. "Caltrain's History," *Caltrain General Information*, (Nov. 7, 2000), http://www.cal-train.com/caltrain/caltrain_history.html.

(87) Keefe, Kevin P., ed. "Only in California?," *Trains*, (Apr. 1995), p.21.

(88) Caltrain. "Caltrain's Bicycle Access/Success," *Caltrain General Information*, (Jan. 16, 2002), http://www.caltrain.com/caltrain/bike_access.html.

(89) Caltrain, "Caltrain's History," http://www.caltrain.com/caltrain/caltrain_history.html.

(90) Caltrain. "Caltrain Locomotives," *Caltrain General Information*, (June 30, 2000), http://www.caltrain.com/caltrain/locomotives.html.

(91) Caltrain. "Caltrain Adds Luggage Racks to Cars," *Caltrain General Information*, (Oct. 18, 2001), http://www.caltrain.com/caltrain/Callug.html.

(92) Sebree, G. Mac. "The trains to the planes," *Trains*, (Oct. 2001), pp.24-25.

(93) Bay Area Rapid Transit. "More than 100,000 ride new BART extension in first week," *BART Press Releases*, (June 30, 2003), http://www.bart.gov/news/press/news_8590.asp.

(94) Planning and Conservation League. "Livable Communities Transportation Proposal," *Maintaining and Strengthening Environmental Laws in California*, (May 11, 2000), http://www.pcl.org/transportation/livable.html.

(95) Ayerdi, Maria. "Transbay Terminal Facts and Figures," *Mayor's Office of Business & Economic Development*, (no date), http://www.mtc.dst.ca.us/projects/transbay/transbay_terminal.htm.

(96) Hamm, Andrew F. "Caltrain turns to Monterey," *Silicon Valley/San Jose Business Journal*, (Sept. 9, 2002), http://sanjose.bizjournals.com/sanjose/stories/2002/09/09/story1.html?t=printable.

(97) Planning and Conservation League, "Livable Communities," http://www.pcl.org/transporta-tion/livable.html.

(98) Hamm, "Caltrain turns," http://sanjose.bizjournals.com/sanjose/stories/2002/09/09/story1.ht-ml?t=printable.

(99) Hamm, "Caltrain turns," http://sanjose.bizjournals.com/sanjose/stories/2002/09/09/story1.ht-ml?t=printable.

(100) Hamm, "Caltrain turns," http://sanjose.bizjournals.com/sanjose/stories/2002/09/09/story1.ht-ml?t=printable.

(101) Caltrain. "The Stork Delivers Caltrain's New Baby," *Caltrain.com - News 2003*, (no date), http://www.caltrain.com/news_2003_new_baby.html.

(102) Caltrain, "Caltrain's History," http://www.caltrain.com/caltrain/caltrain_history.html.

(103) Caltrain. "Signal a 'Go' for Caltrain Thanks to CTX Construction Project," *Caltrain.com - News 2003*, (no date), http://www.caltrain.com/news_2003_ctx_construction_project.html.

(104) Caltrain, "Signal a 'Go,'" http://www.caltrain.com/news_2003_ctx_construction_project.html.

(105) Sebree, "Caltrain to build," p.32.

(106) "Governor's Transportation Initiative Projects: Bay Area," *Governor Gray Davis Traffic Congestion Relief Plan*, (April 2000), p.1.

(107) California Intercity High-Speed Rail Commission, "Executive Summary," http://www.tran-sitinfo.org/HSR/ex_sum.html.

(108) California High-Speed Rail Authority, "Ridership," http://www.cahighspeedrail.ca.gov/busi-ness_plan/index.html.

(109) Caltrain. "Weekend Shutdown for Construction Moves Ahead," *What's New*, (Jan. 18, 2002), http://www.caltrain.com/caltrain/whatsnew/cutback.html.

(110) Shaheen, Susan A., Mollyanne Meyn and Kamill Wipyewski. "U.S. Shared-Use Vehicle Survey Findings: Opportunities and Obstacles For CarSharing & Station Car Growth," *Gocarlink.com*, (Apr. 2003), http://www.gocarlink.com.

(111) CarLink II. "Overview of Research," *Gocarlink.com*, (no date), http://www.gocar-link.com/about/research.htm.

(112) Caltrans. "CT Study Finds 'CarSharing' Eases Stress, Promotes Flexible Travel, Cuts Pollution," *Caltrans CT News*, (July 2000), http://www.dot.ca.gov/ctnews/july00/.

(113) Adame, Jaime. "Sharing cars eases commute crunch," *Contra Costa Times*, (no date), http://www.gocarlink.com/about/articles/cctimes.htm.

(114) Adame, "Sharing cars eases," http://www.gocarlink.com/about/articles/cctimes.htm.

(115) CarLink II. "Frequently Asked Questions," *Gocarlink.com*, (no date), http://www.gocar-link.com/about/faqs3.htm.

(116) Caltrans, "CT Study Finds," http://www.dot.ca.gov/ctnews/july00/

(117) CarLink II, "Frequently Asked," http://www.gocar-link.com/about/faqs3.htm.

(118) Forsman, Theresa. "Car-Sharing: Is It the Next Colossus of Roads?," *BusinessWeek Online*, (Dec. 1, 2000), http://www.businessweek.com:/print/smallbiz/content/nov2000/sb2000121_155.htm.

(119) Forsman, "Car-Sharing: Is It," http://www.businessweek.com:/print/smallbiz/con-tent/nov2000/sb2000121_155.htm.

(120) Forsman, "Car-Sharing: Is It," http://www.businessweek.com:/print/smallbiz/con-tent/nov2000/sb2000121_155.htm.

(121) Shaheen, "U.S. Shared-Use Vehicle Survey," http://www.gocarlink.com.

(122) Metra. "Commuter Rail Ridership Sets Record For 3rd Year In A Row," *Metra News*, (no date), http://www.metrarail.com/News/record.html.

(123) Metra. "Commuter rail posts 20-year ridership record," *Metra News*, (Feb. 16, 2001),
http://www.metrarail.com/News/press-release-02-16-01.html.

(124) Metra, "Commuter Rail Ridership Sets Record," http://www.metrarail.com/News/record.html.

(125) Metra. "Metra dedicates new Great Lakes Station in North Chicago," *Metra News Release*, (May 29, 2003), http://metrarail.com/Press_Releases/press-release-05-29a-03.html.

(126) Metra. "Metra Directors Approve Preliminary 2002 Budget," *Metra Press Release*, (Oct. 12, 2001), http://metrarail.com/Press_Releases/press-release-10-12-01.html.

(127) Metra. "Final 2002 Program and Budget," *Metrarail.com*, (Nov. 2001), http://www.metra-rail.com.

(128) Metra. "Improvements continue with commuters' help," *Metra On The (Bl) Level*, (Jan./Feb. 2002), http://metrarail.com/OTBL/index.html.

(129) Metra. "Ground broken for new Pingree Road Metra station in Crystal Lake," *Metra News Release*, (June 9, 2003), http://metrarail.com/Press_Releases/press-release-06-09-03.html.

(130) Metra, "Ground broken for new Pingree," http://metrarail.com/Press_Releases/press-release-06-09-03.html.

(131) Metra. "Metra ridership sets another record," *Metra Press Release*, (Feb. 15, 2002), http://metrarail.com/Press_Releases/press-release-02-15-02a.html.

(132) Metra, "Metra Directors Approve," http://metrarail.com/Press_Releases/press-release-10-12-01.html.

(133) Ingles, J.David. "Metra:Best Commuter Train," Trains, (July 1993), pp.38-45.

(134) Metra. "Metra expansion gets federal push," *Metra Press Release*, (Nov. 5, 2001), http://metrarail.com/Press_Releases/press-release-11-05-01.html.

(135) Metra. "Metra Grateful For Endorsement Of Service Expansion In President Bush's Proposed 2002 Budget," *Metra News*, (Apr. 10, 2001), http://www.metrarail.com/News/press-release-04-10-01.html.

(136) Ingles, "Metra: Best Commuter," pp.38-45.

(137) Glischinski, Steven. "A Tale of Twin Cities," *Trains*, (Oct. 1986), p.24-36.

(138) Metra. "Metra To Replace Old Locomotives With $79.4 Million Order," *Metra News*, (Jan. 12, 2001), http://www.metrarail.com/News/press-release-01-12-01.html.

(139) Metra, "Metra To Replace," http://www.metrarail.com/News/press-release-01-12-01.html.

(140) Haswell, Anthony. "My ride on the Rock," *Trains*, (Mar.1983), pp.37-46.

(141) Metra, "Commuter rail posts," http://www.metrarail.com/News/press-release-02-16-01.html.

(142) Metra. "Plans announced for renovation of Metra's Randolph Street Station," *Metra Press Release*, (Feb. 15, 2002), http://metrarail.com/Press_Releases/press-release-02-15-02b.html.

(143) Blaszak, Michael W. "Illinois Central:A railroad for the Nineties," *Trains*, (Aug.1992), pp.32-40.

(144) Ingles, "Metra: Best Commuter," pp.38-45.

(145) Ingles, J. David. "ICG's garage sale," *Trains*, (Mar. 1988), pp.34-35.

(146) Ingles, "ICG's garage sale," pp.34-35.

(147) Metra, "Commuter rail posts," http://www.metrarail.com/News/press-release-02-16-01.html.

(148) Sebree, G. Mac. "Randolph Street being redone," *Trains*, (July 2002), p.29.

(149) Metra, "Plans announced for renovation," http://metrarail.com/Press_Releases/press-release-02-15-02b.html.

(150) Metra, "Commuter rail posts," http://www.metrarail.com/News/press-release-02-16-01.html.

(151) Ingles, J.David. "Down at the depot," *Trains*, (May 1992), p.7.

(152) Metra. "MetraMarket, A Major Retail, Restaurant Attraction, Planned By Metra, U.S. Equities For West Loop Train Station," *Metra News*, (Apr. 20, 2001), http://www.metrarail.com/News/press-release-04-20-01.html.

(153) Metra, "MetraMarket," http://www.metrarail.com/News/press-release-04-20-01.html.

(154) Metra, "MetraMarket," http://www.metrarail.com/News/press-release-04-20-01.html.

(155) Schneider, Paul D. "The second coming of Chicago Union Station," *Trains*, (Feb.1992), pp.26-28.

(156) Stephens, Bill, ed. "Amtrak, Metra team up to study Chicago Union Station expansion options," *Trains NewsWire*, (Dec.6, 2000), http://www.trains.com/news/news.shtml.

(157) Cantillon, Kathleen. "Major Mixed-Use Redevelopment Plans for Union Station Announced," *Amtrak News Release*, (Feb. 7, 2002), http://amtrak.com/press/atk20020207029.html.

(158) Janota, Laura. "Transit dreams draw ire," *Daily Herald*, (May 8, 1992), p.5.

(159) Hanna, Janan. "Train brings world to suburbs," *Chicago Tribune*, (Aug.20, 1996), p.B1.

(160) Ingles, J.David. "Ready or not, here we come," *Trains*, (Nov.1996), pp.26-27.

(161) Ingles, "Ready or not," pp.26-27.

(162) Metra, "Metra Grateful For Endorsement," http://www.metrarail.com/News/press-release-04-10-01.html.

(163) Metra, "Commuter Rail Ridership Sets Record," http://www.metrarail.com/News/record.html.

(164) Valdez, Jerry and Morgan Lyons. "Trinity Railway Express Service into Downtown Fort Worth," *DART News Release*, (Nov. 30, 2001), http://www.dart.org/news.asp?ID=322.

(165) Rieder, Robert A. "Electric Interurban Railways," *The Handbook of Texas Online*, (Dec. 4, 2002), http://www.tsha.utexas.edu/handbook/online/articles/view/EE/eqe12.html.

(166) Wilson, Beth. "Reconnecting Dallas-Fort Worth," *Rail*, (Fall 2000), pp.24-28.

(167) Dallas Area Rapid Transit. "Trinity Railway Express Vehicle Information," *Riding DART*, (Jan. 2002), http://dart.org/riding.asp?zeon=trevehicles.

(168) Dallas Area Rapid Transit. "Bond Election," *DART Newsroom*, (no date), http://www.da-rt.org/newsroommain.asp?zeon=annualreport.

(169) Wilson, "Reconnecting Dallas," pp.24-28.

(170) Valdez, "Trinity Railway Express Service into Downtown," http://www.dart.org/ne-ws.asp?ID=322.

(171) Valdez, "Trinity Railway Express Service into Downtown," http://www.dart.org/ne-ws.asp?ID=322.

(172) Sebree, G. Mac. "Texas likes its railroads big," *Trains*, (Jan. 2002), p.33.

(173) Valdez, "Trinity Railway Express Service into Downtown," http://www.dart.org/ne-ws.asp?ID=322.

(174) Hirano, Steve. "Commuter Rail Fever Hits U.S. Transit Agencies," *Metro*, (April 2002), pp.26-31.

(175) Valdez, "Trinity Railway Express Service into Downtown," http://www.dart.org/ne-ws.asp?ID=322.

(176) Trinity Railway Express. "Fort Worth Intermodal Transportation Center," *Trinity Railway Express*, (Jan. 12, 2002), http://www.trinityrailwayexpress.org/itcpage.html.

(177) Valdez, Jerry and Morgan Lyons. "Trinity Railway Express Dedicates Intermodal Transportation Center," *DART News Release*, (Jan. 14, 2002), http://www.dart.org/ne-ws.asp?ID=338.

(178) Valdez, "Trinity Railway Express Dedicates," http://www.dart.org/news.asp?ID=338.

(179) Hirano, "Commuter Rail Fever Hits," p.31.

(180) Hirano, Steve, ed. "Study: DART rail stations add value to nearby properties," *Metro*, (April 2003), p.14.

(181) Lyons, Morgan and Estela Hernandez. "New study shows DART rail stations add value to nearby properties," *DART News Release*, (Jan. 28, 2003), http://www.dart.org/news.asp?ID=451.

(182) Hilton, *The Electric Interurban*, pp.337-338.

(183) Middleton, William D. *South Shore: The Last Interurban*. (San Marino, CA:Golden West Books,1970), p.31.

(184) Hilton, *The Electric Interurban*, pp.337-338.

(185) Middleton, *South Shore*, pp.9-10.

(186) Middleton, *South Shore*, pp.21-22.

(187) Middleton, *South Shore*, p.25.
(188) Middleton, *South Shore*, p.27.
(189) Middleton, *South Shore*, p.28.
(190) Middleton, *South Shore*, p.31.
(191) Middleton, *South Shore*, pp.31-35.
(192) Middleton, *South Shore*, pp.46-47.
(193) Middleton, *South Shore*, pp.42,46.
(194) Middleton, *South Shore*, p.46.
(195) Middleton, *South Shore*, p.151.
(196) Middleton, *South Shore*, pp.75,145.
(197) Middleton, *South Shore*, p.145.
(198) Middleton, *South Shore*, p.87.
(199) Middleton, *South Shore*, p.89.
(200) Middleton, *South Shore*, p.91.
(201) Middleton, *South Shore*, p.143.
(202) Ingles, J.David. "The Venango River boys and their electric train," *Trains*, (July 1985), pp.16-17.
(203) Ingles, J.David. "Profiles of the Class 1's," *Trains*, (Apr.1991), pp.18-21.
(204) Middleton, *South Shore*, pp.108-115.
(205) Stewart, William B. "The lesson of the last interurban," *Passenger Train Journal*, (July 1977), pp.7-11.
(206) Wilson, Beth. "The Venerable South Shore," *Rail*, (Spring 2001), p.34.
(207) Northern Indiana Commuter Transportation District. "History of the South Shore Rail Passenger Service," *NICTD South Shore History*, (Dec. 20, 1999), http://www.nictd.com/history/his-tory.html.
(208) Middleton, William D. "New cars for the South Shore...finally," *Trains*, (Jan.1982), pp.48-50.
(209) Wilson, "The Venerable," p.35.
(210) Morgan, David P., ed. "Instead of Insull," *Trains*, (Jan.1985), pp.4,8.
(211) Wilson, "The Venerable," p.37.
(212) Ingles, J.David, ed. "Private to public," *Trains*, (Apr.1991), p.7.
(213) Ingles, "Private to public," p.7.
(214) Keefe, Kevin P. "South Bend, not Switzerland," *Trains*, (Feb.1993), p.16.
(215) Wilson, "The Venerable," p.58.

(216) Northern Indiana Commuter Transportation District. "History of the Northern Indiana Commuter Transportation District," *NICTD Company History*, (Dec. 6, 2000), http://www.nic-td.com/history/nictdhistory.html.

(217) Wilson, "The Venerable," pp.36-37,39.

(218) Wilson, "The Venerable," p.54.

(219) Wilson, "The Venerable," p.39,55.

(220) Sebree, G. Mac. "New Wires for the South Shore," *Trains*, (Apr. 2002), p.29.

(221) Wilson, "The Venerable," pp.55,60.

(222) Northern Indiana Commuter Transportation District. "West Lake County Corridor," *Major Investment Study*, (Mar. 2001), http://www.nictd.com.

(223) Wilson, "The Venerable," p.59.

(224) Northern Indiana Commuter Transportation District. "West Lake," http://www.nictd.com.

(225) Northern Indiana Commuter Transportation District. "West Lake," http://www.nictd.com.

(226) Northern Indiana Commuter Transportation District. "West Lake," http://www.nictd.com.

(227) Wilson, "The Venerable," p.54.

(228) Vranich, *Derailed*, pp.218,219.

(229) Amtrak. "Amtrak 2001 Strategic Business Plan," *Amtrak.com*, (no date), http://www.am-trak.com.

(230) Nissenbaum, Paul. "Amtrak: Shaping a New Transportation Vision with Rail," *Rail*, (Spring 2001), pp.8-10.

(231) Zeilinger, Chris. "What's on the Capitol's Rail Manifest This Spring?," *Rail*, (Spring 2001), pp.62-63.

(232) Ellsbree, Amy. "Amtrak: Redefining Rail Travel," *Rail*, (Fall 2000), pp.8-10.

(233) Amtrak. "Amtrak Facts & Figures," *Amtrak News & Views*, (no date), http://www.am-trak.com/news/pr/factsheettmp.html.

(234) Amtrak, "Amtrak Facts," http://www.am-trak.com/news/pr/factsheettmp.html.

(235) Amtrak, "Amtrak Facts," http://www.am-trak.com/news/pr/factsheettmp.html.

(236) Vranich, *Derailed*, p.28.

(237) Vranich, *Derailed*, p.79.

(238) Vranich, *Derailed*, p.78.

(239) Johnston, Bob. "Beating the drums," *Trains*, (Jan.1996), pp.24-27.
(240) Johnston, Bob. "Wiring the NEC is not so easy," *Trains*, (Jan.1998), pp.21-22.
(241) Frailey, Fred. "Nothing like it in the United States," *Trains*, (Mar.1985), pp.50-51.
(242) Keefe, Kevin P. "High speed, Swedish style," *Trains*, (Mar.1992), pp.5-10.
(243) Johnston, Bob. "Bombardier sues Amtrak over Acela delays" *Trains*, (Feb. 2002), p.30.
(244) Bogren, Scott. "With Much Fanfare, Amtrak Launches Acela Express," *Rail*, (Fall 2000), p.14.
(245) Phillips, Don. "Full Speed Ahead?," *Washington Post National Weekly Edition*, (Sept. 25, 2000), p.19.
(246) Phillips, "Full Speed," p.19.
(247) Cummings, Cecilia and Karen Dunn. "Amtrak Rolls Out More Acela Express Frequencies," *Amtrak News & Views*, (June 26, 2001), http://www.amtrak.com/news/archive/atk01112.html.
(248) Amtrak. "High Speed Rail Initiatives," *Amtrak.com*, (no date), http://www.am-trak.com/press/hsr-index.html.
(249) Bogren, "With Much Fanfare," p.14.
(250) Amtrak, "Amtrak 2001 Strategic," http://www.amtrak.com.
(251) Hirano, Steve, ed. "Amtrak suspends Acela service amid equipment problems," *Metro*, (Sept./Oct. 2002), p.14.
(252) Ryerson, "California's Capitol idea," pp.24-25.
(253) Ryerson, "California's Capitol idea," pp.24-25.
(254) Vranich, *Derailed*, p.99.
(255) Ryerson, "California's Capitol idea," pp.24-25.
(256) Lustig, David. "GM's F59 diesel goes Hollywood," *Trains*, (Dec. 1994), pp.17-18.
(257) Johnston, Bob. "States show Amtrak the way," *Trains*, (July 1997), p.42.
(258) Caltrans. "Bakersfield Amtrak Passenger Station Opens As Real Yankee Doodle Dandy," *Caltrans CT News*, (July 2000), http://www.dot.ca.gov/ctnews/july00/.
(259) Graham, Vernaé and Jennifer McMahon. "California Transportation Network Choking," *Amtrak News & Views*, (Mar. 6, 2001), http://www.amtrak.com/news/archive/atk0142.html.

(260) Duke, Donald. *Santa Fe...The Railroad Gateway to the American West*. (San Marino, CA: Golden West Books, 1995, Vol.1.), pp.247-249.

(261) Vranich, *Derailed*, p.99.

(262) Stephens, Bill, ed. "Amtrak's Pacific Surfliner to make inaugural revenue run on May 26," *Trains NewsWire*, (May 24, 2000), http://www2.trains.com/trains/news/news.shtml.

(263) Amtrak, "High Speed Rail Initiatives," http://www.amtrak.com/press/hsr-index.html.

(264) Stephens, Bill, ed. "Amtrak officially launches Pacific Surfliner service with sleek new train," *Trains NewsWire*, (June 7, 2000), http://www2.trains.com/trains/news/news.shtml.

(265) Stephens, "Amtrak officially launches Pacific Surfliner," http://www2.trains.com/tra-ins/news/news.shtml.

(266) Graham, "California Transportation Network," http://www.amtrak.com/news/archive/atk01-42.html.

(267) Planning and Conservation League, "Livable Communities," http://www.pcl.org/transporta-tion/livable.html.

(268) Planning and Conservation League, "Livable Communities," http://www.pcl.org/transporta-tion/livable.html.

(269) Graham, "California Transportation Network," http://www.amtrak.com/news/archive/atk01-42.html.

(270) Johnston, Bob. "For Amtrak, a step forward, and back," Trains, (May 1996), p.15.

(271) Johnston, Bob. "Showdown for Amtrak," *Trains*, (Jan.1995), p.43.

(272) Amtrak, "High Speed Rail Initiatives," http://www.amtrak.com/press/hsr-index.html.

(273) Johnston, Bob. "Which vision for Amtrak?" *Trains*, (June 1996), p.40.

(274) Welsh, Joe. "Talgos paving way for true High Speed Rail," *Trains*, (Feb.1997), pp.70-72.

(275) Cupper, Dan. "For high-speed rail, a practical twist," *Trains*, (Sept.1993), pp.30-32.

(276) Cupper, Dan. "Talgo:from D.C.to Washington State," *Trains*, (June 1994), pp.14-16.

(277) Welsh, "Talgos paving way," pp.70-73.

(278) Bogren, Scott. "Talgo: A Key Partner In The Cascade's Success," *Rail*, (Spring 2001), p.23.

(279) Amtrak, "High Speed Rail Initiatives," http://www.amtrak.com/press/hsr-index.html.

(280) Zeitz, Ron. "Excess Success In The Northwest," *Rail*, (Spring 2001), p.22.

(281) Zeitz, "Excess Success," p.21.

(282) Johnston, Bob. "Talgo prepares to conquer the West," *Trains*, (June 1997), pp.17-18.

(283) Zeitz, "Excess Success," p.19.

(284) Zeitz, "Excess Success," pp.18-52.

(285) Zeitz, Ronald A. "A Return Trip for Regional Rail Service," *Rail*, (Fall 2000), p.17.

(286) Blaszak, Michael W. "Out of one railroad, two," *Trains*, (Oct. 1992), pp.36-43.

(287) Blaszak, Michael W. "Union Pacific integrates its old rival," *Trains*, (Apr. 1997), p.45.

(288) Zeitz, "A Return Trip," pp.16-49.

(289) Zeitz, "A Return Trip," p.19.

(290) Stephens, Bill, ed. "Contract awarded for Illinois positive train control test project," *Trains NewsWire*, (June 28, 2000), http://www.trains.com/news/news.shtml.

(291) Stephens, Bill, ed. "Union Pacific crews tackling higher-speed improvements in Illinois," *Trains NewsWire*, (June 14, 2001), http://www.trains.com/Content/Dynamic/Articles/000/000/0-01/164kbahy.asp.

(292) Bogren, Scott. "Amtrak and St. Louis Close to Deal for New Station," *Rail*, (Spring 2001), p.58.

(293) Stephens, Bill, ed. "Report says Chicago-St. Louis high-speed corridor would be safe," *Trains NewsWire*, (July 26, 2000), http://www.trains.com/news/news.shtml.

(294) Zeitz, "A Return Trip," pp.16-49.

(295) Johnston, Bob. "Decentralization on tap," *Trains*, (Sept. 1994), p.17.

(296) Hirano, Steve, ed. "BRT more cost-efficient than LRT, says GAO study," *Metro*, (Nov./Dec. 2001), p.12.

(297) Millar, William W. "Time to Invest is Now," *Rail*, (Spring 2001), pp.12-13.

(298) National Association of Railroad Passengers. "NARP-Hotline #220," *Narprail*, (Dec.7, 2001), http://www.narprail.org/hot220.htm.

(299) Hirano, Steve. "A double dip for more money, more riders," *Metro*, (Jan. 2003), p.20.

(300) "RTD opens new light-rail station," *Denver Post*, (Feb.15, 1996), p.3B.

(301) Southeastern Pennsylvania Transportation Authority. "SEPTA History," (1982), pamphlet.

(302) Southeastern Pennsylvania Transportation Authority, "SEPTA History," pamphlet.

(303) Southeastern Pennsylvania Transportation Authority, "SEPTA History," pamphlet.

(304) Southeastern Pennsylvania Transportation Authority. "The History of Trolley Cars & Routes in Philadelphia," (1982), pamphlet.

(305) Southeastern Pennsylvania Transportation Authority. "Trolley Celebrates 109 Years in Philly," *SEPTA Online*, (Dec. 2001), http://www.septa.org/promo.

(306) Southeastern Pennsylvania Transportation Authority. "Fiscal Year 2002 Capital Budget," *Fiscal Years 2002-2013 Capital Program and Comprehensive Plan*, (June 21, 2001), http://www.septa.com.

(307) Southeastern Pennsylvania Transportation Authority,"Fiscal Year 2002 Capital," http://www.septa.com.

(308) Southeastern Pennsylvania Transportation Authority."SEPTA Five-Year Plan Progress Report," *SEPTA Online*, (1999), http://www.septa.com/reports/99reportB.html.

(309) Southeastern Pennsylvania Transportation Authority,"Fiscal Year 2002 Capital," http://www.septa.com.

(310) Southeastern Pennsylvania Transportation Authority."Norristown High Speed Line," (Mar. 5, 1984), letter.

(311) Horachek, John D. "The receiver was an optimist," *Trains*, (Oct. 1982), pp.34-45.

(312) Middleton, William D. "Bullets: bowing out in style," *Trains*, (Nov. 1986), p.23.

(313) Middleton, "Bullets," p.23.

(314) Middleton, "Bullets," pp.22-23.

(315) Southeastern Pennsylvania Transportation Authority,"Fiscal Year 2002 Capital," http://www.septa.com.

(316) Perez, August and Assoc., Architects. *The Last Line:A Streetcar Named St. Charles*. (Gretna, LA: Pelican Publishing Company,1973), p.35.

(317) Perez, *The Last Line*, p.35.

(318) Perez, *The Last Line*, p.35.
(319) New Orleans Regional Transit Authority. "Today's Streetcar," *Today's Streetcar*, (no date), http://www.regionaltransit.org/todayssc.html.
(320) New Orleans Regional Transit Authority. "Historical Brief," *St. Charles Streetcar Line*, (no date), http://www.regionaltransit.org/schisbrf.html.
(321) New Orleans Regional Transit Authority. "Riverfront Streetcar Line," *Riverfront Streetcar Line*, (no date), http://www.regionaltransit.org/rfscl.html.
(322) Boulard, Garry. "New Orleans reintroduces streetcars," *Metro*, (Nov./Dec. 2001), p.13.
(323) Sebree, G. Mac. "Crescent City comeback," *Trains*, (Dec. 2001), p.29.
(324) Boulard, "New Orleans reintroduces," p.13.
(325) Donze, Frank. "Streetcar barn to be built off Canal," *New Orleans Times-Picayune*, (Dec. 19, 2001), http://www.nola.com/archives/t-p/index.ssf?/newsstory/o_rta19.html.
(326) New Orleans Regional Transit Authority. "The Streetcars," *Canal Streetcar Project*, (no date), http://www.regionaltransit.org/canal/scars.html.
(327) Boulard, "New Orleans reintroduces," p.13.
(328) Donze, "Streetcar barn," http://www.nola.com/archives/t-p/index.ssf?/newsstory/o_rta19.html.
(329) Donze, Frank. "Streetcar project runs on empty," *New Orleans Times-Picayune*, (Nov. 21, 2002), http://www.nola.com/archives/t-p/index.ssf?/newsstory/o_rail21.html.
(330) Donze, "Streetcar project runs," http://www.nola.com/archives/t-p/index.ssf?/newsstory/o_rail-21.html.
(331) Boulard, "New Orleans reintroduces," p.13.
(332) Williams, Leslie. "City, RTA teaming up to rebuild Canal Street," *NORTA News*, (July 11, 2003), http://www.regionaltransit.org/news/?item=new_orleans_rta_news_7-03.
(333) Bogren, Scott. "New Orleans to Add to Streetcar Service," *Rail*, (Fall 2000), p.34.
(334) Donze, "Streetcar project runs," http://www.nola.com/archives/t-p/index.ssf?/newsstory/o_rail-21.html.
(335) Boulard, "New Orleans reintroduces," p.13.
(336) Stauss, Ed. "Capitol Trolley," *Rail Classics*, (Nov.1987), pp.30-55.

(337) Booth, Michael. "A Year On Track," *Denver Post*, (Oct.8, 1995), pp.1B, 6B.

(338) Regional Transportation District. "Transit Planning History," *RTD-Denver.com*, (no date), http://www.rtd-denver.com/History/index.html.

(339) Katz, Alan. "RTD battle looms," *Denver Post*, (Jan.17, 1995), pp.1B,4B.

(340) Katz, "RTD battle looms," p.1B.

(341) Associated Press. "Public owed RTD refund, auditors say," *Colorado Springs Gazette Telegraph*, (Feb.2, 1995), p.B6.

(342) Booth, "A Year On Track," pp.1B,6B.

(343) Booth, "A Year On Track," pp.1B,6B.

(344) Raabe, Steve. "Parking squeeze predicted," *Denver Post*, (Feb.12, 1997), p.8C.

(345) Booth, "A Year On Track," pp.1B,6B.

(346) Booth, "A Year On Track," pp.1B,6B.

(347) Blue, Mary. "Let local vote decide local issues," *Denver Post*, (Jan. 20, 2002), p.3D.

(348) Booth, "A Year On Track," pp.1B,6B.

(349) "RTD offers discount," *Denver Post*, (July 23, 1995), p.2C.

(350) Anton, Genevieve. "Romer backs pursuing grant for light rail," *Colorado Springs Gazette*, (Nov.19, 1997), p.NEWS1.

(351) Gavin, Jennifer. "State may pick up highway slack," *Denver Post*, (Feb.8, 1997), p.13A.

(352) Katz, Alan. "Littleton trying to revive city core," *Denver Post*, (Aug.3, 1997), pp.1A,27A.

(353) Robey, Renate. "Traffic jams stacking up," *Denver Post*, (June 1, 1997), pp.1A,16A.

(354) Marsella, Cal. "Yes: RTD plan can break highway gridlock," *Denver Post*, (Feb. 24, 2002), pp.1E,4E.

(355) Leib, Jeffrey. "Southwest line has year of rail success," *Denver Post*, (July 10, 2001), pp.1B,3B.

(356) Bogren, Scott. "Denver Light-Rail Line Draws More Passengers," *Rail*, (Fall 2000), p.14.

(357) Marsella, "Yes: RTD plan can," pp.1E,4E.

(358) Leib, Jeffrey. "RTD approves FasTracks," *Denver Post*, (Nov. 19, 2003), pp.1A,9A.

(359) Regional Transportation District. "Construction Projects and Studies," *RTD-Denver.com*, (no date), http://www.rtd-denver.com/Projects/index.html.

(360) Barnes-Gelt, Susan. "Denver needs to get on board," *Denver Post*, (Nov. 19, 2003), p.7B.

(361) Marsella, Cal. "Cash detour," *Rocky Mountain News*, (Feb. 8, 2003), pp.1B,19B.

(362) Regional Transportation District. "Transit Oriented Development," *RTD-Denver.com*, (no date), http://www.rtd-denver.com/TOD/index.html.

(363) Regional Transportation District, "Transit Planning History," http://www.rtd-denver.com/His-tory/index.html.

(364) Regional Transportation District, "Transit Planning History," http://www.rtd-denver.com/His-tory/index.html.

(365) McMahon, Thomas. "Light Rail Breathes Life Back into Suburbs," *Metro*, (Nov./Dec. 2002), pp.60-64.

(366) McMahon, "Light Rail Breathes Life," pp.60-64.

(367) Butler, Mary. "U.S. 36 projects moving forward," *Boulder Daily Camera*, (Jan. 12, 2002), http://cfapps.bouldernews.com/printpage/index.cfm.

(368) Leib, Jeffrey. "RTD to seek sales-tax hike for rail," *Denver Post*, (Mar. 2, 2001), pp.1A,6A.

(369) Leib, Jeffrey. "Report touts FasTracks as economic boon," *Denver Post*, (Aug. 19, 2003), p.3B.

(370) Lofholm, Nancy and Jeffrey Leib. "Metro commute gets longer," *Denver Post*, (June 5, 2002), http://www.denverpost.com/cda/article/print/0,1674,36%7E169%7E653347,00.html.

(371) Leib, Jeffrey. "RTD aims to keep rail plan at top speed," *Denver Post*, (Mar. 31, 2002), pp.1B,8B.

(372) Regional Transportation District. "About T-REX," *T-REX: Transportation Expansion Project*, (no date), http://www.trexproject.com/about.asp.

(373) Regional Transportation District, "About T-REX," http://www.trexproject.com/about.asp.

(374) Leib, Jeffrey. "Mousetrap finally finished; financing dragged work out," *Denver Post*, (Dec. 17, 2003), p.2B.

(375) Leib, "RTD to seek," pp.1A,6A.

(376) Regional Transportation District. "Project Design," *T-REX: Transportation Expansion Project*, (no date), http://www.trexproject.com/site_channels/project_design/project_design_lrh.asp.

(377) Leib, Jeffrey. "RTD weighs options for key corridor," *Denver Post*, (May 31, 2002), http:// www.denverpost.com/Stories/ 0,1413,36%7E53%7E644391,00.html?search=filter.

(378) Kenosha Transit Commission. "HarborPark History," *HarborPark*, (no date), pamphlet.

(379) Kenosha Transit Commission. "HarborPark Kenosha, Wisconsin," *HarborPark Kenosha, Wisconsin*, (Sept. 1997), http://myexecpc.com/~coken2/masterplan2.htm.

(380) Bogren, Scott. "Mid-American Streetcar Revival," Rail, (Fall 2000), p.35.

(381) Kenosha Transit Commission. "Frequently Asked Questions," *A Guide To HarborPark: Kenosha's New Lakefront Neighborhood*, (no date), pamphlet.

(382) Sandler, Larry. "Kenosha approves rail system that uses classic streetcars," *Milwaukee Journal Sentinel*, (Oct. 6, 1997), p.5B.

(383) Bogren, "Mid-American," pp.34-35.

(384) Bogren, "Mid-American," pp.34-35.

(385) Kenosha Transit Commission, "HarborPark Kenosha," http://myexecpc.com/~coken2/master-plan2.htm.

(386) Brovsky, Cindy. "Webb set for final year," *Denver Post*, (June 28, 2002), http://www.den-verpost.com/cda/article/print/0,1674,36%7E53%7E700621,00.html.

(387) Vranich, *Derailed*, pp.118-119.

(388) Leib, Jeffrey. "United, airline group opposed to Air Train," *Denver Post*, (Sept.12, 1997), p.2D.

(389) Snel, Alan. "Denver, RTD both pursue DIA rail land," *Denver Post*, (Sept.5, 1997), p.3B.

(390) "Rail where it counts," *Denver Post*, (July 21, 2002), http://www.denverpost.com/cda/article/print/0,1674,36%7E417%7E742877,00.html.

(391) Jones, William C.and Noel T.Holley. *The Kite Route: The Story Of The Denver And Interurban Railroad*. (Boulder, CO:Pruett Publishing,1986), p.67.

(392) Overton, Richard C. *Burlington Route: A History of the Burlington Lines*. (New York, NY: Alfred A. Knopf, Inc., 1965), p.274.

(393) Jones, *The Kite Route*, p.11.

(394) Jones, *The Kite Route*, p.96.

(395) Jones, *The Kite Route*, p.146.

(396) Jones, *The Kite Route*, p.147.

(397) Jones, *The Kite Route*, pp.136-140,147.
(398) Jones, *The Kite Route*, p.147.
(399) Jones, *The Kite Route*, p.148.
(400) Jones, *The Kite Route*, p.149.
(401) Jones, *The Kite Route*, p.153.
(402) Overton, *Burlington Route*, p.357.
(403) Jones, *The Kite Route*, p.153.
(404) Morson, Berny. "Dream growing for transit revolution," *Rocky Mountain News*, (May 18, 2002), p.30A.
(405) McGrath, Gareth. "Trains here soon?" *Denver Post*, (Oct.13, 1995), pp.1A, 22A.
(406) Downs, *Stuck In Traffic*, p.151.
(407) Cortez, Angela. "Foes of Happy Canyon plan unify," *Denver Post*, (Mar.13, 1997), p.2B.
(408) Martinez, Julia C. "RTD pushes state rail plan," *Denver Post*, (June 12, 2003), pp.1B,5B.
(409) Rebchook, John. "Rerouting rail," *Rocky Mountain News*, (Oct. 25, 2003), p.6C.
(410) Ingles, J.David. "New Wings for the Armour Yellow fleet," *Trains*, (July 1993), pp.14-16.
(411) Starcic, Janna. "High-Speed Success Overseas Hasn't Come to the U.S.," *Metro*, (May 2002), p.39.
(412) Hirano, Steve, ed. "Increased transit use reduces smog, energy dependence," *Metro*, (Sept./Oct. 2002), p.11.
(413) Starcic, "High-Speed Success Overseas," p.40.
(414) Starcic, "High-Speed Success Overseas," pp.38-42.

BIBLIOGRAPHY

Adame, Jaime. "Sharing cars eases commute crunch," *Contra Costa Times*, (no date), http://www.gocarlink.com/about/articles/cctimes.htm.

Amtrak. "Amtrak 2001 Strategic Business Plan," *Amtrak.com*, (no date), http://www.amtrak.com.

Amtrak. "Amtrak Facts & Figures," *Amtrak News & Views*, (no date), http://www.amtrak.com/news/pr/factsheettmp.html.

Amtrak. "High Speed Rail Initiatives," *Amtrak.com*, (no date), http://www.amtrak.com/press/hsr-index.html.

Anton, Genevieve. "Romer backs pursuing grant for light rail," *Colorado Springs Gazette*, (Nov.19, 1997), pp.NEWS1,NEWS3.

Associated Press. "How Bush Budget Allocates Spending for Transportation," *Railroad News Network*, (Apr. 10, 2001), http://railroadnews.net/news/4-10.html.

Associated Press. "Mexico City to partly ban cars to ease smog," *Colorado Springs Gazette Telegraph*, (Dec.10, 1995), p.A29.

Associated Press. "Public owed RTD refund, auditors say," *Colorado Springs Gazette Telegraph*, (Feb.2, 1995), p.B6.

Association of American Railroads. "America's Wheels: The Railroads," (Nov. 1977), pamphlet.

Ayerdi, Maria. "Projects: Caltrain Downtown Extension/Transbay Terminal," *Mayor's Office of Business & Economic Development*, (no date), http://www.ci.sf.ca.us/site/moed_page.asp?id=5639.

Ayerdi, Maria. "Transbay Terminal Facts and Figures," *Mayor's Office of Business & Economic Development*, (no date), http://www.mtc.dst.ca.us/projects/transbay/transbay_terminal.htm.

Bailey, Mark W. "IC's Iowa Division rebounds," *Trains*, (July 1997), pp.24-25.

Barnes-Gelt, Susan. "Denver needs to get on board," *Denver Post*, (Nov. 19, 2003), p.7B.

Bay Area Rapid Transit. "More than 100,000 ride new BART extension in first week," *BART Press Releases*, (June 30, 2003), http://www.bart.gov/news/press/news_8590.asp.

Bennett, James. "Taste for trucks costs us plenty," *Denver Post*, (Sept.5, 1995), p.13A.

Blaszak, Michael W. "Illinois Central:A railroad for the Nineties," *Trains*, (Aug.1992), pp.32-40.

Blaszak, Michael W. "Out of one railroad, two," *Trains*, (Oct. 1992), pp.36-43.

Blaszak, Michael W. "The road of misfortune," *Trains*, (Sept.1992), pp.54-63.

Blaszak, Michael W. "Union Pacific integrates its old rival," *Trains*, (Apr. 1997), p.45.

Blue, Mary. "Let local vote decide local issues," *Denver Post*, (Jan. 20, 2002), p.3D.

Bogren, Scott. "Amtrak and St. Louis Close to Deal for New Station," *Rail*, (Spring 2001), p.58.

Bogren, Scott. "Denver Light-Rail Line Draws More Passengers," *Rail*, (Fall 2000), p.14.

Bogren, Scott. "Mid-American Streetcar Revival," *Rail*, (Fall 2000), pp.34-35.

Bogren, Scott. "New Orleans to Add to Streetcar Service," *Rail*, (Fall 2000), pp.32-34.

Bogren, Scott. "Talgo: A Key Partner In The Cascade's Success," *Rail*, (Spring 2001), pp.22-23.

Bogren, Scott. "With Much Fanfare, Amtrak Launches Acela Express," *Rail*, (Fall 2000), p.14.

Booth, Michael. "A Year On Track," *Denver Post*, (Oct.8, 1995), pp.1B,6B.

Boulard, Garry. "New Orleans reintroduces streetcars," *Metro*, (Nov./Dec. 2001), p.13.

Brovsky, Cindy. "Webb set for final year," *Denver Post*, (June 28, 2002), http://www.denverpost.com/cda/article/print/0,1674,36%7E53%7E700621,00.html.

Bryant, Elizabeth. "$28 million slated for Colo.transit," *Denver Post*, (July 17, 1997), p.2B.

Butler, Mary. "U.S. 36 projects moving forward," *Boulder Daily Camera*, (Jan. 12, 2002), http://cfapps.bouldernews.com/printpage/index.cfm.

California High-Speed Rail Authority. "A Comprehensive Approach to Intercity Rail," *Final High-Speed Train Plan*, (no date), http://www.cahighspeedrail.ca.gov/business_plan/index.html.

California High-Speed Rail Authority. "A High-Speed Train System Action Plan," *Final High-Speed Train Plan*, (no date), http://www.cahighspeedrail.ca.gov/business_plan/index.html.

California High-Speed Rail Authority. "Benefits of High-Speed Trains," *Final High-Speed Train Plan*, (no date), http://www.cahighspeedrail.ca.gov/business_plan/index.html.

California High-Speed Rail Authority. "Building a High-Speed Train Network," *Final High-Speed Train Plan*, (no date), http://www.cahighspeedrail.ca.gov/business_plan/index.html.

California High-Speed Rail Authority. "Executive Summary," *Final High-Speed Train Plan*, (no date), http://www.cahighspeedrail.ca.gov/business_plan/index.html.

California High-Speed Rail Authority. "Funding and Building the System," *Final High-Speed Train Plan*, (no date), http://www.cahighspeedrail.ca.gov/business_plan/index.html.

California High-Speed Rail Authority. "How Californians View the High-Speed Train Project," *Final High-Speed Train Plan*, (no date), http://www.cahighspeedrail.ca.gov/business_plan/index.html.

California High-Speed Rail Authority. "Ridership and Revenue," *Final High-Speed Train Plan*, (no date), http://www.cahighspeedrail.ca.gov/business_plan/index.html.

California High-Speed Rail Authority. "What is a High-Speed Train System?," *Final High-Speed Train Plan*, (no date), http://www.cahighspeedrail.ca.gov/business_plan/index.html.

California Intercity High-Speed Rail Commission. "Executive Summary," *High Speed Rail Summary Report & 20-Year Action Plan*, (Feb. 24, 1998), http://www.tran-sitinfo.org/HSR/ex_sum.html.

Caltrain. "Caltrain Adds Luggage Racks to Cars," *Caltrain General Information*, (Oct. 18, 2001), http://www.caltrain.com/caltrain/Callug.html.

Caltrain. "Caltrain Announces Baby Bullet Stops," *Caltrain.com - News 2003*, (no date), http://www.caltrain.com/news_2003_baby_bullet_stops.html.

Caltrain. "Caltrain Facilities and Statistics," *Caltrain General Information*, (July 15, 1999), http://www.caltrain.com/caltrain/caltrain_statistics.html.

Caltrain. "Caltrain Locomotives," *Caltrain General Information*, (June 30, 2000), http://www.cal-train.com/caltrain/locomotives.html.

Caltrain. "Caltrain San Francisco to Gilroy," *Caltrain General Information*, (Dec. 15. 1997), http://www.caltrain.com/caltrain/caltrain_overview.html.

Caltrain. "Caltrain Shuttles," *Caltrain General Information*, (May 29, 2001), http://www.cal-train.com/caltrain/caltrain_shuttles.html.

Caltrain. "Caltrain to Operate New Fare Structure; Adopts POP," *Caltrain.com - News 2003*, (no date), http://www.caltrain.com/news_2003_new_fare_structure_pop.html.

Caltrain. "Caltrain Zones," *Caltrain General Information*, (Apr. 24, 2000), http://www.cal-train.com/caltrain/caltrain_zones.html.

Caltrain. "Caltrain's Bicycle Access/Success," *Caltrain General Information*, (Jan. 16, 2002), http://www.caltrain.com/caltrain/bike_access.html.

Caltrain. "Caltrain's Bicycle Program," Caltrain General Information, (May 23, 2001), http://www.caltrain.com/caltrain/caltrain_bikes.html.

Caltrain. "Caltrain's History," *Caltrain General Information*, (Nov. 7, 2000), http://www.cal-train.com/caltrain/caltrain_history.html.

Caltrain. "CarLink II," *Caltrain General Information*, (Jan. 18, 2002), http://www.cal-train.com/caltrain/carlink2.html.

Caltrain. "Quarterly Capital Program Status Report: Baby Bullet," *Caltrain General Information*, (Mar. 31, 2001), http://www.caltrain.com/caltrain/quart_bullet.html.

Caltrain. "Quarterly Capital Program Status Report: Other," *Caltrain General Information*, (Mar. 31, 2001), http://www.caltrain.com/caltrain/quart_other.html.

Caltrain. "Quarterly Capital Program Status Report: Right of Way," *Caltrain General Information*, (Mar. 31, 2001), http://www.caltrain.com/caltrain/quart_row.html.

Caltrain. "Signal a 'Go' for Caltrain Thanks to CTX Construction Project," *Caltrain.com - News 2003*, (no date), http://www.caltrain.com/news_2003_ctx_construction_project.html.

Caltrain. "Staying on Track for the Future: Caltrain Construction Continues," *Caltrain.com - News 2003*, (no date), http://www.caltrain.com/news_2003_construction_continues.html.

Caltrain. "The Stork Delivers Caltrain's New Baby," *Caltrain.com - News 2003*, (no date), http://www.caltrain.com/news_2003_new_baby.html.

Caltrain. "Weekend Shutdown for Construction Moves Ahead," *What's New*, (Jan. 18, 2002), http://www.caltrain.com/caltrain/whatsnew/cutback.html.

Caltrans. "Bakersfield Amtrak Passenger Station Opens As Real Yankee Doodle Dandy," *Caltrans CT News*, (July 2000), http://www.dot.ca.gov/ctnews/july00/.

Caltrans. "CT Study Finds 'CarSharing' Eases Stress, Promotes Flexible Travel, Cuts Pollution," *Caltrans CT News*, (July 2000), http://www.dot.ca.gov/ctnews/july00/.

Cantillon, Kathleen. "Major Mixed-Use Redevelopment Plans for Union Station Announced," *Amtrak News Release*, (Feb. 7, 2002), http://amtrak.com/press/atk20020207029.html.

CarLink II. "Frequently Asked Questions," *Gocarlink.com*, (no date), http://www.gocar-link.com/about/faqs3.htm.

CarLink II. "How CarLink II Works," *Gocarlink.com*, (no date), http://www.gocarlink.com/how_it_works/index.htm.

CarLink II. "Overview of Research," *Gocarlink.com*, (no date), http://www.gocarlink.com/about/re-search.htm.

Carnahan, Ann. "Danger rises on south stretch of I-25," *Rocky Mountain News*, (Oct.8, 1995), pp.4A,6A.

Carstens, Harold H., ed. *Traction Planbook, 2nd Edition*. (New Jersey: Carstens), 1968.

"Changing Direction: Federal Transportation Spending in the 1990s," *Surface Transportation Policy Project*, (no date), http://www.transact.org/Reports/Cd/exec%20summary.htm.

Claiborne, William. "Imagine London Without the Tube – Imagine L.A. With It," *Washington Post National Weekly Edition*, (Mar. 3, 1997), p.31.

Claytor, W.Graham, Jr. "Amtrak's future may depend on a Transportation Trust Fund," *Trains*, (April 1990), pp.26-27.

Cortez, Angela. "$2.9 million goes to buy open space," *Denver Post*, (June 11, 1997), p.2B.

Cortez, Angela. "Foes of Happy Canyon plan unify," *Denver Post*, (Mar.13, 1997), p.2B.

Cummings, Cecilia and Karen Dunn. "Amtrak Rolls Out More Acela Express Frequencies," *Amtrak News & Views*, (June 26, 2001), http://www.amtrak.com/news/archive/atk01112.html.

Cupper, Dan. "For high-speed rail, a practical twist," *Trains*, (Sept.1993), pp.30-32.

Cupper,Dan. "Hot wheels:the new American Flyer." *Trains*, (June1996), pp.24-26.

Cupper, Dan. "Talgo:from D.C.to Washington State," *Trains*, (June 1994), pp.14-16.

Dallas Area Rapid Transit. "Bond Election," *DART Newsroom*, (no date), http://www.da-rt.org/newsroommain.asp?zeon=annualreport.

Dallas Area Rapid Transit. "Trinity Railway Express Vehicle Information," *Riding DART*, (Jan. 2002), http://dart.org/riding.asp?zeon=trevehicles.

Davis, Leslie. "A Smooth Road Ahead to Reauthorization?," *Metro*, (Feb./Mar. 2003), pp.20-28.

Dolzall, Gary W. "The first 38 miles: the racetrack," *Trains*, (Aug.1988), pp.38-49.

Donze, Frank. "Streetcar barn to be built off Canal," *New Orleans Times-Picayune*, (Dec. 19, 2001), http://www.nola.com/archives/t-p/index.ssf?/newsstory/o_rta19.html.

Donze, Frank. "Streetcar project runs on empty," *New Orleans Times-Picayune*, (Nov. 21, 2002), http://www.nola.com/archives/t-p/index.ssf?/newsstory/o_rail21.html.

Dorin, Patrick. *Commuter Railroads: A Pictorial Review Of The Most Traveled Railroads*. (New York:Bonanza Books),1957, revised 1970.

Downs, Anthony. *Stuck In Traffic: Coping With Peak Hour Traffic Congestion*. (Washington, D.C.:The Brookings Institution, and Cambridge, Mass.:The Lincoln Institute of Land Policy), 1992.

Doxey, John. "California High-Speed Rail Rolls onto 2004 Ballot," *Environment News Service*, (Sept. 24, 2002), http://www.ens-news.com/ens/sep2002/2002-09-24-03.asp.

Drury, George H. "Commuter railroads," *Trains*, (Mar.1992), pp.22-23.

Duke, Donald. *Santa Fe...The Railroad Gateway to the American West*. (San Marino, CA: Golden West Books, 1995), Vol.1.

Eddy, Mark. "Dirty air no longer sullies Denver's reputation," *Denver Post*, (Feb.18, 1997), p.8A.

Ellsbree, Amy. "Amtrak: Redefining Rail Travel," *Rail*, (Fall 2000), pp.8-10.

Ewegen, Bob. "Transportation coalition falls apart," *Rocky Mountain News*, (Feb. 1, 2003), p.21B.

Forsman, Theresa. "Car-Sharing: Is It the Next Colossus of Roads?," *BusinessWeek Online*, (Dec. 1, 2000), http://www.businessweek.com:/print/smallbiz/content/nov2000/sb2000121_155.htm.

Frailey, Fred. "Nothing like it in the United States," *Trains*, (Mar.1985), pp.50-51.

Frailey, Fred. "The Corridor you seldom see," *Trains*, (Mar.1985), pp.40-53.

Gavin, Jennifer. "State may pick up highway slack," *Denver Post*, (Feb.8, 1997), p.13A.

Glischinski, Steven. "A Tale of Twin Cities," *Trains*, (Oct. 1986), p.24-36.

Gormick, Greg. "GO keeps on growing," *Passenger Train Journal*, (April 1988), p.36.

"Governor's Transportation Initiative Projects: Bay Area," *Governor Gray Davis Traffic Congestion Relief Plan*, (April 2000), p.1.

Graham, Vernaé and Jennifer McMahon. "California Transportation Network Choking," *Amtrak News & Views*, (Mar. 6, 2001), http://www.amtrak.com/news/archive/atk0142.html.

Grantier, Virginia. "Douglas, Elbert growth rate lead U.S.," *Denver Post*, (Mar.8, 1996), pp.1A,19A.

Greve, Frank. "Traffic pushing the panic button for many in U.S.," *Denver Post*, (Aug.13, 1997), pp.2A,15A.

Gunnell, John. "The '50s on track," *Old Cars Weekly News & Marketplace*, (Aug.3, 1995), pp.19,24.

Hamm, Andrew F. "Caltrain turns to Monterey," *Silicon Valley/San Jose Business Journal*, (Sept. 9, 2002), http://sanjose.bizjournals.com/sanjose/stories/2002/09/09/story1.html?t=printable.

Hanna, Janan. "Train brings world to suburbs," *Chicago Tribune*, (Aug.20, 1996), pp.B1,B6.

Hansen, Peter A. "Positive Train Control," *Trains*, (Jan.2001), pp.70-77.

Harborpark-Kenosha, Wisconsin: A new waterfront community. (Columbia, MD: LDR Inter-national), 1997.

Haswell, Anthony. "My ride on the Rock," *Trains*, (Mar.1983), pp.37-46.

Hemphill, Mark W., ed. "MARC adds line; tower fixed up," *Trains*, (Feb. 2002), p.24.

Henry, John. "I-25 NOW because it's long overdue," *Colorado Springs Gazette Telegraph*, (Oct.20, 1995), p.3.

Hilton, George W. & John F. Due. *The Electric Interurban Railways In America*. (Stanford, CA: Stanford University Press), 1960.

Hirano, Steve. "A double dip for more money, more riders," *Metro*, (Jan. 2003), p.20.

Hirano, Steve. "Commuter Rail Fever Hits U.S. Transit Agencies," *Metro*, (April 2002), pp.26-31.

Hirano, Steve, ed. "Amtrak suspends Acela service amid equipment problems," *Metro*, (Sept./Oct. 2002), p.14.

Hirano, Steve, ed. "BRT more cost-efficient than LRT, says GAO study," *Metro*, (Nov./Dec. 2001), p.12.

Hirano, Steve, ed. "Increased transit use reduces smog, energy dependence," *Metro*, (Sept./Oct. 2002), p.11.

Hirano, Steve, ed. "Study: DART rail stations add value to nearby properties," *Metro*, (April 2003), p.14.

Horachek, John D. "The receiver was an optimist," *Trains*, (Oct. 1982), pp.34-45.

Ingles, J.David. "Capitols connections..." *Trains*, (July 1992), pp.68-70.

Ingles, J.David. "Down at the depot," *Trains*, (May 1992), p.7.

Ingles, J. David. "ICG's garage sale," *Trains*, (Mar. 1988), pp.34-35.

Ingles, J. David. "Kenosha, Wis., to debut new streetcar line in June," *Trains NewsWire*, (May 17, 2000), http://www2.trains.com/trains/news/news.shtml.

Ingles, J.David. "Metra:Best Commuter Train," *Trains*, (July 1993), pp.38-45.

Ingles, J.David. "New Wings for the Armour Yellow fleet," *Trains*, (July 1993), pp.14-16.

Ingles, J.David. "Profiles of the Class 1's," *Trains*, (Apr.1991), pp.18-21.

Ingles, J.David. "Ready or not, here we come," *Trains*, (Nov.1996), pp.26-27.

Ingles, J.David. "South Shore for sale," *Trains*, (Mar.1989), p.9.

Ingles, J.David. "The Venango River boys and their electric train," *Trains*, (July 1985), pp.16-17.

Ingles, J.David. "Whatever happened to the Rock Island?" *Trains*(Mar.1983), pp.31-36.

Ingles, J.David, ed. "California Allocation," *Trains*, (Feb.1992), p.19.

Ingles, J.David, ed. "Private to public," *Trains*, (Apr.1991), p.7.

Jacobs, Timothy, ed. *The Great Railroads of North America*. (New York: Barns & Noble), 1992.

"Jam nation: Study sees longer commutes," *MSNBC*, (Sept. 30, 2003), http://www.ms-nbc.com/m/pt/printthis_main.asp?storyID=973844.

Janota, Laura. "Transit dreams draw ire," *Daily Herald*, (May 8, 1992), pp.1,5.

Johnston, Bob. "Beating the drums," *Trains*, (Jan.1996), pp.24-27.

Johnston, Bob. "Bombardier sues Amtrak over Acela delays" *Trains*, (Feb. 2002), p.30.

Johnston, Bob. "Decentralization on tap," *Trains*, (Sept. 1994), pp.16-17.

Johnston, Bob. "For Amtrak, a step forward, and back," *Trains*, (May 1996), pp.12-16.

Johnston, Bob. "Safe at any speed," *Trains*, (June 2002), p.30.

Johnston, Bob. "Showdown for Amtrak," *Trains*, (Jan.1995), pp.40-49.

Johnston, Bob. "States show Amtrak the way," *Trains*, (July 1997), pp.36-43.

Johnston, Bob. "Talgo prepares to conquer the West," *Trains*, (June 1997), pp.17-18.

Johnston, Bob. "Which vision for Amtrak?" *Trains*, (June 1996), pp.34-40.

Johnston, Bob. "Wiring the NEC is not so easy," *Trains*, (Jan.1998), pp.21-22.

Jones, William C. and Noel T. Holley. *The Kite Route: The Story Of The Denver And Interurban Railroad*. (Boulder, CO:Pruett Publishing),1986.

Kasindorf, Martin. "The bullet train concept is picking up speed," *USA Today*, (Oct. 11, 2002), p.7A.

Katz, Alan. "Littleton trying to revive city core," *Denver Post*, (Aug.3, 1997), pp.1A,27A.

Katz, Alan. "RTD battle looms," *Denver Post*, (Jan.17, 1995), pp.1B,4B.

Keefe, Kevin P. "Commuter lines expand," *Trains*, (Feb.1995), p.24.

Keefe, Kevin P. "High speed, Swedish style," *Trains*, (Mar.1992), pp.5-10.

Keefe, Kevin P. "South Bend, not Switzerland," *Trains*, (Feb.1993), p.16.

Keefe, Kevin P., ed. "Doubling up," *Trains*, (Mar. 1995), p.27.

Keefe, Kevin P., ed. "Only in California?," *Trains*, (Apr. 1995), p.21.

Kelly, Guy. "RTD gears up for next light rail," *Rocky Mountain News*, (Nov.13, 1995), p.20A.

Kelly, Guy. "RTD wary about asking for tax hike," *Rocky Mountain News*, (Nov.17, 1995), p.5A.

Kenosha Transit Commission. "Frequently Asked Questions," *A Guide To HarborPark: Kenosha's New Lakefront Neighborhood*, (no date), pamphlet.

Kenosha Transit Commission. "HarborPark History," *HarborPark*, (no date), pamphlet.

Kenosha Transit Commission. "HarborPark Kenosha, Wisconsin," *HarborPark Kenosha, Wisconsin*, (Sept. 1997), http://myexecpc.com/~coken2/masterplan2.htm.

Kenosha Transit Commission. "Kenosha, WI Electric Streetcar Project," *New York City Subway*, (no date), http://www.nycsubway.org/./us/kenosha/index.html.

Kenosha Transit Commission. "Kenosha's Electric Transportation Journey," *HarborPark Kenosha, Wisconsin*, (no date), http://myexecpc.com/~coken2/streethistory.html.

Knox, Noelle. "Gas guzzlers drive request to ditch law," *Denver Post*, (Mar.3, 1997) p.2A.

Koch, Wendy and Vic Ostrowidzki. "At 40, U.S.highway system showing its age," *Denver Post*, (Nov.24, 1995), p.41A.

Koch, Wendy and Vic Ostrowidzki. "Pathway to future smooth?," *Denver Post*, (Nov.24, 1995) p.56A.

Kokmen, Leyla. "Tiny chip not just a token," *Denver Post*, (Aug.21, 1997), pp.1C,7C.

Komarow, Steven. "Magnetic train vows super speed," *USA Today*, (July 6, 2001), http://www.calmaglev.org/documents/usa_today_07062001.html.

Koontz, Doug. "Frederick, MD., back on the map," *Trains*, (July 2002), pp.28-29.

Kube, Kathi. "What's old is new at a transit line near you," *Trains*, (Aug. 2004), p.24.

Kunz, Richard."The Last Abandonment (and other notes)," *Passenger Train Journal*, (June 1989), pp.35-37.

Kunz, Richard."Toronto: H(arbourfront) + S(padina) = C(ontroversy)," *Passenger Train Journal*, (April 1988), pp.32-35.

Layton, Lyndsey. "And, You Don't Have to Look for Parking," *Washington Post National Weekly Edition*, (Apr. 23-29, 2001), p.34.

Layton, Lyndsey. "Leaving the Driving to Someone Else," *Washington Post National Weekly Edition*, (May 8, 2000), p.29.

Leib, Jeffrey. "Airport courts rail prize," *Denver Post*, (Apr. 29, 2002), http://www.denverpost.com/cda/article/print/0,1674,36%7E33%7E576742,00.html.

Leib, Jeffrey. "Mousetrap finally finished; financing dragged work out," *Denver Post*, (Dec. 17, 2003), p.2B.

Leib, Jeffrey. "Report touts FasTracks as economic boon," *Denver Post*, (Aug. 19, 2003), p.3B.

Leib, Jeffrey. "RTD aims to keep rail plan at top speed," *Denver Post*, (Mar. 31, 2002), pp.1B,8B.

Leib, Jeffrey. "RTD approves FasTracks," *Denver Post*, (Nov. 19, 2003), pp.1A,9A.

Leib, Jeffrey. "RTD to seek sales-tax hike for rail," *Denver Post*, (Mar. 2, 2001), pp.1A,6A.

Leib, Jeffrey. "RTD to seek tax hike for more rail," *Denver Post*, (May 22, 2002), http://www.denverpost.com/cda/article/print/ 0,1674,36%7E53%7E626974,00.html.

Leib, Jeffrey. "RTD weighs options for key corridor," *Denver Post*, (May 31, 2002), http://www.denverpost.com/Stories/ 0,1413,36%7E53%7E644391,00.html?search=filter.

Leib, Jeffrey. "Southwest line has year of rail success," *Denver Post*, (July 10, 2001), pp.1B,3B.

Leib, Jeffrey. "United, airline group opposed to Air Train," *Denver Post*, (Sept.12, 1997), p.2D.

Lofholm, Nancy and Jeffrey Leib. "Metro commute gets longer," *Denver Post*, (June 5, 2002), http://www.denverpost.com/cda/article/print/ 0,1674,36%7E169%7E653347,00.html.

Lustig, David. "Commuter rail comes to Los Angeles," *Trains*, (Nov. 1992), pp.34-36.

Lustig, David. "GM's F59 diesel goes Hollywood," *Trains*, (Dec. 1994), pp.17-18.

Lustig, David. "Santa Fe rides the waves," *Trains*, (Mar.1993), pp.18-19.

Lyons, Morgan and Estela Hernandez. "New study shows DART rail stations add value to nearby properties," *DART News Release*, (Jan. 28, 2003), http://www.dart.org/news.asp?ID=451.

Lyons, Morgan and Estela Hernandez. "Trinity Railway Express Connects Dallas and Fort Worth," *DART News Release*, (Nov. 21, 2001), http://www.dart.org/news.asp?ID=318.

Marsella, Cal. "Cash detour," *Rocky Mountain News*, (Feb. 8, 2003), pp.1B,19B.

Marsella, Cal. "Yes: RTD plan can break highway gridlock," *Denver Post*, (Feb. 24, 2002), pp.1E,4E.

Martinez, Julia C. "RTD pushes state rail plan," *Denver Post*, (June 12, 2003), pp.1B,5B.

Maryland Department of Transportation. "Commuter Rail Fact Sheet," *State Railroad Administration*, (no date), letter.

Maryland Department of Transportation. *Maryland State Rail Plan*. (version 5),1980.

Maryland Mass Transit Administration. "A Message from Governor Parris N. Glendening," *Marc Train*, (no date), http://www.mtamaryland.com/ marc/marc_gov.htm.

Maryland Mass Transit Administration. "Governor Glendening, Lt. Governor Kennedy Townsend Chart New Course For Mass Transit In Maryland," *Strategic Plan*, (Dec. 7, 2000), http://www.mtamaryland.com/news/strategic%20plan/strategic_plan_today.htm.

Maryland Mass Transit Administration. "MARC Frequently Asked Questions," *Marc Train*, (no date), http://www.mtamaryland.com/marc/marc_faq.htm.

Maryland Mass Transit Administration. "The Mass Transit Administration Today," *Strategic Plan*, (no date), http://www.mtamaryland.com/aboutmta/strategicplan/strategic_plan_today.htm.

McGrath, Gareth. "Trains here soon?" *Denver Post*, (Oct.13, 1995), pp.1A,22A.

McMahon, Thomas. "Light Rail Breathes Life Back into Suburbs," *Metro*, (Nov./Dec. 2002), pp.60-64.

Metra. "Commuter rail posts 20-year ridership record," *Metra News*, (Feb. 16, 2001), http://www.metrarail.com/News/press-release-02-16-01.html.

Metra. "Commuter Rail Ridership Sets Record For 3rd Year In A Row," *Metra News*, (no date), http://www.metrarail.com/News/record.html.

Metra. "Creating capacity for further growth," *Final 2002 Program and Budget*, (Nov. 2002), http://metrarail.com.

Metra. "Final 2002 Program and Budget," *Metrarail.com*, (Nov. 2001), http://www.metrarail.com.

Metra. "Ground broken for new Pingree Road Metra station in Crystal Lake," *Metra News Release*, (June 9, 2003), http://metrarail.com/Press_Releases/press-release-06-09-03.html.

Metra. "Improvements continue with commuters' help," *Metra On The (Bl) Level*, (Jan./Feb. 2002), http://metrarail.com/OTBL/index.html.

Metra. "Metra dedicates new Great Lakes Station in North Chicago," *Metra News Release*, (May 29, 2003), http://metrarail.com/Press_Releases/press-release-05-29a-03.html.

Metra. "Metra Directors Approve Preliminary 2002 Budget," *Metra Press Release*, (Oct. 12, 2001), http://metrarail.com/Press_Releases/press-release-10-12-01.html.

Metra. "Metra expansion gets federal push," *Metra Press Release*, (Nov. 5, 2001), http://metra-rail.com/Press_Releases/press-release-11-05-01.html.

Metra. "Metra Grateful For Endorsement Of Service Expansion In President Bush's Proposed 2002 Budget," *Metra News*, (Apr. 10, 2001), http://www.metrarail.com/News/press-release-04-10-01.html.

Metra. "Metra ridership sets another record," *Metra Press Release*, (Feb. 15, 2002), http://metra-rail.com/Press_Releases/press-release-02-15-02a.html.

Metra. "Metra To Replace Old Locomotives With $79.4 Million Order," *Metra News*, (Jan. 12, 2001), http://www.metrarail.com/News/press-release-01-12-01.html.

Metra. "MetraMarket, A Major Retail, Restaurant Attraction, Planned By Metra, U.S. Equities For West Loop Train Station," *Metra News*, (Apr. 20, 2001), http://www.metrarail.com/News/press-release-04-20-01.html.

Metra. "Plans announced for renovation of Metra's Randolph Street Station," *Metra Press Release*, (Feb. 15, 2002), http://metrarail.com/Press_Releases/press-release-02-15-02b.html.

Meyer, Michael D. and Eric J. Miller. *Urban Transportation Planning: A Decision-Oriented Approach.* (New York: McGraw-Hill), 1984.

Middleton, William D. "Bullets: bowing out in style," *Trains*, (Nov. 1986), pp.22-23.

Middleton, William D. "New cars for the South Shore...finally," *Trains*, (Jan.1982), pp.48-50.

Middleton, William D. *South Shore: The Last Interurban.* (San Marino, CA: Golden West Books), 1970.

Millar, William W. "Time to Invest is Now," *Rail*, (Spring 2001), pp.12-13.

Miller, Ken. "Fight over cleaner air clouded by rival views," *Denver Post*, (Nov.16, 1996), pp.19A-22A.

Miller, Ken. "States search for ways to reduce ozone levels," *Denver Post*, (Nov.16, 1996), pp.19A-24A.

Miller, Ken. "Sunshine, toxic 'broth' form ozone," *Denver Post*, (Nov.16, 1996), pp.25A-26A.

Miniclier, Kit. "Amtrak line may detour," *Denver Post*, (Mar.1, 1997), pp.1A,11A.

Miniclier, Kit. "City's new light rail service enjoying heavy patronage," *Denver Post*, (Apr. 2, 2000), p.15A.

Mochari, Ilan. "Upstarts: CarSharing," *Inc Magazine*, (Feb. 1, 2001), http://www.inc.com/se-arch/21824-print.html.

Morgan, David P., ed. "Instead of Insull," *Trains*, (Jan.1985), pp.4,8.

Morson, Berny. "Dream growing for transit revolution," *Rocky Mountain News*, (May 18, 2002), pp.29A-30A.

Mulligan, Hugh. "U.S. high-speed train huffs, puffs behind Europe's," *Colorado Springs Gazette*, (July 27, 2003), p.TRAVEL5.

National Association of Railroad Passengers. "NARP-Hotline #187," *Narprail*, (Apr.20, 2001), http://www.narprail.org/hot187.htm.

National Association of Railroad Passengers. "NARP-Hotline #220," *Narprail*, (Dec.7, 2001), http://www.narprail.org/hot220.htm.

National Association of Railroad Passengers. "NARP-Hotline #225," *Narprail*, (Jan.11, 2002), http://www.narprail.org/hot225.htm.

National Association of Railroad Passengers. "NARP-Hotline #232," *Narprail*, (Mar.1, 2002), http://www.narprail.org/hot232.htm.

New Orleans Regional Transit Authority. "900 Series Perley Thomas," *Today's Streetcar*, (no date), http://www.regionaltransit.org/900seris.html.

New Orleans Regional Transit Authority. "Carrollton Barn Renovations," *Canal Streetcar Project*, (no date), http://www.regionaltransit.org/canal/barnren.html.

New Orleans Regional Transit Authority. "Historical Brief," *St. Charles Streetcar Line*, (no date), http://www.regionaltransit.org/schisbrf.html.

New Orleans Regional Transit Authority. "Historical Perspective," *Canal Streetcar Project*, (no date), http://www.regionaltransit.org/canal/histpers.html.

New Orleans Regional Transit Authority. "Introduction," *Canal Streetcar Project*, (no date), http://www.regionaltransit.org/canal/intro.html.

New Orleans Regional Transit Authority. "Introduction," *St. Charles Streetcar Line*, (no date), http://www.regionaltransit.org/intro.html.

New Orleans Regional Transit Authority. "News and Developments," *Canal Streetcar Project*, (no date), http://www.regionaltransit.org/canal/newsndev.html.

New Orleans Regional Transit Authority. "Rail and Track Construction," *Canal Streetcar Project*, (no date), http://www.regionaltransit.org/canal/trax.html.

New Orleans Regional Transit Authority. "Riverfront Streetcar Line," *Riverfront Streetcar Line*, (no date), http://www.regionaltransit.org/rfscl.html.

New Orleans Regional Transit Authority. "Riverfront Streetcars," *Canal Streetcar Project*, (no date), http://www.regionaltransit.org/rfscars.html.

New Orleans Regional Transit Authority. "The Route," *Canal Streetcar Project*, (no date), http://www.regionaltransit.org/canal/route.html.

New Orleans Regional Transit Authority. "The Stations," *Canal Streetcar Project*, (no date), http://www.regionaltransit.org/canal/stations.html.

New Orleans Regional Transit Authority. "The Streetcars," *Canal Streetcar Project*, (no date), http://www.regionaltransit.org/canal/scars.html.

New Orleans Regional Transit Authority. "Tips on Riding the St. Charles Streetcar," *How to Ride the Streetcar*, (no date), http://www.regionaltransit.org/howtorsc.html.

New Orleans Regional Transit Authority. "Today's Streetcar," *Today's Streetcar*, (no date), http://www.regionaltransit.org/todayssc.html.

New York Times News Service. "Denver voters look at light-rail to ease rush-hour congestion," *Colorado Springs Gazette*, (Nov.3, 1997), p.NEWS2.

Nissenbaum, Paul. "Amtrak: Shaping a New Transportation Vision with Rail," *Rail*, (Spring 2001), pp.8-10.

Northern Indiana Commuter Transportation District. "History of the Northern Indiana Commuter Transportation District," *NICTD Company History*, (Dec. 6, 2000), http://www.nictd.com/his-tory/nictdhistory.html.

Northern Indiana Commuter Transportation District. "History of the South Shore Rail Passenger Service," *NICTD South Shore History*, (Dec. 20, 1999), http://www.nictd.com/history/history.html.

Northern Indiana Commuter Transportation District. "South Shore Express Mortgage," *Featured Information*, (Nov. 17, 2003), http://www.nictd.com/info/featured.htm.

Northern Indiana Commuter Transportation District. "West Lake County Corridor," *Major Investment Study*, (Mar. 2001), http://www.nictd.com.

Overton, Richard C. *Burlington Route: A History of the Burlington Lines*. (New York, NY: Alfred A. Knopf, Inc.), 1965.

Pearlstine, Norman. "1907," *Life*, (Winter 1996 Special), p.23.

Pearlstine, Norman. "1958," *Life*, (Winter 1996 Special), p.95.

Pederson, Eldor O. *Transportation in Cities*. (Elmsford, NY: Pergamon Press, Inc.), 1980.

Perez, August and Assoc., Architects. *The Last Line: A Streetcar Named St. Charles*. (Gretna, LA: Pelican Publishing Company),1973.

Perez-Pena, Richard. "An M.T.A.Card That Can Pay for Your Sandwich," *New York Times*, (Jan.22, 1996), p.B12.

Perez-Pena, Richard. "U.S.Is Faulted on Rules To Make Railways Safer," *New York Times*, (Feb.25, 1996), p.12.

Phillips, Don. "Acela makes impressive debut," *Denver Post*, (Dec. 12, 2000), p.7A.

Phillips, Don. "Full Speed Ahead?," *Washington Post National Weekly Edition*, (Sept. 25, 2000), p.19.

Phillips, Don. "Riding the Troubled Rails of Amtrak," *Washington Post National Weekly Edition*, (Aug.28 - Sept.3, 1995), pp.20-21.

Pikes Peak Historical Street Railway Foundation. *Heritage Trolley System Feasibility Study/Master Plan:For The Colorado Springs Metro Area*. (Denver:Kimley-Horn and Assoc., Inc.), Aug.1995.

Planning and Conservation League. "Glossary of Terms," *Maintaining and Strengthening Environmental Laws in California*, (no date), http://www.pcl.org/zev/zev_news.html.

Planning and Conservation League. "Livable Communities Transportation Proposal," *Maintaining and Strengthening Environmental Laws in California*, (May 11, 2000), http://www.pcl.org/trans-portation/livable.html.

"Pueblo-Denver rail studied," *Denver Post*, (Feb.24, 1997), p.3B

Raabe, Steve. "Parking squeeze predicted," *Denver Post*, (Feb.12, 1997), pp.1C,8C.

"Rail where it counts," *Denver Post*, (July 21, 2002), http://www.denverpost.com/cda/article/print/0,1674,36%7E417%7E742877,00.html.

Rebchook, John. "Rerouting rail," *Rocky Mountain News*, (Oct. 25, 2003), pp.1C,6C.

"Record Transportation Spending Tilts Toward New Roads," *Surface Transportation Policy Project*, (Mar. 22, 2000), http://www.transact.org/Reports/Cd/pressrel.htm.

Regional Transportation District. "About T-REX," *T-REX: Transportation Expansion Project*, (no date), http://www.trexproject.com/about.asp.

Regional Transportation District. "Construction Projects and Studies," *RTD-Denver.com*, (no date), http://www.rtd-denver.com/Projects/index.html.

Regional Transportation District. "Project Design," *T-REX: Transportation Expansion Project*, (no date), http://www.trexproject.com/site_channels/project_design/project_design_lrh.asp.

Regional Transportation District. "Transit Oriented Development," *RTD-Denver.com*, (no date), http://www.rtd-denver.com/TOD/index.html.

Regional Transportation District. "Transit Planning History," *RTD-Denver.com*, (no date), http://www.rtd-denver.com/History/index.html.

Rieder, Robert A. "Electric Interurban Railways," *The Handbook of Texas Online*, (Dec. 4, 2002), http://www.tsha.utexas.edu/handbook/online/articles/view/EE/eqe12.html.

Robey, Renate. "Traffic jams stacking up," *Denver Post*, (June 1, 1997), pp.1A,16A.

"RTD offers discount," *Denver Post*, (July 23, 1995), p.2C.

"RTD opens new light-rail station," *Denver Post*, (Feb.15, 1996), p.3B.

Rutkowski, Charles. "The Rebirth of a Grand and Glorious Station," *Rail*, (Spring 2001), pp.40-49.

Ryerson, Victor D. "California's Capitol idea," *Trains*, (Mar.1992), pp.24-25.

Sandler, Larry. "Kenosha approves rail system that uses classic streetcars," *Milwaukee Journal Sentinel*, (Oct. 6, 1997), p.5B.

Schiermeyer, Carl. "San Diego ridership plummets." *Passenger Train Journal*, (June 1989), pp.10-11.

Schmollinger, Steve. "California's hidden valley." *Trains*, (Jan.1993), pp.34-43.

Schneider, Paul D. "In the violet hour," *Trains*, (Mar.1983), pp.22-30.

Schneider, Paul D. "On The MARC," *Trains*, (Jan.1994), pp.51-56.

Schneider, Paul D. "The second coming of Chicago Union Station," *Trains*, (Feb.1992), pp.26-28.

Schultz, Jeffrey T. "The Cascadia Corridor begins to emerge," *Trains*, (Oct.1993), p.36.

Sebree, G. Mac. "Baltimore to double its rail system," *Trains*, (Sept. 2002), p.30.

Sebree, G. Mac. "Caltrain to build four-track raceway," *Trains*, (Aug. 2002), p.32.

Sebree, G. Mac. "Crescent City comeback," *Trains*, (Dec. 2001), p.29.

Sebree, G. Mac. "GO Transit bulges with riders," *Trains*, (Sept. 2001), p.25.

Sebree, G. Mac. "New Wires for the South Shore," *Trains*, (Apr. 2002), p.29.

Sebree, G. Mac. "Randolph Street being redone," *Trains*, (July 2002), p.29.

Sebree, G. Mac. "Record Chicago commuter spending," *Trains*, (Nov. 2001), pp.28-29.

Sebree, G. Mac. "Texas likes its railroads big," *Trains*, (Jan. 2002), p.33.

Sebree, G. Mac. "The trains to the planes," *Trains*, (Oct. 2001), pp.24-25.

Selden, Andrew C. "How to get Amtrak out of the woods," *Trains*, (Jan.1986), pp.24-30.

Shaheen, Susan A. and Kamill Wipyewski. "Applying Integrated ITS Technologies To CarSharing System Management: A CarLink Case Study," *Gocarlink.com*, (Apr. 2003), http://www.gocar-link.com.

Shaheen, Susan A., Mollyanne Meyn and Kamill Wipyewski. "U.S. Shared-Use Vehicle Survey Findings: Opportunities and Obstacles For CarSharing & Station Car Growth," *Gocarlink.com*, (Apr. 2003), http://www.gocarlink.com.

Simon, El. "Amtrak's Holiday Crunch," *Trains*, (Dec.1993), pp.78-81.

Smallwood, Charles, and Warren E. Miller, and Don DeNevi. *The Cable Car Book*. (New York: Bonanza Books), 1980.

Smerk, George M. "A 'Hollywood' for Hollywood," *Railfan and Railroad*, (May 1987), pp.24-27.

Snel, Alan. "Denver, RTD both pursue DIA rail land," *Denver Post*, (Sept.5, 1997), pp.1B,3B.

Southeastern Pennsylvania Transportation Authority."Fiscal Year 2002 Capital Budget," *Fiscal Years 2002-2013 Capital Program and Comprehensive Plan*, (June 21, 2001), http://www.septa.com.

Southeastern Pennsylvania Transportation Authority."Light Rail Project Update," *SEPTA Online*, (no date), http://www.septa.org/news/light_rail.htm.

Southeastern Pennsylvania Transportation Authority."Norristown High Speed Line," (Mar. 5, 1984), letter.

Southeastern Pennsylvania Transportation Authority. "Route 15 Girard Avenue Light Rail Project,"*SEPTA Online*, (Oct. 24, 2002), http://www.septa.org/news/lightrail.html.

Southeastern Pennsylvania Transportation Authority. *SEPTA Annual Report*, 1982-1983.

Southeastern Pennsylvania Transportation Authority."SEPTA Five-Year Plan Progress Report," *SEPTA Online*, (1999), http://www.septa.com/reports/99reportB.html.

Southeastern Pennsylvania Transportation Authority."SEPTA History," (1982), pamphlet.

Southeastern Pennsylvania Transportation Authority."The History of Trolley Cars & Routes in Philadelphia," (1982), pamphlet.

Southeastern Pennsylvania Transportation Authority."Trolley Celebrates 109 Years in Philly," *SEPTA Online*, (Dec. 2001), http://www.septa.org/promo.

Starcic, Janna. "High-Speed Success Overseas Hasn't Come to the U.S.," *Metro*, (May 2002), pp.38-42.

Stauss, Ed. "Capitol Trolley," *Rail Classics*, (Nov.1987), pp.30-55.

Stephens, Bill. "FRA pushes train control," *Trains*, (Oct.1994), pp.18-18b.

Stephens, Bill, ed. "Amtrak, Metra team up to study Chicago Union Station expansion options," *Trains NewsWire*, (Dec.6, 2000), http://www.trains.com/news/news.shtml.

Stephens, Bill, ed. "Amtrak officially launches Pacific Surfliner service with sleek new train," *Trains NewsWire*, (June 7, 2000), http://www2.trains.com/trains/news/news.shtml.

Stephens, Bill, ed. "Amtrak, St.Louis near accord on new train station," *Trains NewsWire*, (Dec.6, 2000), http://www.trains.com/news/news.shtml.

Stephens, Bill, ed. "Amtrak's Pacific Surfliner to make inaugural revenue run on May 26," *Trains NewsWire*, (May 24, 2000), http://www2.trains.com/trains/news/news.shtml.

Stephens, Bill, ed. "Commuter rail ridership hits all-time high in 2000," *Trains NewsWire*, (Apr. 4, 2001), http://www.trains.com/Content/Dynamic/Articles/000/000/000/918pyjxj.asp.

Stephens, Bill, ed. "Contract awarded for Illinois positive train control test project," *Trains NewsWire*, (June 28, 2000), http://www.trains.com/news/news.shtml.

Stephens, Bill, ed. "Regional higher-speed rail networks advance in Washington," *Trains NewsWire*, (Oct.18, 2000), http://www.trains.com/news/news.shtml.

Stephens, Bill, ed. "Report says Chicago-St.Louis high-speed corridor would be safe," *Trains NewsWire*, (July 26, 2000), http://www.trains.com/news/news.shtml.

Stephens, Bill, ed. "Union Pacific crews tackling higher-speed improvements in Illinois," *Trains NewsWire*, (June 14, 2001), http://www.trains.com/Content/Dynamic/Articles/000/000/0-01/164kbahy.asp.

Sterngold, James. "Betting on Rails in the Realm of Cars," *New York Times*, (Jan. 15, 1996), p.A9.

Stewart, William B. "The lesson of the last interurban," *Passenger Train Journal*, (July 1977), pp.7-11.

Strong, Catherine. "Truck-sales boom may lead to fines over fuel economy," *Denver Post*, (May 6, 1997), p.10C.

Thomas, Jeff. "I-25 plan sounds good on the Hill," *Colorado Springs Gazette Telegraph*, (Sept.21, 1995), p.B1.

Thoms, William E. "Is the clock running down for U.S.rail commuters?" *Trains*, (Oct.1983), pp.30-35.

Thoms, William E. "When Amtrak runs the 5:45," *Trains*, (Apr. 1993), p.24.

"Traffic Congestion Driven By Sprawl," *Surface Transportation Policy Project*, (Nov. 16, 1999), http://www.transact.org/Reports/constr99/release.htm.

TransIT Services of Frederick County. "Frederick MARC Shuttle Service," *TransIT*, (no date), http://www.co.frederick.md.us/govt/transit/newmarcshut.htm.

Trinity Railway Express. "Fort Worth Intermodal Transportation Center," *Trinity Railway Express*, (Jan. 12, 2002), http://www.trinityrailwayexpress.org/itcpage.html.

Twigg, Bob and Tom Curley. "Attention turns to rail safety," *USA Today*, (Feb.19, 1996), p.3A.

Valdez, Jerry and Morgan Lyons. "Trinity Railway Express Dedicates Intermodal Transportation Center," *DART News Release*, (Jan. 14, 2002), http://www.dart.org/news.asp?ID=338.

Valdez, Jerry and Morgan Lyons. "Trinity Railway Express Service into Downtown Fort Worth," *DART News Release*, (Nov. 30, 2001), http://www.dart.org/news.asp?ID=322.

Vranich, Joseph. *Derailed: What Went Wrong And What To Do About America's Passenger Trains*. (New York, NY: St. Martin's Press), 1997.

Washington Post. "Amtrak derails some daily service," *Denver Post*, (Apr.7, 1995), p.7A.

Waters, Kathryn D. "History of MARC," *Maryland Mass Transit Administration Transit Profiles*, (no date), http://www.mtamaryland.com/aboutmta/transit_profile.cfm.

Welsh, Joe. "Talgos paving way for true High Speed Rail," *Trains*, (Feb.1997), pp.70-73.

Williams, Larry. "Transportation plans laid out," *Denver Post*, (Mar.13, 1997), p.2A.

Williams, Leslie. "City, RTA teaming up to rebuild Canal Street," *NORTA News*, (July 11, 2003), http://www.regionaltransit.org/news/?item=new_orleans_rta_news_7-03.

Wilson, Beth. "Reconnecting Dallas-Fort Worth," *Rail*, (Fall 2000), pp.24-28.

Wilson, Beth. "The Venerable South Shore," *Rail*, (Spring 2001), pp.32-61.

Yates, Brock. "An American Love Affair," *Life*, (Winter 1996 Special), pp.11-14.

Yenne, Bill, ed. *The Great Railroads Of North America*. (New York:Barnes & Noble Books),1992.

Young, Ricky. "RTD raises fares for businesses, too," *Denver Post*, (July 28, 1997), pp.1A,9A.

Young, Ricky. "RTD's Klein goes to the vote," *Denver Post*, (Aug.12, 1997), p.1B.

Zeilinger, Chris. "Record Federal Investment in Passenger Rail," *Rail*, (Fall 2000), pp.52-53.

Zeilinger, Chris. "What's on the Capitol's Rail Manifest This Spring?," *Rail*, (Spring 2001), pp.62-63.

Zeitz, Ron. "Excess Success In The Northwest," *Rail*, (Spring 2001), pp.18-52.

Zeitz, Ronald A. "A Return Trip for Regional Rail Service," *Rail*, (Fall 2000), pp.16-49.

Printed in the United States
55123LVS00003B/98